FIGHTING TOXIC IGNORANCE

FIGHTING TOXIC IGNORANCE

Origins of the Right to Know about Workplace Health Hazards

Alan Derickson

ILR PRESS
AN IMPRINT OF CORNELL UNIVERSITY PRESS   ITHACA AND LONDON

Copyright © 2025 by Cornell University

All rights reserved. Except for brief quotations in a review, this book, or parts thereof, must not be reproduced in any form without permission in writing from the publisher. For information, address Cornell University Press, Sage House, 512 East State Street, Ithaca, New York 14850. Visit our website at cornellpress.cornell.edu.

First published 2025 by Cornell University Press

Library of Congress Cataloging-in-Publication Data

Names: Derickson, Alan author.
Title: Fighting toxic ignorance : origins of the right to know about workplace health hazards / Alan Derickson.
Description: Ithaca : ILR Press, an imprint of Cornell University Press, 2025. | Includes bibliographical references and index.
Identifiers: LCCN 2024021858 (print) | LCCN 2024021859 (ebook) | ISBN 9781501780196 paperback | ISBN 9781501780189 hardcover | ISBN 9781501780219 pdf | ISBN 9781501780202 epub
Subjects: LCSH: Industrial hygiene—United States—History—20th century. | Disclosure of information—United States—History—20th century. | Work environment—United States—History—20th century. | Occupational diseases—Risk factors—United States—History. | Health risk communication—United States—History—20th century. | Communication in industrial safety—United States—History—20th century.
Classification: LCC HD7654 .D47 2025 (print) | LCC HD7654 (ebook) | DDC 363.110973—dc23/eng/20240827
LC record available at https://lccn.loc.gov/2024021858
LC ebook record available at https://lccn.loc.gov/2024021859

For Rosalia, Hugo, and Vivian

Contents

Acknowledgments	ix
Abbreviations	xi
Introduction: Somebody Had to Fight	1
1. A Very General Ignorance	7
2. Wider Use of Existing Knowledge	35
3. The Path of Self-Correction	59
4. A Matter of Increasingly Public Record	86
5. No Need to Alarm Employees	107
6. New Worker-Oriented Counter-Institutions	125
Epilogue: Turning the Tide on Toxic Chemical Ignorance	148
Notes	155
Index	201

Acknowledgments

It is a pleasure to acknowledge those who have helped to bring this project to completion. I obviously could not have produced this work without the help of numerous individuals and institutions. It is gratifying to note that many of these creditors have seen fit to provide similar aid to my previous studies over the course of decades. It is less pleasant to acknowledge that I am surely failing to remember to thank some others worthy of recognition.

Penn State University has consistently supported my research, both during my thirty years of employment and even in retirement. I am especially indebted to Paul Clark and my other colleagues in the School of Labor and Employment Relations for various contributions. At the Penn State Libraries, the staffs of the Historical Collections and Labor Archives and the Interlibrary Loan Service were unfailingly and patiently helpful on countless occasions.

Archivists and librarians elsewhere came to my assistance in ways that often went well beyond the call of duty. I appreciate the efforts of the conscientious staff members at the Kheel Center for Labor-Management Documentation, Cornell University; the Manuscripts and Archives Department, Hagley Museum and Library; the National Archives II; the Pennsylvania State Archives; the Farmworker Documentation Project, University of California, San Diego; the Schlesinger Library, Harvard University; the Detre Library and Archives, Heinz History Center; the Archives and Modern Manuscripts Program, National Library of Medicine; the Kislak Center for Special Collections, University of Pennsylvania; the Archives and Special Collections, University of Montana; the Archives and Services Center, University of Pittsburgh; the Manuscripts Division, Chicago History Museum; the University Archives and Special Collections, University of Massachusetts, Boston; the Archives and Special Collections, University of California, San Francisco (UCSF); the Archives, Youngstown Historical Center of Industry and Labor; the Manuscripts Division, Rhode Island Historical Society; the Special Collections and University Archives, Rutgers University; and the Technical Data Center, Occupational Safety and Health Administration (OSHA). Jim Quigel at Penn State, Erin Hurley at UCSF, Robb Turnage at OSHA, and Tamar Brown and Zoe Hill at Harvard were especially helpful in my archival expeditions.

To the Toxic Docs online database, created by David Rosner, Gerald Markowitz, and Merlin Chowkwanyun and based at Columbia University and the

City University of New York, I owe a particular debt of gratitude. For a project like this one, whose central question is problematic access to information about toxic chemicals, the ready availability of such a resource that so strikingly embodies the principle of transparency is truly exemplary.

Generous encouragement, advice, and good humor came from friends and colleagues. I am glad to have the chance to thank Peter Agree, Dan Berman, Barry Castleman, Brian Derickson, Rick Engler, Abby Ginzberg, Barbara Jenkins, Chuck Levenstein, and Josiah Rector. The endnotes in this volume make clear my indebtedness to and respect for many historians and other scholars whose work has guided me. At Cornell University Press, I benefited from the expertise of Jim Lance, Bethany Wasik, and others behind the scenes. I very much profited from the copyediting delivered by Kalie Hyatt and her colleagues at KnowledgeWorks Global. Besides the mysterious anonymous reviewers for the press, various incarnations and portions of the work in progress benefited from critical readings by Ted Brown, David Rosner, Jim Weeks, and Nan Woodruff. Useful criticism also came from participants in discussions at meetings of the Labor and Working-Class History Association and the Working Class Studies Association. These colleagues' insights unquestionably strengthened my analysis and saved me from errors of all sorts.

As always, my immediate family delivered the most sustained and sustaining support for this endeavor. My daughters Katherine and Elizabeth have continued to be stalwart (and seemingly uncritical) supporters of my work. I am happy to dedicate this book to their children. In myriad ways large and small, my wife Margaret Ellen has kept me going on this trek. She offered many astute editing suggestions and much else of great value. I am very grateful for her commitment to this part of our partnership.

Abbreviations

AALL	American Association for Labor Legislation
ACGIH	American Conference of Governmental Industrial Hygienists
AJPH	*American Journal of Public Health*
ALLR	*American Labor Legislation Review*
BLS	US Bureau of Labor Statistics
COSH	Committee/Coalition on Occupational Safety and Health
DLS	US Division of Labor Standards
DoL	US Department of Labor
GPO	US Government Printing Office
ICWU	International Chemical Workers Union
JAMA	*Journal of the American Medical Association*
LaPIC	Labels and Precautionary Information Committee
MCA	Manufacturing Chemists' Association
NIOSH	National Institute for Occupational Safety and Health
NYDoL	New York Department of Labor
OCAW	Oil, Chemical and Atomic Workers International Union
OSHA	US Occupational Safety and Health Administration
PhilaPOSH	Philadelphia Area Project on Occupational Safety and Health
PHS	US Public Health Service
RG	Record Group
USW	United Steelworkers of America

FIGHTING TOXIC IGNORANCE

INTRODUCTION
Somebody Had to Fight

> I felt somebody had to fight for some of these conditions because I despise working in the area I am working. I felt somebody has got to fight. It is a hurting feeling just seeing what is going on. It is a hurting feeling seeing my older men dying.
>
> —Eugene Pughsley, 1975

Eugene Pughsley's determination to fight over hazardous conditions came from his long experience working around the coke ovens at the Inland Steel Company plant in East Chicago, Indiana. He had spent many years enveloped in clouds of the toxic chemicals emitted from the ovens. He had seen his coworkers, the vast majority African Americans like himself, dying of cancer with alarming frequency. By 1975, when he testified in Washington, DC, in support of a strong US Occupational Safety and Health Administration (OSHA) standard on exposure to coke oven emissions, in all probability he was aware of the epidemiological discovery that those who spent five years or more laboring atop the ovens were ten times more likely to die from lung cancer than other steelworkers. But besides his primary interest in eradicating this lethal threat, Pughsley, along with other coking worker witnesses at the regulatory hearings, was fighting for access to crucial information. Pughsley told OSHA officials about his employer's refusal to reveal the results of periodic employee medical examinations. He pointed out that plant management gave no warnings about the respiratory hazards present in the coking department. Like countless other workers before and after him, Pughsley was struggling to eradicate dangerous ignorance.[1]

There was much at stake in the fight over the right to know about workplace hazards. As a rank-and-file activist who watched his comrades sicken and die, Pughsley had one compelling vantage point on the meaning of denial of lifesaving facts. By the 1970s, other vantages provided compelling evidence of a critical situation. In 1972, the US Department of Health, Education, and Welfare estimated that occupational disease killed up to 100,000 Americans a year. A few years later, that agency announced that it had already identified 19,000 commercial substances with known toxic effects, including more than four hundred carcinogens. Because the vast majority of these substances entered the nation's workplaces under one of almost 100,000 opaque trade names, federal authorities concluded that about 90 percent of the tens of millions of the nation's workers exposed to toxic chemicals had no meaningful information about the risks they were facing. Long before these revelations, close observers of working conditions understood that ignorance of hazards exacted a heavy human toll.[2]

Asymmetric access to information exacerbated the jeopardy of frontline workers throughout the recent COVID-19 pandemic. The fast-food industry, employer of more than four million Americans, where workers function in close proximity to one another and to customers, has been one especially risk-filled environment. A University of California, Los Angeles (UCLA) study conducted in 2021 in Los Angeles County, where nine in ten fast-food employees are people of color, found that most employers failed to comply with a state requirement to notify potentially exposed workers within one business day of learning of a confirmed case of COVID-19 at the worksite. According to the UCLA investigators, "Workers described deliberate obfuscation of potential exposure, which they experienced as a frightening ignorance of a health threat." In some instances, food-service staff learned of their risk only when sick coworkers returned to the job and revealed the cause of their absence. One of the issues that led workers at the Amazon warehouse in Staten Island, New York, to organize a union in early 2022 was the refusal of management to acknowledge the occurrence of COVID-19 cases at their facility. The failure of managers to alert employees that a colleague had either tested positive or fallen ill with the virus has represented a dangerous denial of vital information.[3]

As the historian Robert Proctor has observed, "Ignorance has many friends and enemies." This has certainly been the case with respect to unawareness of occupational disease. The existing historical literature has delivered several accounts of the behavior of the friends of ignorance, mainly in and around the business community. As analyses of asbestos, beryllium, vinyl chloride, and other workplace health hazards have shown, the creators and perpetuators of ignorance as a strategic ploy have engaged in a variety of machinations, often with success. To a great extent, as David Michaels, who directed OSHA during President Barack Obama's administration, put it, "Doubt is their product." Michaels and other scholars have emphasized that manipulation of science is central to the manufacture of doubt. By obstructing and distorting research and by influencing the distribution and interpretation of scientific findings, powerful friends of ignorance have, in a sense, endeavored to dam up the headwaters of the flow of information regarding toxins encountered at the worksite. Historians, journalists, and social scientists have helpfully illuminated the conspiratorial and other efforts of these forces and their blighting effects.[4]

In contrast, this book focuses on the enemies of ignorance. Since the turn of the twentieth century, a diverse aggregation of individuals and organizations has sought to expand the knowledge of at-risk workers. Working-class advocates of democratic transparency were driven by fears of disability or death. Sympathetic outside supporters were animated by humanitarian concern for the well-being of vulnerable workers, particularly the workers of color and immigrants who have disproportionately endured the worst working conditions. For both those activists directly at risk and their sympathetic allies, toxic ignorance had become something that they could not ignore. Previous historical works have appropriately emphasized the widespread victimization resulting from ignorance; however, the central thesis here is that there has also been a long history of resistance to victimization.

It would be a mistake to examine the partisans of transparency in isolation from their opponents. Unsurprisingly, the relations between labor and capital were highly conflictual on this fraught issue. Although many disputes played out within the confines of the employment relationship itself, the main battlefield was that of public policy and administration. This is not the first work to consider the battles waged in the public arena between the friends and enemies of ignorance of toxic hazards, but it is the first to examine those contests across a wide range of occupational health hazards, at national and subnational levels, and over the span of several decades. One striking pattern that emerges from this overview is the support that secretive corporate interests found from public health authorities. With notable exceptions, guardians of the public health guarded the proprietary interests of employers on critical aspects of the dissemination of facts about hazards and their ill effects. Against this tendency, there stood opposition and at times fierce antagonism from governmental officials in labor agencies. The state thus served not so much to mediate class conflict as to provide a setting in which to conduct it. (Alas, this book will not settle the larger question of the role of the state in advanced capitalist society. The presence of a substantial contingent of proworker governmental actors does, however, lend support to that school of thought stressing the relative autonomy of the state from absolute control by the dominant class.)[5]

Complementing the historical work emphasizing the damming up of scientific headwaters, this project explores the downstream situation in order to determine how much information flowed so far as to reach workers at risk. To that end, it investigates the availability of messages found on warning labels and placards; the provision of oral precautionary alerts and instructions; and the distribution of flyers, pamphlets, and other educational materials.

This study covers roughly the first three-quarters of the twentieth century, up through the moment when a full-blown national movement arose to establish a strong legal right to know about occupational hazards. Although there is no straight line of continuous incremental development that culminated in this movement, there were unmistakable continuities in activists' concerns and in their reform agenda. In seeking at least to identify all the significant contributors and contributions to this quest for greater transparency, this book uncovers a number of previously unrecognized participants in this marathon struggle. Many of these individuals resided within the lower and middle levels of state and federal bureaucracies. Others inhabited relatively obscure corners of the labor movement or of academia. All possessed a willingness to confront powerful forces that had an interest in workers' ignorance.

Chapter 1 deals with the first systematic attempts to assess and redress the problem of workers' and employers' nonrecognition of hazardous toxic chemicals, especially lead and arsenic, during the Progressive Era. Three leading industrial states mounted deep investigations into the extent and causes of occupational disease. These investigations revealed a large and growing array of poorly understood threats, particularly to the sizable non-English-speaking segment of the workforce. This interval witnessed the conscientious interventions of Alice Hamilton, whose actions demonstrated that she was not only the founding mother of American occupational medicine but also the grandmother of the right-to-know movement.

Chapter 2 analyzes the bureaucratic infighting over control of the dissemination of information that raged from the 1910s through the 1940s. At both the state and national levels, labor and health agencies competed fiercely, especially in the pivotal 1930s. Led by the US Public Health Service, the health institutions made it a cardinal principle to preserve opacity, which was part of a strategy of accommodating employers in order to maintain access to research sites. Governmental labor officials saw their mission as democratizing access to lifesaving information for workers in jeopardy. Although labor agencies, especially in the state of New York, did manage to dispense a good deal of warning material to the endangered, their adversaries won a clear-cut victory in this turf fight.

Chapter 3 takes up the private regime constructed in the post–World War II years by the Manufacturing Chemists' Association. As its main informational activity, this trade association sought to protect its member firms from legal liabilities by devising and promoting a set of warning labels for containers of toxic chemicals. On the political front, the association aggressively strove to forestall government regulation at either the state or federal level. Where the industry could not prevent public intervention, it pressed, with much success, to encode its minimal labeling scheme into law.

Chapter 4 discusses the labor movement's growing resistance to the not-quite-hegemonic privatized system of the chemical manufacturers and their allies. Protests by the United Steelworkers of the refusal of state health officials to turn over reports of hazard surveillance activities led to corrective legislation in Pennsylvania that carved out an unprecedented right to hazard knowledge. Although thwarted in their demands for similar state-held information about poisonous pesticides, the United Farm Workers Organizing Committee made effective use of the issue of withheld facts in building support for its organizing drives. At the insistence of organized labor and its progressive allies, the landmark Occupational Safety and Health Act of 1970 incorporated a number of breakthrough provisions extending workers' epistemic rights.

Chapter 5 assesses the problematic implementation of the 1970 legislation. The tortuous, protracted process of promulgating OSHA regulations often frustrated champions of transparency. Setting standards for carcinogens like asbestos and coke oven emissions, as well as for other severe hazards, forced advocates of employee enlightenment into a series of confrontations with intractable opposition from formidable employer interests. Despite their frustrations, these encounters in the bureaucratic arena did yield some significant gains, including requirements that the methods of delivering warnings extend beyond the placement of labels and placards to encompass training and instruction of employees.

Chapter 6 is devoted to the emergence of the national right-to-know movement. OSHA had only a brief honeymoon with progressives. The limitations of reliance on federal administrative capacity reinforced a predisposition for collective self-help among activists. The critical development in bringing a new movement to life was the founding of a network of local and state coalitions that united union leaders, rank-and-file activists, and health and legal professionals. The product of delicate class-bridging negotiations, these organizations effectively harnessed and created militant energy.

The epilogue to this book briefly sketches the advances made in the 1980s by the right-to-know movement. It delineates the main components in initiatives at the local, state, and federal levels and their positive results. Reforms included the issuance of the long-delayed federal Hazard Communication Standard in 1983, which mandated dissemination of basic warning information. The epilogue also suggests the need for further study of the challenges of assuring that workers are aware of on-the-job risks that might kill them.

Beyond whatever it may add to our understanding of the history of occupational health, this study seeks to help illuminate the larger question of rights to knowledge of hidden dangers. Philosopher Lani Watson recently observed that epistemic rights "play an increasingly important role in our lives and communities and yet they often go unnoticed, disregarded and unprotected." The struggles over the right to know about workplace hazards suggest that establishing and protecting such entitlements require sustained collective action and that they may come only after a very long gestation period.[6]

1

A VERY GENERAL IGNORANCE

> **It is universally recognized as the moral duty of every civilized state to secure and publish information of vital importance to all citizens to promote safety and health.**
> —Illinois Legislature, 1907

The well-meaning lawmakers in Illinois were wrong with regard to one important type of health information. There was no universal recognition of a moral duty to disseminate workplace hazard information as of 1907. There was no public policy reflecting such a commitment. The concerns animating this aspirational claim in Illinois and elsewhere in America, however, were beginning to bear fruit at that moment. Inquiries and observations by numerous public and private actors in the early twentieth century elevated the principle of transparency regarding occupational health hazards. These interventions marked an advance toward the distant goal of fully informing the public and especially at-risk workers about these dangers. The Progressive Era witnessed the first significant, if halting, steps toward the establishment of a right of American workers to know about the health risks they encountered on the job.

By the turn of the twentieth century, the industrial development of the United States had brought with it both the exacerbation of old hazards of occupational and work-related disease and the generation of new hazards. Many types of deleterious dusts, fumes, vapors, gases, and liquids often contaminated the environment of factories, mills, and other worksites. These chemical threats were supplemented by biological and physical agents of disease. A sizable share of the nation's diverse workforce exposed to these myriad risks existed in an especially precarious state of structural vulnerability to illness, disability, and death. Mass immigration from southern and eastern Europe and other nonindustrial areas meant that language barriers, nativist and racist prejudices, and discriminatory job assignments, as well as a lack of industrial work experience, intensified the vulnerability of millions of foreign-born laborers. Many native-born workers, especially those of color, also could not avoid suffering. Revelations of the mounting toll in morbidity and mortality from lead and arsenic poisoning and other work-induced afflictions placed the widespread nonrecognition of workplace hazards on the reform agenda of some reformers in the first quarter of the twentieth century. Legislative, regulatory, and other actions by states brought a modicum of enlightenment to a fraction of the most endangered workers and produced a body of policy-relevant knowledge for future initiatives.[1]

Exploratory work by government officials began in earnest in the first decade of the century. In 1907, Massachusetts set up a system of medical inspection that encompassed working conditions. Inspectors reported numerous situations involving both exposure to toxic chemicals and the health consequences thereof. Elliott Washburn's 1908 visit to a factory that produced patent leather yielded the observation that employees were almost constantly inhaling intoxicating naphtha fumes. According to Washburn, "'Naphtha drunks' were said to be not uncommon among the workers. The minors at work were all Italians, young and rugged, recently landed." Inspectors found lead hazards in several industries. At Massachusetts General Hospital, they located eighteen cases of lead poisoning among men engaged in making rubber. In 1909, the State Board of Health official William Hanson reported, "Inasmuch as a great proportion of the rubber workers are foreigners—Poles, Italians, etc.—the patients themselves may not understand fully the nature of the trouble for which they are treated." To address the "general ignorance among employers and employees," he recommended the placement of warning notices in conspicuous places in the rubber factories. Hanson also expressed dismay at the plight of metal polishers who inhaled toxic dusts, many of whom "do not realize the danger to which they are exposed." Just as it had pioneered factory safety inspections in the 1870s, Massachusetts broke new ground by entering the area of monitoring health risks.[2]

Subsequent efforts in three other states proved to be more extensive and intensive. Investigations in Illinois, New York, and Ohio all gathered a wealth of data on both emerging and well-entrenched hazards. The first of these got underway in Illinois in 1909. The key figure in this inquiry was Alice Hamilton, not only the mother of American occupational medicine but also arguably the grandmother of the right-to-know movement. A veteran of Chicago's Hull House settlement, Hamilton later became the first woman to hold a faculty position at Harvard. She brought both a Progressive reformist sensibility, with its faith in bureaucratic structures and processes, and a commitment to rigorous fieldwork to her role as the chief investigator for the Illinois Commission on Occupational Diseases. Focusing her energies on the preeminent hazard of lead poisoning, she visited 304 workplaces, several health-care institutions, and countless workers' homes. She found that immigrant men comprised the majority of the thousands of workers inhaling and ingesting lead on the job across about twenty industries and trades. In her autobiography, *Exploring the Dangerous Trades*, Hamilton reflected on the makeup of the contingent that applied enamel to bathtubs and other sanitary ware: "They were almost always foreigners, Bulgarians, Serbs, Poles, Italians, Hungarians, who had come to this country in the search for a better life." She learned that in many instances management gave employees neither warnings about the threat they faced nor guidance about avoiding that threat. Based on conversations with managers, she attributed much of this failing to the managers' own lack of knowledge: "We found . . . a very general ignorance of the hygiene of the lead trades on the part of the employers. In Europe and England employers have been carefully trained in industrial hygiene, but here they have been taught nothing." The labor force in smelters, paint shops, storage battery plants, and white-lead factories followed the pattern of recent arrivals from agrarian societies. Hamilton told a joint session of the American Economic Association and the American Association for Labor Legislation in December 1910 that "only the most ignorant and helpless foreigners seek employment in the white lead or lead smelting works." For the notorious white-lead production facilities, she urged the posting of "simple instructions in different languages," a suggestion she reiterated for other contaminated working environments. She characterized as merely the tip of the iceberg the total of 578 cases of lead-induced disease discovered by various methods. Her own examinations of 148 Slavic enamelers determined that almost two-thirds had a definite or probable diagnosis of lead poisoning. Hamilton noted that "the majority of physicians keep no record of their cases; some do not even attempt to keep the names if these are foreign and hard to catch." This formative experience much strengthened her dedication to advocacy for the most vulnerable migrant laborers. The experience also forged an abiding commitment to the worker's right to know about health risks. Based on her interactions with lead-exposed cut-glass workers, she maintained, "It is essential that the workmen understand what it is they are using, and for this purpose simple statements explaining the facts should be displayed."[3]

Hamilton's coworkers pursued hazards other than lead that menaced the workforce in Illinois. The physician Emery Hayhurst's visits to eighty-nine brass foundries involved inspections of conditions and roughly two hundred interviews with workers and managers. Those inspections produced evidence of widespread intoxication with the disorder commonly known as the brass chills or brass shakes, a problem caused by inhalation of metal fumes. Hayhurst's tour of zinc smelters similarly brought to light the prevalence of the neuromuscular ailment called the smelter shakes, which resulted from uncontrolled air contamination. The workforce in both industries was largely composed of international migrants. Hayhurst concluded that very few of the Polish men who dominated the smelter crews spoke or understood English. This obviously posed an obstacle to ascertaining the presence and nature of occupational disease. The communication barrier also posed an obstacle to determining the state of the workers' knowledge of the risks they faced. Unlike his colleague Hamilton, who attempted to surmount these difficulties, Hayhurst apparently failed to delve into the extent to which English-speaking managers understood hazards and warned their subordinates of them. The same disregard for this question of knowledge and ignorance characterized the investigation of painters' gastrointestinal and respiratory illnesses resulting from turpentine exposure, a study in which Hayhurst also participated. In contrast, when Walter Haines, Matthew Karasek, and George Apfelbach inspected five steel mills around Chicago, they called attention to the efforts of management, especially at Illinois Steel Company (a US Steel Corporation subsidiary) to educate employees about threats by use of oral and printed messages. At the massive South Works of Illinois Steel, the warning signs around furnaces and other areas where carbon monoxide lurked appeared in English, Hungarian, Russian, Polish, and Czech. The report by Karasek and his wife Stella Karasek on the injurious effects of the hazards of photoengraving called attention to dermatological conditions caused by chromic acid and instances of acute cyanide poisoning. The Karasek team criticized the fact that in the forty photo studios evaluated, "there were no posters, instructions or warnings to the employees regarding poisonous and dangerous chemicals; neither were labels present on any of the bottles containing potassium cyanide or other chemicals used."[4]

The report sent to the governor by the Illinois Commission on Occupational Diseases in January 1911 embraced a right-to-know perspective to a considerable extent. To be sure, the commission declared a preference for controlling health hazards more systematically through engineering controls such as ventilation and enclosure. Nonetheless, it asserted the value of greater dissemination of information, insisting that "much can be accomplished by the wide publication and posting in shops of the dangers attending particular processes of manufacture and the best means of preventing injuries." The commission's secretary, University of Chicago professor Charles Henderson, made clear that union leaders had requested "brief, plain, practical directions for the working men in different trades so that they may be able to avoid disease." Thus, the group put forth a few recommendations for the display of warning posters and the issuance of instructions on recognizing and avoiding health risks.

The commission couched its recommendation for further investigation of the occupational disease problem in dark terms. "A policy of concealment and of obstinacy in willful ignorance," the commissioners warned insinuatingly, "is a folly unworthy of our noble commonwealth." They maintained that the public interest required that "evil and harmful conditions shall be brought to light, that workmen may be taught their dangers."[5]

The Illinois commission's report went into some detail in specifying the ameliorative measures sought. Its draft occupational disease law required the posting of hazard warning notices in conspicuous places and that notices contain information on methods of preventing disease. The provision on notices also mandated that "in addition to English they shall be printed in such other language or languages as may be necessary to make them intelligible to the employees." This proposal for multilanguage messages picked up on the suggestions made by Hamilton and her fellow investigators as well as the established practice of US Steel, a prominent and prestigious firm. Such a commitment was not unprecedented in Illinois public policy. In 1909, the state had enacted a law requiring that "poisonous and noxious fumes or gases and dust injurious to health, arising from any process, shall be removed as far as practicable." Although "practicable" was a term vague enough to undercut the law's impact, of relevance here is the requirement that notices spelling out the basic provisions of the act in languages other than English be posted in workplaces. The commissioners' report suggested warning notices, albeit only in English, for both employers and employees that addressed various lead hazards. The reformers indicated that these could serve as templates for delivering guidance on other hazards. Illinois legislators immediately passed a bill that charged employers with the responsibility of displaying multilanguage signs to apprise their labor force of the dangers of lead and other toxic substances. But with a sizable share of immigrant workers illiterate in their native languages, this measure could have only limited effectiveness. Taken together, however, the actions of the Illinois commission constituted significant beginning steps toward the democratizing of access to occupational health hazard information.[6]

A catastrophic fire in the Triangle Shirtwaist Factory in New York City on March 25, 1911, prompted a systematic state evaluation of working conditions across the state. This evaluation soon extended far beyond the issue of fire safety. As in Illinois, the New York State Factory Investigating Commission found itself dealing largely with the inordinate risks of industrialization borne by those newly arrived from preindustrial homelands. Without the funds needed to conduct medical screening of large numbers of workers and former workers, the staff of the commission focused on the types of disease that exhibited unmistakable, distinctive symptoms and disorders that could produce valid reports from either the victims themselves or other nonmedical observers. This orientation placed lead and the other heavy metals at the center of attention.[7]

New York State harbored an abundance of lead hazards. An investigative crew led by the economics professor Edward Pratt inspected several lead-filled establishments in New York City where immigrants from southern and eastern Europe were joined by a contingent of men of African descent from Barbados. Some who understood the threat used bandanas or rags to try to intercept high concentrations of dust and fumes, with limited success. Pratt's group determined that workers took these protective actions even though their managers seldom gave them warnings in any form. These investigators learned that only seventeen of ninety poisoning victims had received any hazard instruction. Pratt concluded that "one of the things which must be done . . . in stamping out lead poisoning is to instruct the rank and file of workers in lead as to the danger of the poison in which they are working and the methods of prevention." At the commission's hearings in late 1911, the physician for the National Lead Company plant in Brooklyn contended that he had discovered few lead poisoning cases but conceded that he could not communicate with most of his patients. At one of the world's largest glass works, the investigators Charles Graham-Rogers and John Vogt observed in the manufacture of leaded glass that "none of the workers exposed to the danger are aware of it, and as they understand very little English, it is hard to make them understand." Graham-Rogers and Vogt found in their inspection tour that "in many instances the proprietors themselves are unaware of the presence of lead in the material used, or the danger therefrom." Management at a storage-battery production facility in Niagara Falls denied that there was intoxication among its largely foreign-born workforce of about three hundred. Yet the admission by the company's chief engineer W. L. Bliss that this "class of work isn't congenial to American taste" implied the existence of a possible problem.[8]

The Factory Investigating Commission's field staff, along with its witnesses at public hearings, illuminated the unhealthful conditions of exposure to a number of hazards besides lead and the general failure to alert employees to those hazards. Chemical manufacturing unleashed a host of perils, new and old, upon a workforce three-quarters of which had been born in either Italy or Poland. A review of working conditions and employment relations in 359 chemical factories led the commission to a dismal assessment: "In no other industry is a knowledge of the poisonous substances which are handled so necessary to the worker; but in no other industry is the ignorance of the worker as to the character of . . . substances with which he works so complete." George Price, the commission's director of investigation, excoriated those responsible for the plight of "the large number of unskilled, densely ignorant foreign laborers who are employed in extremely dangerous processes. Taking advantage of this ignorance of the worker and subjecting him to conditions fraught with fearful danger to his life may be characterized as the peculiar reproach of the chemical trade." Price maintained that these international migrants were "not regarded as 'white'" by their employers. His tour of dozens of production facilities left him convinced that warnings delivered in the workers' native languages were a rarity: "There is very little attempt made on the part of managers to instruct the foreign laborer in the dangers of the materials with which he works or the inevitable peril to his life consequent on certain processes. Very few printed notices or precautions are posted in the native languages of the workers." He believed any warnings came from an ulterior motive: "Whatever notices or cards are found in the chemical establishments do not seem to serve as a means of instruction, but rather as an extenuation for the manufacturer, placing the onus upon the employee in case of a suit for damages." Henry Carnegie testified that his job shoveling bleach into drums at Hooker Electro-Chemical Company subjected him to such intense doses of the respiratory irritant chlorine that he could only labor for brief intervals; spilled materials ate his shoes at the rate of a pair every week or two. Neither Carnegie nor two coworkers who also testified at hearings on October 4, 1912, received any hazard avoidance instructions from Hooker management. Vogt visited a site where the ancient poison arsenic was used by a staff of Polish, Italian, and Russian Jewish migrants to manufacture the colorant Paris green. The shop had neither a ventilation system nor any warning signs. The language barrier thwarted the attempt by Vogt and Graham-Rogers to ascertain whether exposure to the arsenic impurities in zinc was sickening the foreign-born workers in four galvanizing plants they visited. However, the investigators came away with the definite conclusion that workers were unaware of the risks involved. Vogt testified before the commission that a "policy of indifference and concealment" prevailed in the nascent chemical industry. The manager who oversaw production of muriatic acid at Niagara Alkali Company testified that his subordinates wrapped flannel around their mouths even though acid vapors posed no hazard to them. Commission investigators who toured his facility, however, found the air quality "unbearable for two minutes" and considered exposed workers "poorly protected." The physician Antonio Stella's work among immigrants gave him insight into one of the ways that problems remained somewhat concealed across a range of dusty occupations. Stella advised the commission that dust-generating industrial tasks gave his Italian, Greek, Slavic, and Spanish patients silicosis or silico-tuberculosis. He contended that remigration of the disabled to their homelands led to underestimation of the prevalence of these disorders.[9]

The lessons from the wealth of information gathered by the New York commission prompted a number of reform recommendations. Edward Pratt expressed doubt that more than 10 percent of lead-exposed workers could read warning signs, all of which were printed only in English. Pratt advocated for the display of multilanguage warning posters and that "some person acquainted with the languages of the various nationalities . . . personally interview each man and instruct him" in safe practices. Besides these corrective actions to be undertaken by employers, Pratt urged that the state Department of Labor launch "a campaign of education among the workers in industries in which lead in any form is used, by means of circulars printed in different languages and by means of talks and lectures before groups of workers in the factories and trade union meetings." His colleagues Price, Vogt, and Graham-Rogers concurred in these recommendations. The commission itself broadened this suggestion to encompass educational publications on other hazards as well. Perhaps more important, the commission proposed legislation for structural reforms to strengthen the capacity of the state labor department to expand the right to know.[10]

The New York legislature quickly put this progressive plan into law. The legislation of March 28, 1913, created a new Division of Industrial Hygiene with authority to investigate and regulate occupational health problems. The granting of direct general regulatory authority to state labor administrators was an important departure that facilitated the development of public policy and practice. Business owners had to post state regulations or digests thereof in hazardous locations, in whatever languages the authorities deemed appropriate. The reorganized Department of Labor was obligated to hire an inspector capable of speaking and writing in at least five languages other than English.[11]

In implementing this reform, the New York labor department embraced a firm commitment to disseminate hazard information. State Labor Commissioner James Lynch observed that the reform law meant that his department "should become a larger educational agent." Lynch welcomed the opportunity. To be sure, the fledgling efforts of the understaffed Division of Industrial Hygiene to deal with a few hazards brought no immediate transformative enlightenment in the endangered ranks. Nonetheless, Progressives in New York had managed to establish an important beachhead in the early stage of the struggle for transparency.[12]

The final major state study of the decade took place in Ohio in 1913 and 1914. The State Board of Health carried out this project, under the leadership of Emery Hayhurst, a veteran of the Illinois investigation. Field investigators, almost all of whom were physicians, evaluated conditions in more than one thousand establishments, mainly in the state's sprawling manufacturing sector.

The Board of Health reporting guidelines unfortunately conflated workers' mental capacity and their possession of knowledge in a way that put nativistic condescension out in the open. Staff were told to characterize "the type of workers, whether intelligent, responsible, and capable of understanding instructions or whether an ignorant and usually non-English speaking class." Despite this prejudice and other limiting factors, the survey did manage to throw a good deal of light on right-to-know matters related to hazard exposures and their health effects.[13]

The Ohio inquiry consistently pursued the question of whether management conveyed hazard information to at-risk employees. Of 43 iron foundries, where silicosis posed a common threat, only 8 delivered any disease-prevention instructions. No health warnings were given in 92 of 106 brass foundries, where lead commonly contaminated the working environment. Intermittent commentary on workforce composition adhered to the prescribed terminology, noting the presence of "more or less ignorant foreigners, non-English speaking" in many metal-grinding establishments, where managers in only 10 of 64 places gave any warnings. The Board of Health assessed risks at 25 junk-processing sites, 17 of which relied upon "ignorant foreigners" to endure exposure to lead and other toxic substances. "There were no instructions or health placards in any of the establishments," the state agents reported, "including those which brought the workers in contact with poisonous metals and fumes." The Hayhurst team did not explore the degree to which this failure to inform resulted from managerial lack of understanding of the hazard. They did not explain why most firms failed to inform their employees about serious, well-known risks. In the same vein, their review of 1,060 workplaces contained not a word of criticism of the substance of the health messages posted on any warning signs, even though investigators were charged with reporting "wrongful instructions." This oversight contrasted starkly with the numerous critical comments about employees' personal hygiene and other behavior.[14]

The Ohio assessors gained relatively little insight into the incidence of occupational diseases. Interviews with uninformed workers yielded evidence of symptoms but limited understanding of the causation of their illnesses. Here again, the language barrier operated to curtail the gathering of data. The State Board of Health did not take this opportunity to use its medical expertise to combat ignorance. The fieldworkers were instead forbidden to enlighten those being observed about the causes and nature of their problems. Hayhurst stated plainly that "investigators were carefully instructed . . . not to pass opinions upon working conditions to employees, nor to express to any employee who was questioned or examined any opinions concerning his or her state of health as determined by the physician-investigator." At least in part, this restriction may have stemmed from the fact that investigators were not authorized to conduct a thorough physical examination but instead had to confine themselves to cursory observations of the workers' appearance, usually an insufficient basis for an authoritative diagnosis. Superficial comments that a group of employees looked pale or unhealthy recurred in the survey report.[15]

Hayhurst's mandate from the Ohio General Assembly extended to making remedial recommendations. His report declined to advocate any strong legislative measures, such as banning certain uses of lead or requiring ventilation systems or other engineering controls. "As most of the problems concerned have to do with education and the creation through appeal and psychological means of a receptive and subsequently active state of mind of the masses concerned," he argued, "it does not appear that much legislation is necessary." In a sense, a vague commitment to education (for which Progressives had great, sometimes uncritical, enthusiasm) and increased receptivity became a means of deflecting interest away from more substantial reforms. The state's lawmakers had already provided an inviting opening for new right-to-know protections. In 1913, Ohio addressed the lead hazard by requiring that employers post warning signs in all the languages needed to reach their employees effectively and that they have interpreters hold monthly informational meetings on the dangers of lead. Extension of this precedent to arsenic, mercury, benzene, and other recognized threats would have been a natural move for Hayhurst at this juncture. Instead of support for using the force of law to help enlighten the diverse workforce in that way, this state health official placed his hopes for dissemination of information on a voluntaristic approach. The only recommendation relevant to mandatory production of knowledge of occupational disease was a proposal for reporting cases of occupational disease to the Board of Health. This idea drew on the long-established public health policy of requiring clinicians to make case reports of certain infectious diseases. By 1901, all states forced doctors to notify health authorities of cases of specified communicable disorders seen among their patients.[16]

Progressives had great confidence in the unique capability of scientific experts, in and out of government, to solve the social problems of industrializing America. Reacting to the recent report of the Illinois commission, the University of Iowa economics professor Paul Peirce envisioned organized scientism bringing societal enlightenment: "It is to agencies such as these—commissions, clinics, medical inspectors, and compulsory examinations and reports—and to the wide-spread publicity of their findings that we must look for guidance toward the prevention of unnecessary industrial disease." The American Medical Association hastened to agree with Peirce's prescription. Reformers considered the ignorance of occupational health hazards exhibited by the medical profession and by state agents to be especially troubling. Hayhurst's support for mandatory reporting of cases aimed to tackle those deficiencies by utilizing a standard public health procedure to orient the medical profession to the existence of an underrecognized issue. By the time of the issuance of the Ohio survey report, a national campaign led by the American Association for Labor Legislation (AALL) was well under way for obligatory reporting by physicians of their cases of major occupational disorders. An affiliate of the International Association for Labor Legislation, the AALL saw as an integral part of its mission the importation of European reforms. In this case, Great Britain's adoption in 1895 of a legal requirement for physicians to report lead, phosphorus, and arsenic poisoning and anthrax served as the exemplar of progress. Six years later, the British parliament added mercury poisoning to the list. Discussion at the association's December 1910 annual meeting noted the unfortunate extent of medical ignorance that the Illinois commission had recently discovered and the cost of that ignorance. The group decided to promote a model bill as one of its top legislative priorities. The AALL proposition sought to make reportable the five conditions enumerated in Britain, as well as compressed air illness.[17]

The following year, six states—Connecticut, New York, California, Michigan, Illinois, and Wisconsin—adopted this measure, or slight variations thereof. None of these laws limited access to the information thus provided, opening the possibility that knowledge might trickle down to workers and their unions. In recounting the recent successes, John Andrews, the association's secretary, indicated that one of the aims of the legislation was "to secure for public use a regular supply of information from those who should be best informed upon the subject." Andrews expressed hope that the governmental agents would supplement this data by following up with investigations of the disorders revealed. He also appealed to the medical profession to use its unique potential to create broader societal understanding. His article in the April 15, 1911, issue of the *Journal of the American Medical Association* shrewdly relied on one of the profession's own authorities: "'Medical men alone,' said Dr. William Hanson of the Massachusetts Board of Health, 'are in a position to make the best use of facts obtained concerning the sanitary conditions of premises where men and women work; . . . and to collect and make proper use of all facts and data, including morbidity and mortality statistics, pertaining to occupational hygiene.'" Two more states—New Jersey (where the state federation of labor instigated reform) and Maryland—passed disease-reporting legislation in 1912.[18]

Beyond the behavior of individual clinicians in private practice, Progressives looked to systematic action by organizational players. Faith in modern organizations (generally government, academic, and corporate bureaucratic structures) as appropriate agents for producing and distributing scientific knowledge guided this endeavor. In 1912, W. Gilman Thompson, a professor of medicine at Cornell University Medical College who would soon publish a pioneering textbook in the field, urged not only further education of physicians in the recognition of occupational disease but also a more inclusive initiative targeting rank-and-file chemical workers. Thompson encouraged the New York Section of the American Chemical Society to have its member firms provide danger signs and printed directions for handling toxic chemicals and that they set up workers' committees to help implement the educational program. At the same time, Andrews nudged the New York Department of Labor to publish and distribute "short industrial disease leaflets for workers" and assured his contact in the department that Thompson and his colleagues "would be very glad to prepare the leaflets." Proceeding simultaneously on a separate track, the AALL's Committee on Industrial Diseases started preparing its own leaflets and other literature.[19]

Unions were one component of civil society that reformers understood could play a pivotal role in expanding workers' knowledge. In 1909, C.-E. A. Winslow challenged organized labor to do more to inform its membership. In Winslow's view, the unions had "almost wholly failed to grasp the magnificent opportunity, which should be theirs, of bringing to the individual worker that knowledge of sanitary science which will enable him . . . to maintain a maximum of health and efficiency." George Price played a singular role in helping the labor movement take on this issue. Price came to the New York State Factory Investigating Commission from the Joint Board of Sanitary Control, a novel institution set up to deal with health and safety issues in New York City's garment industry. The board was the outcome of demands of the International Ladies Garment Workers Union, a group whose membership base was largely comprised of immigrants from eastern and southern Europe, especially Jews and Italians. Under the auspices of the Joint Board of Sanitary Control, Price gave workplace lectures on industrial poisons and factory sanitation. In addition, Andrews sought out physicians to make presentations on industrial hygiene to labor organizations.[20]

Progressives looked to company doctors as the contingent within the medical profession with the most potential for delivering hazard information to rank-and-file workers. Social reformers in the early twentieth century had inordinate faith in the ability of professional expertise to mediate class relations, and this faith extended to medical expertise in the industrial setting. The period witnessed considerable growth in the number of physicians and surgeons serving either directly on the staff of business firms or as contractors with them. Delivery of health services by employers constituted one component of a welfare capitalist system that expanded the employment relationship through the provision of a wide range of goods and services—housing, recreational facilities, pensions, profit sharing, and much else. The risk-filled transportation, extractive, and manufacturing sectors in particular added medical professionals to render curative, screening, and preventive services. Delivery of each of these types of service afforded opportunities to inform workers of their exposure to health threats and how they might avoid those threats.[21]

The challenges for the company doctors often began with their own ignorance. Without any specialized training in occupational medicine, these practitioners generally had much to learn about the nature and causes of the ailments presented by their patients. Harry Mock, medical director at Sears, Roebuck and Company, acknowledged the deficiencies of many supposed specialists, who frequently had no awareness of even prevalent and well-known work-induced diseases such as lead poisoning. "Ignorance such as this," Mock complained in 1919, "is inexcusable.... Unfortunately, the reputations of many company physicians in the past have been of the lowest standard professionally." His assessment of the standing of this group was shared by Alice Hamilton, who contended that "for a surgeon or physician to accept a position with a manufacturing company was to earn the contempt of his colleagues." To help uplift his fellows to competence and respectability, Mock produced a major textbook. His *Industrial Medicine and Surgery* contributed both an overview of occupational diseases and basic guidance for conducting a practice in this embryonic specialty. The tome offered a short checklist on the dispensing of hazard warnings: "Have you carefully instructed the management and employees in all hazards represented by their work and the best means of prevention? Are new employees instructed in the same before going to work?" Alerting the newly hired obviously dealt most straightforwardly with the paramount aim of primary prevention of disease.[22]

Their place in the managerial structure of the firm sometimes made it difficult for company doctors to share information. The main tasks of most doctor-managers were performing preemployment and periodic screening examinations and reviewing the cases of sick employees. Notifying those examined of a diagnosis of an occupational disease and suggesting ameliorative steps to limit or reverse the condition constituted the main teaching moment available. In these situations, a fundamental tension existed between divulging and concealing information, especially regarding employees who might use diagnostic reports as evidence in lawsuits or workers' compensation claims. At an eastern lead smelter that Alice Hamilton toured as a federal consultant, she met a company doctor who viewed his immigrant patients with contempt and was "always ready to fend off a damage suit by certifying that the victim had heart disease." She maintained that in general in her early experience "secrecy was ... part of the doctor's loyalty to his employer. Of course, I found this to be a very great obstacle. It was not only secrecy toward the men, but toward the public and toward me." Hamilton's interactions with company physicians in places that made the toxic explosive trinitrotoluene (TNT) left her dismayed. In contrast with the information sharing of physicians associated with Britain's Ministry of Munitions, US physicians were "for the most part ignorant and indifferent, or secretive at the behest of their employers, who thought that frankness might frighten the men away." Josephine Bates of the National Civic Federation found that two medical contractors stopped getting patient referrals after they told victims of mercury poisoning the real cause of their maladies and advised them to avoid further exposure. Hamilton and Bates lent credence to the cynical view that the company doctor's real patient was the company. Hamilton's brand of Progressivism plainly did not embrace the naïve view that reformers could somehow ignore class interest.[23]

Yet a fraction of these managerial agents overcame or overlooked their employer's interest in nondisclosure. Some practitioners operated in organizations that tolerated or even embraced a measure of transparency. The policy of Norton Company, an abrasives manufacturer with a state-of-the-art program, was to share diagnostic information with the dust-exposed employees regularly examined. Under its standard procedure, Norton physicians even advised workers whose health was somewhat compromised to leave their jobs. The American Telephone and Telegraph physician C. H. Watson endorsed sending examination findings to the employee's own doctor. The Life Extension Institute in New York City promoted its screening services to businesses as a modern efficiency measure and maintained that annual employee examinations were as necessary as "inspection of other machinery." The institute reported outcomes not only to its corporate clients but also to the physician designated by the individual examined for major problems or directly to the examinee for minor problems.[24]

Government officials promoted disclosure of medical evidence. The US Public Health Service (PHS) endorsed an open approach by company physicians. The PHS surgeon Joseph Schereschewsky announced in 1914 that major industrial enterprises were accepting a "duty to minimize the effects of ignorance and carelessness in the production of sickness." Schereschewsky believed that proper medical management should extend to advising workers of their physical condition. His colleague C. D. Selby concurred. At the 1918 meeting of the National Safety Council, Selby counseled that "personal talks, especially with the findings of physical examinations, are well received by working people and tend more to impress them than lectures or health bulletins." In a frank characterization based on his survey of 170 plants, Selby described industrial medicine as "a compromise between the ideals of medicine and the necessities of business." The New York Department of Labor in 1916 publicized the British policy that gave lead-exposed workers access to the results of their mandatory annual medical examinations.[25]

Any notification of diagnoses of occupational disease and concomitant hazard control messages usually came as a secondary outcome of employee medical examinations. A much larger concern with nonoccupational disorders animated most such practices. To be sure, a host of illnesses and disabilities that were entirely or at least partly unrelated to work did plague the American labor force in this period, and health information on these conditions was certainly warranted. Even physicians like George Price, who had great sympathy for the precarious plight of workers new to industrialism, pressed the need to encourage personal habits that helped to curb infectious disease. But warnings about hazards lurking in the workplace environment were sometimes drowned out by advice about personal cleanliness, irresponsible spitting, alcohol consumption, and poor eating habits. Thomas Darlington, a physician with the American Iron and Steel Institute, did his best to shift the focus in a 1918 presentation: "Personally I do not believe much in occupational diseases. . . . Phosphorus and lead have been spoken of on many occasions as the most important occupational diseases. In the prevention of such diseases the thing of most importance is the care of the man himself, his personal hygiene, his home, and his surroundings." Darlington held that teaching workers to brush their teeth would help them prevent heart disease and advocated sending nurses into employees' homes to provide instructions. He asserted that proper handwashing would virtually eliminate lead poisoning. Close attention to self-care amounted to a crusade for Darlington. As a prominent spokesperson for a major industry, he exerted considerable professional influence. The Conference Board of Physicians in Industrial Practice, organized by leading corporate medical men in 1914, promoted a similar agenda. The board published a series of brief, simple "Health Hints" on personal habits, such as proper methods of breathing. This series was not supplemented by one on the prevention of any occupational diseases, including those incurred while breathing toxic dusts, fumes, or gases on the job.[26]

At the worksite, where services actually took place, many company doctors shared this perspective. C. E. Ford, chief surgeon at General Chemical Company, lectured on sexually transmitted diseases but apparently not on dangerous industrial chemicals. A survey of seventy industrial physicians conducted by a team led by Michael Davis as part of the Carnegie Corporation's Americanization Study found that only six of the practitioners concerned themselves with occupational disease among immigrant workers. In contrast, twenty-two dealt with housing matters, twelve with food habits, and ten with personal hygiene.

Davis worried that the language barrier kept company physicians, nurses, and managers from conveying to international migrants the importance of "careful personal habits and cleanliness" in resisting workplace poisons.[27]

In some circumstances, company doctors reductively explained the causation of disorders like lead poisoning, where a mix of environmental and behavioral factors could be at work, as simply the fault of the poisoning victim. Alice Hamilton questioned the judgment of her corporate colleagues: "Strangely enough, in the United States both physicians and laymen connected with lead-smelting plants almost invariably lay far greater stress on the danger of uncleanliness on the part of the workman than on anything in his surroundings." She wondered how men who spent all day "working in clouds of dust . . . are supposed to get leaded from eating their lunch without washing their hands and faces." In her autobiography, she recalled employers' willing embrace of this convenient, medically authorized exoneration: "Many times in the early days I met men who employed foreign-born labor because it was cheap and submissive, and then washed their hands of all responsibility for accidents and sickness in the plant, because, as they would say: 'What can you do with a lot of ignorant Dagoes, Wops, Hunkies, Greasers? You couldn't make them wash if you took a shotgun to them.'" In an individualistic society experiencing a massive influx of workers from poor countries, the dominant theme easily became one of patronizing victim blaming. Adding further weight to this perspective was the widespread belief that germ-infected lower-class immigrants threatened the health of respectable native-born members of society. As Mark Aldrich has observed, with the passage of workers' compensation laws, claims of employee negligence no longer carried legal weight, and it became necessary to rely on education to enforce a sense of victim responsibility. Aldrich also insightfully points out, "No doubt the doctrine that workers were careless . . . meshed nicely with some employers' social Darwinian views and ethnic prejudices." In this context, concentration on personal hygiene often displaced or trivialized industrial hygiene.[28]

Instruction in the English language was another common component of American welfare capitalism in the early twentieth century. Many leading firms where non-English speakers constituted a substantial fraction of the workforce launched language programs. In a large share of cases, the primary incentive was to give international migrants a new sense of national identity and a willingness to become loyal US citizens. And like all other aspects of corporate paternalism, this one aimed to create loyalty to the employer. But Americanizers in the business world also aimed to promote health and safety by improving workers' comprehension of written and oral messages. Mobilization for World

War I and especially the loss of labor to the military draft intensified interest in any program that helped to conserve scarce human resources.[29]

Development of workers' English proficiency attacked a sizable problem. The chorus of commentary in the three state investigations about the difficulties experienced by managers, physicians, and the investigators themselves in communicating with workers in hazardous jobs illuminated a prevalent dangerous situation. In 1911, the US Immigration Commission reported that only slightly more than half of foreign-born employees in manufacturing and mining could speak English. The issue increasingly came to be seen in broader terms: a significant fraction of the immigrant working class was illiterate even in its own native language. Multilanguage warning signs would not reach workers in this predicament. Of the 1,400,000 white immigrants over the age of ten in Pennsylvania in 1910, one-third could not speak English and one-fifth were illiterate in any language. Marion Clark reported in 1918 that only half the approximately 1,600,000 immigrant factory workers in New York could either speak or comprehend the dominant language, and one-quarter were illiterate in their homeland's language. Speaking on "Americanization and Safety" at a state-sponsored safety conference, Clark promoted language training as a "sound business investment" and proposed that every industrial establishment conduct English classes.[30]

Along with public and private schools and various other institutions, many employers taught English to immigrant workers either during or after working hours. International Harvester Company conducted language classes as early as 1904. American Car and Foundry ran separate night sessions for Italians and Slavs at its Berwick, Pennsylvania, operations, enrolling about two hundred students. The state Department of Labor and Industry promoted the railroad equipment manufacturer's program as "combining Americanization with Safety First." Solvay Process Company, an upstate New York chemical manufacturer, gave overall control of its Americanization project to its safety engineer. As might be expected, the Solvay project included an English-language component laden with safety messages. Employers' messages commonly emphasized personal responsibility. One typical lesson for Massachusetts leather workers conveyed this alert: "I must wash my hands and gloves often. If I leave lime on my hands, it will burn me. Handling wet hides makes the floor wet and slippery. If I am not careful, I may slip and fall." Nineteen of the twenty-four lessons in this teaching guide deal with employee carelessness. If nothing else, pupils in their employers' courses learned that individual responsibility was central to Americanization.[31]

The Ford Motor Company created the best-known workplace initiative. The firm started its English School after determining that, to communicate effectively with its diverse army of employees, it would have to translate safety materials into forty-two languages. In 1914, Ford brought in Peter Roberts to install an instructional plan for personnel at its main plant in Highland Park, Michigan. Roberts had become a prominent practitioner in the field by inventing a system used at hundreds of branches of the Young Men's Christian Association (YMCA) and numerous firms, including International Harvester. His system proceeded from the premise that in the context of a polyglot and often illiterate workforce, "the only rational solution of the difficulty is to teach all foreigners employed in hazardous industries enough English to enable them to understand simple instruction, to read simple warnings, and to communicate [with] one with another." His perspective aligned closely with that of Ford management. The company aggressively recruited students for the Roberts program. Inserts in pay envelopes displayed a paternalistic tone: "This School was established for your benefit, and you should be glad of [sic] this opportunity. You must . . . be able to read the safety signs about the plant. There is no excuse for your remaining away from school." In three years, this educational intervention cut the share of Ford workers who could not speak English from 35 percent to 12 percent. The automaker's program served as a model for many others. Detroit employers launched an "English First" initiative, sometimes run by company safety committees. The National Americanization Committee seized on the Detroit developments to proclaim that the movements for English First, Safety First, and America First were synergistically interrelated. Far-reaching publicity hailed the sizable decline in workplace injuries since its implementation. In his 1920 overview *Schooling of the Immigrant*, the product of a study supported by the Carnegie Corporation, Frank Thompson, superintendent of public schools in Boston, lauded the tight focus at the English School: "The Ford classes have emphasized the industrial efficiency aim, such objectives as 'safety first' and ability to understand instructions, more than the citizenship ideal." Workplace language curricula concentrated on prevention of injuries, which were newly covered by workers' compensation laws, not prevention of illnesses, which seldom received coverage under those laws in the 1910s. Nonetheless, gains in English comprehension gave workers the ability to grasp oral and written warnings about health hazards as well.[32]

There was relatively little traffic on Ford's English-only road. Some proponents of Safety First in the business community did reject multilanguage messaging, demanded that all workplace communication be in the dominant American language, and insisted that the foreign-born learn it. A number of members of the emerging cohort of personnel management specialists tested the ability of job applicants to read safety signs and rejected those who failed that test. In 1919, however, when the National Conference on Americanization in Industries, an event attended largely by representatives of industrial companies, voted on the question of requiring employees to attend English classes, the result was one hundred to eight against such a requirement.[33]

Public policy in Pennsylvania did embrace the single-language method in one respect. To be sure, in 1913 Pennsylvania enacted legislation requiring that employers alert workers about lead hazards and how to escape them by posting signs in all languages relevant to the composition of their workforce. But in 1917, the state promulgated a regulation requiring that all members of a workgroup, including the supervisor, be able to speak the same language. The main practical meaning of this rule was to force non-English-speaking workers to conform with the language of their English-speaking superior. The Pennsylvania Industrial Board accompanied the issuance of the regulation with a recommendation that employers encourage those lacking English proficiency to enroll in night classes. The Americanization Bureau of the Pennsylvania Council of National Defense supported wartime mobilization by distributing a syllabus that contained a lesson devoted to deciphering warning signs. This privileging of English-language competency reinforced ethnic segregation in the workplace, with bilingual low-level managers overseeing crews composed of immigrants who shared one native tongue. Pennsylvania officials applied this policy to specific health hazards. They gave employers an obligation to warn workers exposed to the dangerous industrial chemical benzene but avoided declaring any duty to communicate in languages other than English. Similarly, when the Industrial Board put forth standards governing the toxic materials used in making explosives, they imposed no obligation for oral or written communication in multiple languages. Notwithstanding the limitations of this stance, a senior official of the Pennsylvania Department of Labor and Industry insisted that "all workers should be cautioned concerning the hazard of their employment and instructed how to avoid this hazard" in discussing industrial disease in 1922.[34]

Policymakers and public administrators in other jurisdictions departed from the restrictive approach. As previously discussed, the revelations of the investigating commissions in Illinois, New York, and Ohio all immediately brought forth legislative enactments requiring that notices about occupational disease hazards appear in languages appropriate for all those exposed. The AALL's Standard Bill on occupational disease prevention called for this policy. Besides the action taken in Pennsylvania in 1913, at least two other states pursued that strategy as well. The New Jersey legislature in 1914 made employers post signs "in English and in such other languages as the circumstances may reasonably require" that warned of lead hazards and advised as to methods of hazard avoidance. In addition, the law ordered managers to explain the hazards and their avoidance to all employees entering lead-exposed jobs, with "interpreters being provided by the employer, when necessary." In 1916, the Massachusetts State Board of Labor and Industries moved to protect workers exposed to benzene derivatives and explosives by publishing a regulation that demanded the display of notices "in language intelligible to all the workers." This regulation required, among other things, that notices identify the common name of the substance present, indicate the signs and symptoms of poisoning, and provide guidance for disease prevention. This modest reform addressed only one category of hazards and thus did not go so far as a plan suggested four years earlier by the health inspector M. G. Overlock. Overlock proposed that Massachusetts officials create a series of leaflets on a range of industrial disease risks, to be "printed in the several languages used by the employees in the different industries" and distributed by unions.[35]

While encouraging attainment of English proficiency, American firms devised varied modes of communication that went beyond rigid insistence on monolingualism. Both line managers and safety and health staff used various methods to reach their non-English-speaking employees, even when not compelled by law to do so. Foremen and other low-level supervisors learned a smattering of their subordinates' languages or identified an employee to provide translations of warning messages. Some companies sent English-language literature home with employees and counted on the immigrants' children to translate it. Films, slideshows, photographs, and drawings helped to surmount linguistic barriers by illustrating hazardous situations and how to deal with them. The Pennsylvania Railroad relied on slideshows and motion pictures to teach safety to its thousands of Italian-born track maintenance workers. In an appeal to company doctors at a 1917 conference, Alice Hamilton explained that "pictures can be understood by all nationalities." Desperate managers occasionally resorted to gestures or pantomiming to deliver information. The efficacy of these efforts is unclear but was in all probability quite limited.[36]

Beyond piecemeal actions and makeshift improvisations, some employers of endangered workers undertook substantial programs of multilanguage messaging. Cleveland-Cliffs Iron Company printed the safety rule book given to all workers in English, Italian, and Finnish, as did other industrial enterprises. One chemical manufacturer regularly placed warnings written in English, Italian, and Polish in its employees' pay envelopes. The Workmen's Compensation Service Bureau put out a reference volume to guide its corporate clients in preparing signs to warn of dangerous gases and fumes "in [a] language (or languages) understood by all employees." After hearing in 1916 that English-language materials sometimes worked for only a minority of employees, the National

Safety Council produced publications in other languages. However, the council's announcement the following year that its bulletin-board literature was now available in seventeen languages received one cold response. Joseph Schereschewsky of the PHS considered it in the best interests of non-English speakers "not to give them the opportunity for perpetuating their native speech but make them understand that now is the time to become true American citizens and learn the language of this country." Amid wartime patriotic fervor, encouragement of multilingualism was bound to be controversial.[37]

In addition to varied communication strategies and tactics, many employers in the early twentieth century did recognize the inevitable limitations of attempts to prevent disease and trauma by giving out warnings. These business organizations implemented more systematic hazard controls that sometimes obviated the need for dissemination of hazard information. Rather than rely on delivery of imperfect explanations of risks, enlightened management in some firms strove to reengineer the workplace by installing mechanical ventilation, enclosing hazardous processes, and taking other constructive measures. Less farsighted managers put in controls when ordered to do so or otherwise encouraged by public authorities. At a health and safety conference in Syracuse in 1917, Royal Meeker, head of the US Bureau of Labor Statistics (BLS), advised explosives manufacturers that "there are mechanical devices . . . which make it well-nigh impossible for an employee, whether he can read and write and understand the English language or not" to get poisoned by TNT. In his presentation at a 1919 Americanization conference sponsored by the US Department of the Interior, the PHS sanitarian Bernard Newman emphasized technological protections against the threat of occupational diseases, which he contended did more harm to immigrant workers than did traumatic injuries.[38]

Alice Hamilton passed up no chance to promote engineering controls. Both in conversations in the course of her fieldwork and in her reports for the state of Illinois and then for the federal government, Hamilton emphasized those firms that had redesigned their production technology. Hamilton convinced the Pullman Company to curtail the use of lead-based paints on its sleeping and dining cars, replacing those formulations with innocuous or at least less toxic ones. She noted the phasing out of a process of curing rubber goods that involved the dangerous solvent carbon disulfide. She advertised the installation of enclosed, mechanized equipment and the proliferation of wet methods of dust control in lead smelters and refineries. She thus publicized the existence of effective, practicable control measures. Her reliance on invidious comparisons applied moral suasion to laggard employers. While observing the technological improvements present in most lead smelters and refineries, Hamilton characterized two exceptionally dusty facilities as exhibiting "carelessness in management," subverting the careless-worker trope so beloved by many in management. Across many industries, ventilation systems swept away airborne gases, dusts, mists, and fumes before they entered employees' respiratory systems. Increasing substitution of nontoxic materials for toxic ones simply eradicated hazards. From early on, there was in some quarters a recognition that eliminating hazards was better than explaining them.[39]

Any inclination to overcome communication difficulties by adopting engineering controls faced stiff ideological headwinds. The repetition of unfounded claims that most workplace injuries and illnesses resulted from employee carelessness gave cover to a shortsighted resort to minimal warnings about personal behavior, often poorly understood, that absolved employers of further responsibility. In her classic 1910 study *Work-Accidents and the Law*, the attorney Crystal Eastman analyzed 377 industrial accidents and discovered that the injured were wholly or partly at fault in only one-third of the cases. Lucian Chaney and Hugh Hanna of the BLS viewed victim blaming as partly "an ingrained notion inherited from the days when the slightest 'contributory negligence' barred the victim from recovery" of damages. Chaney added that the worker resented the "fundamental injustice in the emphasis placed upon his share in the responsibility for accident losses." Yet the conventional wisdom in management circles continued to concentrate on workers' negligence. In 1917, Arthur Young, director of the American Museum of Safety and a former steel executive, announced that "the general consensus of opinion is that perfection of mechanical safeguarding will contribute not over twenty-five percent of the attainable reduction of accidents." Young attributed most problems to misbehavior of the worker, whose lapses included "failing to wash dangerous dusts from his hands before eating." In a 1917 review of chemical hazards, L. A. DeBlois of E. I. DuPont de Nemours and Company acknowledged but downplayed the value of exhaust ventilation and closed systems. DeBlois, who lamented the prevalence of international migrants in his industry, held that in preserving employee health from toxic chemicals, "the greatest factor is undoubtedly personal cleanliness." From its founding in 1913, the National Safety Council devoted considerable resources to propounding the idea that workers were the main cause of their own difficulties. Victim blaming, which fell with particular force on immigrants and workers of color, undercut corporate decision makers' willingness to invest in promising engineered protections.[40]

United States Steel Corporation was the world's first billion-dollar corporation at its founding in 1901. It set an influential example of a strategy that attempted to balance technological changes with attempts to increase its employees' understanding of the dangers of their workplace. Beginning in 1906, this paragon of welfare capitalism expanded and institutionalized its occupational safety and, to a lesser extent, its occupational health activities. The firm created a hierarchical system of safety committees and a central Bureau of Safety, Sanitation and Welfare to oversee the program. Some observers considered this departure to be the commencement of the Safety First movement in American industry. In a discussion in 1912 about health hazards in the chemical industries, the physician W. Gilman Thompson hailed the steel corporation's work as exemplary and urged that its safety plan be adapted to combat health risks. The corporation certainly made no secret of its activities. At the first meeting of the group that would soon become the National Safety Council, the Illinois Steel attorney R. W. Campbell boasted of the work underway. At the same event, Robert Young, manager of the safety operation at the Illinois subsidiary, followed up by describing the actions targeting the roughly three-fifths of the US Steel workforce who were immigrants. In 1913, a member of the Wisconsin Industrial Commission predicted that within a year, almost all of his state's large manufacturers would have set up a safety organization in the mold of nation's largest steelmaker.[41]

From the outset, US Steel took a multifaceted approach, with a strong commitment to controlling hazards through investing in engineering measures. But management supplemented those advances with education and training programs. Across its many production facilities, the steelmaker used a variety of means to reach and discipline the sizable non-English-speaking fraction of its force regarding on-the-job health and safety risks. As previously noted, the Illinois Commission on Occupational Diseases applauded the company's deployment of multilanguage signs to warn of carbon monoxide hazards at the Illinois Steel South Works in Chicago. Hiring offices at all sites greeted job applicants with hazard warning signs in several languages. The company printed safety rule books in multiple languages. Management distributed the books to all employees and to priests in immigrant communities. Plant superintendents brought in interpreters to interrogate recently hired employees to determine if their supervisors had instructed them about their job hazards and how to avoid them. Although published only in English, the monthly safety bulletin carried "picture stories" of injury episodes. The firm ran English classes at a number of locations using the Roberts curriculum, which gave considerable attention to safety and health topics. The course offered at the National Tube plant in Lorain, Ohio, featured fourteen safety sessions. The general theme of all these communications was the imperative to avoid carelessness, reinforcing the placement of blame on the victim. In his contention that about 90 percent of accidents stemmed from a lack of care, Robert Young reflected the belief that shaped his firm's perspective and that of others in industrial management.[42]

In one innovative initiative, US Steel devised and disseminated a sign that aimed to transmit a hazard message wordlessly. The front cover of the August 1912 safety bulletin displayed a large red disk identified as "The Universal Danger Sign." The company announced that this symbol would now appear "on all warning signs to indicate danger, and for the especial benefit of the foreigner who cannot read. It is hoped this will become as significant as the Red Cross." This simple graphic marker could warn workers approaching an area with a health or safety hazard to stop and obtain additional information. Although undoubtedly of some utility in alerting illiterate steelworkers, the disk image did not achieve its sponsor's ambition of becoming a universally recognized meaningful symbol, one that rivaled the red cross. The steel industry's trade association, however, did embrace the image. The March 1913 issue of the American Iron and Steel Institute magazine featured a color illustration of a blue warning sign in four languages superimposed over the red disk. The National Association of Manufacturers and the American Museum of Safety promoted the circular symbol.[43]

The National Safety Council supported what they termed "the red ball" despite misgivings. At the 1916 annual meeting, a working group on danger signs prefaced its analysis with the acknowledgment that a mere warning emblem had severe limitations: "It is not sufficient to advise a man that danger exists, depending upon him to search for the source of the danger which is not always self-evident." This was a caveat that had particular relevance for minimal warnings about often-invisible health hazards. A survey of the organization's members found that most preferred the skull and crossbones long used on poison bottles. Those in the minority opposed this traditional image and had rejected it as too gruesome; somehow this led the subcommittee on danger emblems to dismiss the majority view. The alternative they proposed incorporated US Steel's red disk, even though the recommendation came after the concession that "the skull and crossbones is undoubtedly the more effective of the two." The recommendation also took no account of the recent invention and distribution by US Steel itself of an electrocution warning sign that contained the objectionable skull and bones. The council adopted as its official Universal Danger or Caution Emblem a design that placed a red disk within a white diamond with a black border and black vertical and horizontal cross lines. This general warning image achieved less than general or lasting acceptance. By the late 1920s, it appears that even the National Safety Council itself had set it aside.[44]

It is difficult to gauge the effects of the public and private efforts to expand workers' awareness of workplace hazards in the early twentieth century.

The Safety First drive took aim at traumatic injuries, not illnesses. The preoccupation with preventing accidents served to perpetuate the obscurity of threats of occupational disease. But increased attention to injury risks probably served to create a heightened sensitivity to risk, one that extended to disease. Government activity to promote broader knowledge of risks was confined to a few states and to a few severe hazards. In New York, the most ambitious information program of the period had limited impact in the near term. In 1919, the Division of Industrial Hygiene's review of the state's chemical industry came to this unhappy conclusion: "The average workman met with in certain chemical plants, in many cases, knows little or nothing of the nature or effect of the substances which he constantly handles, this ignorance being fostered by some manufacturers for the purpose of protecting their secrets from their competitors, or keeping the men in positions which they would refuse to hold if they realized the dangers of their occupations. Many of the materials are referred to only as 'dope,' 'stuff,' 'liquor,' or by initials which have no relation to the name or real composition of the material." Without doubt, the dissemination of a limited amount of warning information did not precipitate any significant movement within the working class, or the immigrant segment thereof, for a right to know more about these threats.[45]

For the minority of wage earners with union representation, some attempts to advance knowledge about work-induced disease did emerge during the Progressive Era. In both coal and metal mining, where international migrants comprised a majority of the workforce, organized labor fought for both workers' compensation and preventive measures to deal with pneumoconiosis in ways that raised consciousness of peril. The Brotherhood of Painters, Decorators, and Paperhangers distributed information on lead poisoning for the benefit of skilled workers in the construction sector. As previously discussed, the International Ladies Garment Workers Union engaged in significant educational activity. Two veterans of the garment workers' Joint Board of Sanitary Control, Harriet Silverman and Grace Burnham, went on in 1921 to found the Workers' Health Bureau. The bureau's primary function was to spread knowledge about occupational disease hazards among the membership of local unions. Agitation by the labor movement definitely brought with it some gains in awareness among the rank and file.[46]

The nonunion majority of the working class in the burgeoning manufacturing sector derived knowledge from varied sources beyond what it gleaned from managers' signs and instructions and government agents' publications. Experienced coworkers advised new hires in situations where they shared a common language. These veterans also shaped a workplace culture that gave rise to well-understood vernacular terms for occupational disorders. A 1913 reference volume advised that in places where dust inhalation from abrasives caused silicosis and silico-tuberculosis, "'grinder's rot,' 'grinder's asthma,' and 'grinder's consumption' are very familiar terms among the industries using grindstones." A Catholic priest whose parishioners included many Polish immigrants employed in the grinding department of a local industrial plant wove a bit of epidemiologically based vocational guidance into a sermon. The cleric encouraged these imperiled men to change jobs after observing that the church cemetery already held the remains of four hundred victims of grinding hazards. But in all probability, the main source of enlightenment for workers at risk was an unfortunate belated one—direct observation of their own and their fellow workers' ailing health.[47]

The strongest evidence of growing awareness among endangered workers comes from their behavior. The most common observable sign of increased knowledge was employee turnover as disease victims and potential victims fled from threats. The very low rates of employee retention in hazardous jobs were, in fact, one of the most frequently noted phenomena of the period. The Massachusetts State Board of Health reported in 1907 that Poles, Greeks, Armenians, and Syrians did not remain for long in tanneries where hides were coated in a nasty mixture of amyl acetate, naphtha, and wood alcohol. Alice Hamilton commented that the lead smelters where many Italian, Greek, and Slavic natives labored experienced monthly turnover of up to 25 percent. In 1916, Hamilton shared with the American Chemical Society her recent inspection of an explosives plant where nitrogen oxide had caused severe respiratory illness among the immigrant labor force. "So many were frightened and quit," she stated, "that the force used to change about every fortnight." Her report to the US Department of Labor on the explosives industry as a whole made clear that this was not an atypical situation. She revealed an industry-wide problem of retention among the immigrants and African Americans consigned to the most unhealthful positions. Hamilton also speculated on a perverse information-denying ramification of the turnover problem amid the tight wartime labor market: "In some plants no instruction at all seems to be given, perhaps for fear of frightening away the men at a time when labor is scarce." Emery Hayhurst's inspectors in Ohio discovered that laborers who produced rubber cement by stirring together benzene, carbon disulfide, and other toxic ingredients in open containers rarely stayed long on the job. "Many workers," Hayhurst reported, "refused to remain more than a day or two." Numerous female cigar makers in that state failed to return after one day exposed to nicotine-laden tobacco dust. In Ohio's lime-manufacturing operations, where immigrants and African Americans predominated, "the majority of the workers were of a changing character." Similar comments recurred throughout this report.[48]

Although the tendency to move on from hazardous jobs contradicted the representation of unskilled immigrants as stupid, nativist disdain colored some responses to this survival maneuver. The new cohort of international migrants was pejoratively dismissed as a "floating population" of drifters. DuPont's manager DeBlois complained that foreign-born employees were "not apt to be steady workers, and all this makes for difficulties in education." The same prejudice rationalized the mobility of African Americans. Hamilton's visit to a dilapidated white-lead plant in Saint Louis in 1911 elicited this observation: "There seems to be little concern for the health of the men, and it is taken for granted that the majority will quit after a few months. As most of them are Negroes this is attributed, not to illness, but to their natural shiftlessness." The churning of labor thus reinforced the stereotype of backward peasants and workers of color as too weak and undisciplined for the rigors of the modern workplace.[49]

High rates of turnover cut both ways regarding the growth of hazard knowledge. Employees who departed took away with them whatever lessons they had learned and left their superiors with the chore of educating their uninformed replacements. Managers who witnessed a steady stream of workers exiting their companies had little incentive to advise new employees unlikely to remain on the job very long, thus setting in motion a downward spiral that reproduced ignorance. When sick employees dropped off a firm's employee list, the company's medical professionals were denied opportunities to gather information from physical examinations or visits to worksite clinics. On the other hand, establishments with revolving doors gained unsavory reputations that gave potential employees enough information to act with caution and seek work elsewhere.[50]

Shortly after the publication of the landmark report of the Illinois Commission on Occupational Diseases, Hamilton's friend Florence Kelley asked her to share her insights with the National Conference of Charities and Corrections. Hamilton's review of the human costs of industrialism for this assemblage of social workers captured many of the dimensions of the toll of occupational health hazards. Besides the lack of knowledge exhibited by workers, employers, and others of this "great and sadly neglected problem of our day," she illuminated the broader reaches of the very general ignorance that prevailed. Her recollection of a visit to one industrial town that relied on recent immigrants cast the breadth of the problem in harsh light: "I do not believe that in any country the distance between peasant and noble is greater than is that between this army of homeless Greeks and Slavs housed in the company shacks of the smelting works, and the American citizen householder of the little town barely a mile away. . . . Perhaps this isolation of the industrial worker is not the only reason for our ignorance about the diseases of industry but certainly it is one reason." This Progressive leader saw that the ignorance about workplace hazards that extended to the general public and to her own well-meaning fellow social reformers was a matter of serious concern. This conscientious perspective, with its sense that professional experts needed to take responsibility for the most vulnerable groups in society, colored much of the incipient effort to extend workplace transparency in the early twentieth century.[51]

2
WIDER USE OF EXISTING KNOWLEDGE

> It is not so easy to understand why we have so long been in ignorance on the subject, why American physicians and sanitarians, to whom all other questions of preventable disease are matters of the greatest interest, should for so long have neglected industrial plumbism, which their colleagues on the other side of the water had so effectively controlled. After all, it is a question for the public health men to solve.
>
> —Alice Hamilton, 1914

When Alice Hamilton called on her colleagues in the American public health community to overcome their ignorance about lead poisoning so that they could move forward to prevent it, she came to them as a consultant to the newly established US Department of Labor (DoL). That is, she was neither an officer of nor an adviser to the nation's preeminent health institution, the US Public Health Service (PHS). Her affiliation was quite telling. That year, the PHS had moved to expand its work in the field of occupational health, an initiative that the service consolidated in 1919 with the creation of an Office of Industrial Hygiene and Sanitation. Yet Hamilton remained committed to the federal labor agency. Upon her retirement from Harvard in 1935, she spurned an offer of employment from the PHS and instead resumed her consulting work with the DoL. As a stalwart partisan for workers' health, Hamilton sided with the group she considered more likely to act forcefully.[1]

Highly respected and richly networked, Hamilton had the social and cultural capital to cross and disregard bureaucratic lines of division. But she stood out as remarkable, if not unique, in that capacity. Throughout the three decades of her consulting career, recurrent battles raged between heath and labor agents at the state and federal levels of government. The crucial engagement that commenced in 1935 has received the careful attention of the historians David Rosner and Gerald Markowitz. These scholars have captured the key distinction between the unabashedly proworker advocacy stance taken by the DoL and the more cautious focus on impartial research adopted by the PHS. The circumscribed purpose here is to explore the implications of this jurisdictional dispute for the availability of occupational health hazard information for workers themselves and their representatives. In exploring these implications, it will be advantageous to examine the history of bureaucratic conflict prior to the New Deal period that began in 1933 and to illuminate the ways that the conflict played out at the state level. The fresh infusion of resources to combat occupational disease provided in the Social Security Act decisively shaped policy and practice in the field for decades to come, but it did not represent a federal takeover. State-level actors remained critical in promoting or constraining the creation and flow of knowledge about hazards. Over the course of this period, proponents of expanding workers' access to information to a more significant extent cast their proposals and demands in terms of rights.[2]

The early involvement of the PHS with occupational and work-related disease was reactive. It was also belated. Although by the 1910s the United States had been engaged in intense industrialization for almost a century, the PHS and its predecessors had done almost no work in that area over that long time. Shortly after its birth in 1910, the US Bureau of Mines (BoM), which had no medical staff, asked the PHS for assistance. The bureau and the service forged what proved to be a durable partnership under which the latter assigned officers to conduct investigations in the extractive sector. Beginning with Special Investigator Samuel Hotchkiss's foray into western coal- and metal-mining districts in 1911, the PHS mounted a series of studies in the 1910s. The most important of these addressed the silicosis plague in hard-rock mining. The reports issued under PHS-BoM joint auspices introduced themes that would continue to be central to its messaging for the next three decades. In a presentation to the American Association for Labor Legislation (AALL) in December 1911, Hotchkiss declared, "Consideration of the subject of occupational diseases cannot confine itself to diseases distinctly attributable to the hazards of occupation. It must of necessity include a much broader field." Thus, Hotchkiss took only passing notice of silicosis, coal workers' pneumoconiosis (which he called "anthrocosis"), and lead poisoning and instead devoted attention to nonoccupational disorders like typhoid fever and hookworm disease. However admirable such breadth of vision might be in a general sense, in this context, it served to perpetuate inattention to a matter that had not received adequate scrutiny. What would sometimes become almost a perverse determination to trivialize the ostensible subject of inquiry appeared at the very outset.[3]

A second early theme that would become a prominent refrain was an inordinate emphasis on the role of miners' personal hygiene and other behavior in disease prevention. In line with views expressed by numerous other sources during the Progressive Era, PHS representatives dwelled on the responsibility of the individual to prevent disease by his or her own action. Here again, a valid truism was deployed with good intentions but with the unfortunate effect of undercutting the importance of more appropriate and systematic preventive measures. In 1916, at the first meeting of the American Association of Industrial Physicians and Surgeons, Joseph Schereschewsky encouraged attendees to assist employees who too often exhibited "indifference, neglect, or ignorance" in maintaining their own health. Schereschewsky held that company doctors were "able powerfully to influence and promote the education of workers in matters of personal hygiene." This claim elicited a skeptical response from George Price of the garment workers' Joint Board of Sanitary Control. Drawing on deep experience, Price warned that "education by the industrial physician is looked upon by employees with some distrust." In his report on health promotion in steel mills, James Watkins echoed his colleague Schereschewsky in suggesting that company doctors teach personal hygiene. However, Watkins provided not only a model pay-envelope insert that told steelworkers to "cut out the booze" but also another on the value of wearing respirators to limit inhalation of harmful dusts on the job. Others in the federal health service pointed out ways to curtail defective habits and to replace them with self-protective ones to reduce occupational health hazards. The team that observed pottery workers recommended a long, detailed list of behavioral changes to help prevent lead poisoning—what, where, and how to eat and drink before, during, and after their shifts; removal of beards and trimming of mustaches; washing of hands and face. During their study of the severe silicosis epidemic around Joplin, Missouri, the PHS surgeon Anthony Lanza and coworker Edwin Higgins gave talks to groups of zinc-lead miners "with emphasis upon the fact that, regardless of any rules or regulations in force, their salvation from pulmonary diseases rested largely with themselves," not with their employers, who could install engineering controls such as mechanical ventilation and water-fed drills.[4]

Although PHS guidance regarding workers' habits did address the control of occupational hazards to some extent, it more often dealt with nonoccupational risks. Lanza and the BoM sanitary engineer Joseph White in 1916 produced a short pamphlet, *How a Miner Can Avoid Some Dangerous Diseases*, that concentrated heavily on avoidance of germs and filth outside the workplace. This BoM pamphlet devoted little space to facts about the respiratory hazards associated with underground exposure to airborne mineral particles. The cursory treatment of the dust threat alerted readers to the risk of tuberculosis and pneumonia but negligently not to the risk of any form of pneumoconiosis. Adding insult to obliviousness, the pamphleteers advised that "a great deal, if not most, of the dust breathing is due to the carelessness on the part of the miner himself." Lanza and White thus reached a sort of perverse synthesis that combined a "big-picture" diversion from occupational disease with a victim-blaming exercise. Beginning with the mobilization for World War I and continuing thereafter, the PHS also devoted much of its attention to warning workers about the debilitating effects of sexually transmitted diseases.[5]

Unlike its cooperation with the mining bureau, no amicable division of chores characterized the relations of the PHS and the federal cabinet-level labor agency established in 1913. The new DoL quickly took steps to attack the challenges of workplace injuries and illnesses in the world's leading industrial economy. Its immediate predecessor, the US Bureau of Labor, had helped to address the epidemic of phosphorus poisoning afflicting employees in the friction-match industry. Within months of its elevation to departmental status, the labor agency's congressional supporters moved to give it a Bureau of Labor Safety. Although focused on the more prominent problem of traumatic injuries, the proposed legislation also authorized the DoL to study occupational diseases and disseminate information on this subject. As the historian Christopher Sellers has observed, this initiative jolted the PHS into much-increased action in the field. The two bills introduced in the House of Representatives to authorize this new bureau triggered a territorial contest that would continue until midcentury. In February 1914, Byron Newton, assistant secretary of the Treasury Department, within which the PHS was located, informed both the Secretary of Labor and the Senate of his opposition. Newton contended that his department had jurisdiction over this problem and the expertise to deal with it. Any DoL program would be an inefficient duplication of effort. At House hearings, advocates for the Bureau of Labor Safety proposal maintained that they envisioned this body serving as a clearinghouse for information on occupational disease. Representative Robert Bremner, sponsor of one of the bills under consideration, asserted that "education is the key to occupational health." The PHS had staked out its claims to authority based primarily on its superior investigative abilities, not its capacity to distribute health information. Hence, it was conceivable at this juncture that the public health agency might confine itself to the scientific research function that it deemed most central to its identity and legitimacy and leave the less-valued function of spreading information to labor agents. Instead, the PHS took a hard line, foreshadowing the rivalry to follow. After passage by the House, this proposition died in the Senate. The Public Health Service had won the first round of the fight.[6]

Federal public health officials endeavored to differentiate themselves from their labor-affiliated rivals by claims of impartiality and objectivity. Whether located in the public sector or the private sector, health professionals, many of whom imagined that they held unique capabilities and opportunities to mediate class relations, commonly took this stance in the early twentieth century. PHS investigators rationalized their unwillingness to divulge the diagnoses of workers observed in field studies by reference to a dedication to impartiality. By 1917, the organization had adopted the policy of not providing examination results to those examined or to their employers. Among other ventures involving mass screening of workers, in two major investigations in the coal industry—one in bituminous fields in the 1920s and another in the anthracite region in the 1930s—the PHS followed this secretive approach. Yet inconsistencies occasionally cropped up during early projects. In its 1918 inquiry in the pottery industry, a project in which more than 1,700 workers received examinations, the PHS did inform those with lead poisoning of their diagnosis and advised them to see a physician of their own choosing. The government physicians kept this information from employers. The pottery workers' case may have been a unique exception, a consequence of the cordial relations between the employers' trade association and the workers' union, the National Brotherhood of Operative Potters. One of the agency's consultants apparently did not believe that such a policy should apply to private parties. Based on his PHS-commissioned survey of 170 industrial firms, C. D. Selby encouraged company doctors attending the 1918 meeting of the National Safety Council to be forthcoming with employees who had undergone workplace examinations. Selby suggested that merely making the effort to share findings would be appreciated by patients. These inconsistencies notwithstanding, the determination of the federal health authority to create for itself a strong identity as an investigatory enterprise gave it an imperative to gain access to research subjects, a privilege that employers could easily deny if they feared that diagnostic evidence could be used against them.[7]

Federal interagency conflict was minimal over the two decades following the defeat of the proposals for a safety and health unit based in the DoL in the mid-1910s. A brief truce held while the DoL operated a Working Conditions Service with PHS assistance during World War I. Even this moment of cooperation occurred only after a failed takeover gambit by the health officials. In the postwar decade, revived efforts to place a safety division in the DoL went nowhere. In expressing opposition to an initiative in 1926, Department of Treasury and PHS leaders contended that they had the problems of occupational disease so well in hand that nothing but wasteful duplication would result from any labor intervention. Secretary of the Treasury Andrew Mellon conceded only that the DoL had a right to deal with traumatic injuries. Defenders of the PHS at this moment again emphasized its function of collecting scientific data, not that of warning workers at risk.[8]

The early days of the New Deal witnessed another moment that illuminated the contrasting orientations of the rival agencies. In February 1934, the Bureau of Labor Statistics offered the committee drafting health and safety provisions for codes of fair competition for the National Recovery Administration a right-to-know proposition for the manufacturing sector. The proposal set this requirement: "All employees shall be instructed in the hazards incidental to the work engaged in, both in regard to the individual and to fellow workers." The short-lived recovery agency apparently never incorporated this radical right into any of its many codes governing an industry or trade. Nonetheless, mere consideration of this audacious proposition represented a suggestive commitment to the principle of transparency.[9]

During the quarter century after 1910, the occasional interventions from any administrative source in Washington remained marginal compared with the work undertaken on an ongoing basis by public agencies of the industrial states. Following the pathbreaking investigatory surveys in Illinois, New York, and Ohio, numerous systematic efforts to come to grips with the emergent issue of occupational disease occurred at the state level of government. New York led the way in building institutional capacity and using it. Of most relevance here, the New York Department of Labor (NYDoL) devised an influential policy of democratizing access to health hazard knowledge and other information related to occupational disease. In this early phase of government action, no two states followed exactly the same path, however. The New York model was hardly hegemonic. An alternative system arose in neighboring Connecticut that bestowed authority on the state's health, not labor, officials and pursued a more restrictive approach to the generation and transfer of information. The divergent patterns forged in New York and Connecticut would each offer definitive guidance for the DoL-PHS rivalry after 1935.

From its founding in 1913, the NYDoL's Division of Industrial Hygiene (renamed the Bureau of Industrial Hygiene in 1924) led the way in promoting workers' knowledge of work-induced health hazards and their adverse effects. Its parent department embraced as a priority its educational role in this area. In 1916, at the first major conference it sponsored, the department's second in command, James Gernon, discussed what he termed "the necessity for educating employers and employees." Gernon posed the issue in emphatic terms: "There are ever changing industrial processes, many of which are productive of industrial hazards and diseases, in the wake of which follow thousands of instances of untold suffering and enormous economic loss. Much of this human waste can be prevented. Of industrial diseases we know far too little and here is offered a wide field for intelligent investigation and endless opportunity for educating all the people." In cooperation with other departmental branches, the industrial hygiene unit produced and distributed posters, pamphlets, and other educational materials. Mass mailings of warning cards on the hazards of lead in English, German, Italian, Polish, Hungarian, and Yiddish went out in

1913 to all locals of the painters' union in the state. By the mid-1920s, the division had added pamphlets for workers covering the risks associated with antimony, arsenic, wood alcohol, chromic acid, mercury, benzene, anthrax, and silicosis. Outreach efforts extended to presentations in workplaces, where a team of lecturers from the Section of Education deployed films, exhibits, and slideshows. In 1917, Lester Roos, one of the Division of Industrial Hygiene's medical inspectors, decried the disproportionate exposure of non-English speakers not only to lead but also to other toxic chemicals. "It is almost impossible to make them understand the dangers in the work in which they are employed," Roos observed, "and it seems to me that something should be done along the lines of education." In his view, this meant primarily promoting the teaching of English. In situations where they could surmount a language barrier or faced none, inspectors like Roos had opportunities to convey warnings orally. In 1923, the division used a radio broadcast to encourage working-class listeners to send in written questions about their occupational health hazards. While maintaining a focus on health threats in the workplace, the state industrial hygienists also issued guidance on general health matters like nutrition.[10]

Besides direct communication with at-risk employees, the Division of Industrial Hygiene and its associates elsewhere in the NYDoL attempted to prevail upon employers to assist in alerting their employees to the health risks they faced. Picking up on Dr. Loos's concern, state officials pressed managers to institute worksite language training for their non-English-speaking laborers. The industrial hygiene group urged managers to do more to instruct all their subordinates about the threats posed by substances like arsenic. In at least one major class of industries fraught with hazards, these urgings took some effect. In 1929, William Burke, a chemical engineer with the Bureau of Industrial Hygiene, found that chemical manufacturers were "becoming awake to the necessity of the proper education of the employees pertaining to the accident and health hazards." Burke noted that prospective employees received notification of the risks they would encounter even before they accepted job offers. Both in its own publications and in selecting employer representatives to discuss their educational programs at annual conferences, the NYDoL publicized managerial best practices. A pamphlet on the health hazards in chemical manufacturing praised an unnamed firm that had adopted the red-disc warning symbol in its plant and that regularly placed instructive messages in English, Italian, and Polish in pay envelopes. One presentation at the department's 1919 safety conference extolled the use of educational movies by numerous prominent companies. Louis Dublin of Metropolitan Life Insurance Company told attendees at the 1924 conference, "Workers must be taught what dangers they must avoid in the course of their everyday employment. When they know more about the hazards of their occupation they will exercise greater care." (Two years earlier, Dublin had published a widely distributed reference work, *Occupation Hazards and Diagnostic Signs*, which struck the same imperative tone: "Workers must be instructed as to the toxicity of the substance handled.") Physician May Mayers of the Bureau of Industrial Hygiene advised company doctors and their superiors that "education of the worker to an intelligent understanding of the hazards to which he is exposed and their prevention is indispensable to proper cooperation between worker and industrial physician."[11]

New York's policy of openness extended to granting workers and their representatives access to data that it held. In 1911, when the state's lawmakers ordered physicians to report cases of selected occupational illnesses to the DoL, that statute placed no restrictions on the sharing of that information. This was also the nature of the legislation in other states in the first wave of such enactments. These laws used the template crafted by the AALL. That crew of Progressive reformers valued the creation of a corpus of evidence on the prevalence and incidence of occupational disease and its utility for government experts more than it valued transparency in making that database widely available to those directly affected. When the AALL joined with the National Civic Federation to study mercury poisoning in the New York metropolitan area (where an inordinate share of the victims were foreign-born workers), their 1912 report on the project looked hopefully to the process set in motion by the recent disease-reporting requirement: "Gradually a body of authoritative data will be collected, showing the conditions of health in the factories and demonstrating the process in industries which call for special regulation." The AALL reformers soon recognized that company doctors were the key constituency for reporting cases and that diligent reporting by those practitioners would likely prove to be disadvantageous to their relations with their employers. Alice Hamilton saw that passage of a reporting law in Illinois had the perverse effect of causing doctors retained by firms with lead hazards to "refuse to admit that any but the most extreme cases are to be called lead poisoning." Hence, the association changed its standard bill to add a clause that aimed to lower the resistance of physicians to submit reports. The 1913 version of the AALL model bill disallowed use of the reports in any legal proceeding. In short order, a number of states adopted into law this revised formulation, including some that retreated from their earlier laws.[12]

New York refused, however, to go along with this denial of transparency. When the state amended its requirements in 1913 to make brass poisoning reportable, it passed over an opportunity to make case reports inadmissible evidence. These reports to the NYDoL served to trigger inspections that gathered corroborating evidence of hazards, evidence that could prove helpful to sickened workers and their unions or lawyers. The state held out as the inadmissibility principle, blessed with an authoritative endorsement from the national group of state officials seeking uniform laws, become predominant after 1913. In a further move to facilitate just resolution of compensation claims, the New York Bureau of Industrial Hygiene made its laboratory services available in the 1920s at cost to physicians attempting to confirm diagnoses in lead-poisoning cases.[13]

The fullest expression of New York's dedication to expanding workers' access to self-protective information came in January 1919 with the issuance of *A Plan for Shop Safety, Sanitation and Health Organization*. This booklet delineated a participative system that challenged the prevailing preoccupation with carelessness. Drawing on the experience of the innovative Joint Board of Sanitary Control in the garment industry, the state labor department criticized the inadequacy of a top-down approach and advocated giving rank-and-file workers a new active role: "The remedy is to educate and interest the worker in safe and sanitary practices. But signs and posters alone are inadequate. Success in such matters can best be attained with the cooperation of employees." In this model, the key mechanism for achieving labor-management cooperation was the active participation of workers' committees in creating and sharing hazard information and acting on this information to solve workplace problems. The committees, composed of members elected by their peers in the workplace, would be designated to receive hazard evidence from management and to discover additional facts on working conditions in their own inspections. They would use their knowledge to propose methods of disease and injury prevention. The extent to which New York companies adopted this innovative and daring approach is, unfortunately, unknown. Nonetheless, this proposal stands out as not only embodying a right to know but even pointing the way toward a right to act.[14]

Beyond their support for voluntary action by employers, New York labor administrators promoted dissemination of occupational health knowledge in at least one recommendation for regulatory change. In 1919 the Division of Industrial Hygiene visited 335 chemical factories, with the express aim of determining whether the state's code of regulations needed amendments. The investigators found a widespread lack of hazard knowledge among a vulnerable workforce in risky jobs. They urged the Industrial Commission to make a number of new rules. One suggestion in particular addressed the pervasive ignorance on the front lines of production: "In all places in which there are handled substances which are poisonous, or are dangerous to health or safety, it shall be mandatory for the employer to fully acquaint the employees with the nature and the properties of the materials being handled. This shall be done by means of posters, printed in the English language, and by verbal instruction when necessary." Whether it became a casualty of the postwar recession or it was simply too radical, this recommendation did not find its way into the state's regulatory arsenal.[15]

Beginning in the 1910s, a number of other industrial states adopted an approach similar to that of New York, basing their occupational health programs in labor agencies and pursuing a policy of promoting openness in sharing information with workers. Developments in New Jersey mirrored those in New York State. At a 1916 symposium on occupational disease held by the American Chemical Society, Newell Gordon of the New Jersey Department of Labor chided employers who refused to divulge known hazards to their laborers. Gordon's department, aware of the findings from his study of conditions in the state's burgeoning munitions industry, stood willing to disseminate warnings but lamented its lack of funding to do so. Two events in the mid-1920s served to increase the agency's role in alerting at-risk workers. In 1924, New Jersey amended its workers' compensation statute to add coverage for a number of occupational diseases. "Until this law was passed," Andrew McBride, the state's commissioner of labor, observed, "it had been a common practice for employers to hire labor ignorant of the nature of the poisonous substances that were being handled and to give workers no more than a cursory, formal warning notice to take care of themselves." The filing of compensation claims triggered investigations by his department, whose representatives gave managers warning notices to be posted and pamphlets to be passed on to those endangered. By 1928, according to McBride, his officers insisted that chemical plants "engage in a strict practice of industrial education for their workers and that this education be intensive and continuous." The second event that illuminated the need to improve the flow of information was quite a dramatic one. The fatal intoxications suffered in 1924 by five Standard Oil of New Jersey employees who manufactured the fuel additive tetraethyl lead precipitated the distribution of warning notices by the state and requirements for advising workers about the hazard. In the wake of this disaster, Commissioner McBride declared that his inspectors were "required to see that these precautionary measures are strictly carried out." Here, as in New York and elsewhere, the availability, at least in principle, of police powers of enforcement distinguished labor department methods from the softer approach generally taken by health officers. But the extent to which the inspectors strictly implemented that mandate is unclear and doubtful in chronically underfunded agencies.[16]

In Wisconsin, the dynamics of change resembled those that operated in New Jersey. During the 1910s, the state drew criticism from unions for its minimal intervention on work-induced illnesses. Then the enactment of workers' compensation for all occupational diseases in 1919 precipitated a modest measure of reform in spreading protective information. In 1921, the state's Industrial Commission issued a general order compelling the disclosure of information. This order commanded that "the employer shall instruct all employees who are required to work where industrial poisons of a hazardous nature are used, stored, or carried regarding the danger connected with their work, the best preventative methods, and the measure for affording assistance to other employees when affected by such poisons." The order was accompanied by a set of warning posters. These came with a warning to employers that "the mere posting of a warning poster is not enough" and that they "must do everything reasonably calculated to instruct their employees fully upon the hazards and the methods of prevention." Both in its compensation reform and in this regulation, Wisconsin took a comprehensive approach, in contrast to the piecemeal, hazard-by-hazard strategy used in some other jurisdictions.[17]

In 1912, Massachusetts transferred the regulation of occupational disease from the Board of Health to a newly created Board of Labor and Industries. The board's lack of resources placed it in a weak position with regard to effecting compliance. This weakness was manifest in the very terminology used in its rules. In 1916, it promulgated "rules and regulations suggested" for advising workers about anthrax and benzene derivatives. In the guidance it offered employers on anthrax, the board set a solicitous tone: "You are urged to apply these suggestions in your establishment in so far as they are applicable to your special line of industry." Shortly thereafter, the agency put out a poster on the dangers of anthrax, without any indication that its display was mandatory. The political-economic situation in this state clearly permitted only very limited, tentative exercise of government authority on what was then a regulatory frontier.[18]

When Pennsylvania created its Department of Labor and Industry in 1913, one of the original components was a Division of Industrial Hygiene and Engineering. By the following year, the division was distributing multilanguage posters devoted to the lead hazard. In addressing the problem of benzene, Pennsylvania's government labor officials insisted on the employer's duty to make subordinates aware of the risks associated with this toxic solvent. As munitions production accelerated with the mobilization for war in 1917, the Department of Labor and Industry required that explosives factories post warnings regarding hazards of acid fumes and asphyxiants. In the postwar period, Francis Patterson, the head of the industrial hygiene unit, proposed moving beyond circumscribed initiatives that dealt with one or a few hazards in a particular industry. At a 1922 conference put together by the PHS, Patterson declared that all workers should be warned about the occupational disease hazards of their jobs and advised how to avoid them. But in the conservative context of the 1920s, the state made no discernible progress toward this objective. In at least one significant instance, the Department of Labor and Industry failed to make available to endangered workers the data that it had gathered. In 1934, the department's Industrial Hygiene Section collected dust data and conducted medical examinations at four plants that made asbestos textiles. Although the examinations determined that one quarter of the employees had asbestosis, no individual received notification of his or her diagnosis. This practice blurred the line between the greater transparency that prevailed where labor officials held information and the opacity favored by their counterparts in health agencies. Like its counterpart in New York, the Pennsylvania labor department sponsored its own series of educational conferences, with those members of the medical profession specializing in occupational disorders as the primary audience. At a session in 1917, the ubiquitous Alice Hamilton called on company doctors to take the lead in educating workers about industrial diseases. Hamilton encouraged reliance primarily on oral messages delivered in the workers' own language and suggested the value of using readily understood pictures.[19]

States in which regulation of occupational disease fell under the control of health agencies tended to follow more conservative policies generally and with regard to transparency specifically. Connecticut epitomized this more secretive approach. That state stood near the opposite end of the political spectrum from New York, which from the 1910s onward grew into a bastion of liberalism with an inclination to protect workers from a range of perils besides those of occupational disease. In contrast, Connecticut welcomed ruthless manufacturers fleeing New York's new limitations on sweatshop operations. Its factory safety inspection was notoriously weak. The conservative workers' compensation law of 1913 accommodated manufacturers and the powerful insurance firms based in Hartford. The 1913 session of the state legislature also forbade the introduction of any physician's mandated report of occupational disease into "any action at law against any employer of such diseased person." After occupying a gray area of overlapping jurisdiction between the Department of Labor and Factory Inspection and the Board of Health, the job of disseminating information on work-induced disease was assigned by statute in 1917 to a newly created Department of Health.[20]

The Connecticut Department of Health set about controlling the flow of information. That physicians' disease reports still went to the labor office for compilation prompted Commissioner of Health John Black and colleague E. K. Root to complain to the governor in 1919. Black and Root contended that, because the Department of Labor and Factory Inspection was "not prepared to consider the problems of industrial hygiene from a scientific point of view," this function should be transferred to his department. Four years later, physicians' case reports were redirected by the legislature to go to the health department. In 1927, that is, fourteen years after New York launched its Division of Industrial Hygiene, Connecticut established a Division of Occupational Diseases within its Department of Health. The department brought in physician Albert Gray, a PHS veteran, to run the unit. Under Gray's direction, the division's primary mission was investigatory, not informational. Modest information transfer activity targeted employers and the medical community and excluded workers. In recounting work done in the year that ended in mid-1930, Gray devoted thirty-one pages to technical studies and one sentence to educational activities. None of the division's recommendations to business management for remedial action dealt with giving at-risk employees any knowledge of their situation. During its initial decade of operation, the unit gave no evidence of having any working relationship with either organized labor or their fellow public servants in the Department of Labor and Factory Inspection. In its preoccupation with serving the needs of business organizations and professional groups, the Division of Occupational Diseases embraced the same adherence to a sort of corporatism without labor that Gray's former employer pursued at this time in its administration of the notorious Picher, Oklahoma, clinic in the Tri-State zinc-lead mining district and in its handling of the controversy over tetraethyl lead.[21]

Safeguarding the database of physicians' case reports remained a concern in Connecticut. In 1929, by which time the state allowed workers' compensation benefits for certain diseases, the legislature explicitly barred from the claims adjudication process any use of mandated physicians' reports. The hallmark principle of secrecy was something to boast about. In his role as chair of the Industrial Hygiene Committee of the Conference of State and Provincial Health Authorities of North America, Stanley Osborn, Connecticut's health commissioner, used his annual report for 1929 to note his state's ability to avoid entanglement in the adversarial compensation process. R. L. Thompson of the PHS applauded Connecticut's stance. Thompson was acutely aware that at the end of the 1920s, only the health agencies in Connecticut, Ohio, and Michigan had authority over occupational diseases and that the activities in the latter two states were quite circumscribed. He delivered both encouragement and a warning to the conference of health officials: "Except for the excellent progress in industrial hygiene in the State of Connecticut, State Departments of Health seem to have entirely neglected this field of public health work. It is believed it cannot be too strongly recommended to the state health officers that unless they take steps to attach this work to their departments it will be located in Departments of Labor or Industry." This exhortation only foreshadowed the promotional campaign that the PHS would mount in the coming years. In 1931, the Connecticut legislature further extended the unavailability of government-held information by blocking the admission of any data gathered in the course of a health department investigation of occupational disease as evidence in any lawsuit or compensation claim. As Gray fought in 1933 to maintain his operation, recently elevated to bureau status but under the stress of budget cuts amid the Great Depression, he emphasized that his organization provided confidential evaluations to many employers that could not be used against them. The contrast between the transparency guiding New York and the opacity across the state line could not have been starker.[22]

The Great Depression set in motion developments that had a profound impact on the role of government in addressing occupational disease. Among the millions of workers displaced by the decade-long economic collapse were many impaired by work-induced illness. Desperate sick and disabled unemployed workers filed a flood of workers' compensation claims and, more commonly, lawsuits for damages where state workers' compensation did not cover disease. The carnage wrought by one disorder alone, silicosis, sent shock waves through the business community. Although examining the full breadth of this crisis is beyond the scope of this book, one reform that resulted from the pressures brought by the discarded members of the working class had a major blighting influence on the nature of public policy on the right to know, an influence that lasted for more than a third of a century.[23]

As a sense of anxiety and even panic beset corporate leaders, those interested in containing losses from occupational disease saw the arrangements in Connecticut as a potential firewall. At its 1934 session, the Conference of State and Provincial Health Authorities heard the fears and desires of the insurance industry articulated by Wesley Graff, safety director of the National Bureau of Casualty and Surety Underwriters. As the representative of forty firms that wrote workers' compensation policies, Graff noted the disturbing rate at which occupational-disease claims had risen in recent years. Without claiming that even one enterprise in any industry had actually failed thus far because of these claims, he asserted, "It is no exaggeration to say that the financial life of many of our most important industries is at stake." Graff appealed to state health leaders to intervene and indicated his group's preference for their involvement over that of labor agencies. In his view, the state "should be kept clear of all legal entanglements" such as providing factual information relevant to compensation claims. He offered this more specific guidance: "The relation between the employer and such occupational disease bureau should be strictly confidential, so that the results of the bureau's investigation of any particular plant will be available only to the management of that plant." Graff pointed to the success of this sort of arrangement in Connecticut. He assured his audience that his own industry was ready to help pass any legislation necessary. The conference's Industrial Hygiene Committee, still chaired by Connecticut's Stanley Osborn, lent its support. The committee urged that "definite provisions should be made that the results of investigations by the health department cannot be used as evidence in connection with any claim for compensation." They repeated the contention that business enterprises would not use the state's expertise without that safeguard. In the assemblage's discussion of the Industrial Hygiene Committee's report, Roy Jones of the PHS reiterated his organization's well-known position and described the assistance that it had given to Connecticut in launching its program. The conferees voted to back the Connecticut model. In its annual report for the year ended June 30, 1934, the Connecticut Bureau of Occupational Diseases called attention to a recent similar endorsement from the American Public Health Association. Albert Gray gloated, "During the past year National and State Trade Associations, Insurance Institutes and Departments of Health in industrial states have displayed great interest in the method used in Connecticut for the administration of occupational disease control." The state's status as the exemplar of conservatism had become well recognized.[24]

By the mid-thirties, representatives of organized capital had another reason to favor Connecticut's system. One early initiative of the New Deal had raised the specter of a fuller commitment to the labor-based alternative identified with New York. Prior to his election to the presidency, Franklin Roosevelt was serving as governor of New York State. He brought with him to Washington his industrial commissioner, Frances Perkins, to serve as secretary of labor. In July 1934, Perkins set up a Division of Labor Standards (DLS) headed by Verne Zimmer, her former subordinate in the NYDoL. The primary aim of this new body was to expand federal involvement in the regulation of hazardous working conditions. Promotion of the New York model under federal auspices could become a nightmare for employers and insurers unwilling, and, in a depressed economy, perhaps simply unable, to bear the human costs of production.[25]

Partisans of health department primacy had their prayers answered by Congress. After the American Medical Association killed an attempt to incorporate a state health insurance plan into economic security legislation, policymakers offered what was essentially a consolation prize in the realm of health affairs. Title VI of the Social Security Act, which became law on August 8, 1935, provided for federal grants to state and local health departments and for additional funding for the PHS to cooperate with state and local authorities in disease investigations. Although the act did not explicitly cite control of occupational diseases as an object of concern, at congressional hearings on the proposal, Surgeon General Hugh Cumming had identified this as a matter in great need of remedial action. Cumming assured the House Ways and Means Committee that, "as an impartial fact-finding body, [his agency's] investigations are accepted by the general public and by both labor and industry." In anticipation of the passage of the security program, A. J. Chesley, secretary of the Conference of State and Provincial Health Authorities, predicted that soon there would be "a better chance for the development of occupational disease control by State departments than ever before."[26]

Chesley was right. With the dire budget constraints imposed by the protracted depression, the lure of federal money immediately induced many states to start, expand, or transfer programs. The PHS undertook a strenuous campaign to guide, train, and otherwise assist state-level officials, especially those just entering the field. Trainees who completed the service's seminar in Washington were sent to Hartford for an orientation to the flagship Connecticut program. Within approximately two years of the approval of the Social Security legislation, twenty-five state health departments were running or planning occupational health offices. In March 1936, Pennsylvania shifted its Division of Industrial Hygiene from the Department of Labor and Industry, leaving behind its coordination with compensation and enforcement activities there. Pennsylvania was participating in a mass exodus. Whereas in the 1920s, twenty-seven state programs were based in labor departments, by the late 1930s, only two remained in that institutional location.[27]

To qualify for federal funding, states had to develop programs with an educational component. But under PHS tutelage and with the Connecticut example on display, these activities tended to be modest. They also targeted managers and health professionals, not at-risk workers. Information aimed at working-class audiences was often marginal or even irrelevant to expanding workers' knowledge about occupational health hazards. Federal officials made available to their grantees a series of pamphlets for which a significant share of the topics chosen were subjects of general health—influenza; appendicitis; and, the perennial favorite, sexually transmitted diseases. This dispersion of focus only reinforced the preexisting orientation of state health agencies, which had long left occupational disorders at the margin.[28]

The PHS maneuvered to instill the code of opacity in embryonic state systems. Rhode Island launched an industrial hygiene program in 1936 and at once conducted a hazard survey. This exercise determined that toxic substances threatened fully one-third of the workers in surveyed establishments. The fledgling Division of Industrial Hygiene in the Department of Public Health hastened to assure business owners who granted access to their premises that its study findings "were to be treated confidentially, and retained so." This policy became entrenched for subsequent field investigations. The Rhode Island department believed that "such a procedure is advised by the U.S. Public Health

Service and by various like agencies that have had meritorious experience in this work." The department vowed to "jealously guard our vouched confidence." In 1940, the PHS offered grantees a manual for administering statewide surveys, with the assurance that this procedural template had proven to be a successful and efficient one. The manual provided a form letter to use to gain access to worksites, which promised that data gathered "will be treated in such a confidential manner that no individual plant findings will be revealed."[29]

Federal consultants managed to attach to the reports of state survey findings recommended prescriptions for gathering and sharing investigative data and other sensitive information. When the Colorado State Board of Health made proposals for hazard control measures after their evaluative exercise (a study that encompassed the irrelevant phenomenon of "venereal diseases"), the PHS influence was evident. The roster of proposed preventive measures did not extend to any dissemination of information to workers at risk. The joint federal-state needs assessment in Utah yielded a similar list of suggestions devoid of any encouragement for delivering warnings or instructions to vulnerable workers. The report from Utah made clear that no findings regarding workplace hazards were divulged to those facing those hazards. This document advocated that recipients of periodic, employer-administered medical examinations be counseled about any nonoccupational disorders discovered. Another chance to normalize the barricading of information came when states pondered reforming their workers' compensation laws to cover diseases. Where legislative changes were being contemplated, the PHS urged state health officials to seize the opportunity to sell their program to employers as a way to avoid potential outlays by assuring the impounding of sensitive data that might aid compensation claimants. In 1941, J. J. Bloomfield and PHS colleague W. M. Gafafer pointed to the arrangement that prevailed in their recent Utah project: "It was decided that all records obtained in the study were to become the property of the Public Health Service, and that all information would be strictly confidential." Bloomfield and Gafafer noted that this strategy had led directly to both the successful formation of a permanent industrial hygiene office in the Utah State Board of Health and the enactment of compensation for selected occupational diseases. Appearing in *Public Health Reports*, the official journal of the PHS, this was a straightforward, authoritative message to state-level grantees. Decision makers in Tennessee got the message. In 1945, that state authorized establishment of an industrial hygiene operation in its Department of Public Health and made the results of its studies and investigations unavailable for any compensation claims or lawsuits.[30]

Not every state chose to fall in line. Wisconsin took federal funds to set up an industrial hygiene unit under its State Board of Health in 1937 but continued to make the fruits of state investigations of hazards available to compensation applicants. Harry Nelson of the Wisconsin Industrial Commission told his peers in the International Association of Industrial Accident Boards and Commissions that "suppression of any pertinent testimony is always dangerous."[31]

For the most part, New York held its ground. But even there, powerful interests fearful of silicosis liability made inroads. In 1936, shortly after the state broadened eligibility for compensation for occupational disease, lawmakers took up a proposal to study dust diseases but bar the admission of any information obtained into any compensation proceeding. The possibility infuriated Frances Perkins. When this measure came under serious consideration, she declared, "There can be no legitimate excuse for a provision that forbids the Industrial Commissioner, who is the administrator of the Workmen's Compensation Act, to utilize any information that will assure the fair and equitable disposition of a pending compensation claim." Over these objections by the former commissioner, this bill became law in mid-1936. Otherwise, however, the nation's leading industrial state remained the citadel of the proworker approach. The Department of Labor's Division of Industrial Hygiene continued to assist compensation administrators in nonpneumoconiosis cases and to aid the federal DLS in training state inspectors in occupational disease issues. The division circumvented the restrictions on use of specific evidence of silicosis by launching an educational campaign on dust disease. The agency also continued to attack other hazards by producing numerous publications and engaging in other forms of outreach aimed at workers and their unions. To reach one sizable cohort of recent immigrants, the division placed fifteen articles in Italian-language newspapers in 1937. The following year, in a bulletin intended to reach not only labor but also management in lead-producing and lead-using establishments, it advised that "each and every applicant for employment should be informed of the special health hazards presented by exposure to lead, [and] the preventive measures available for his protection." At the same time, the division investigated a benzene formulation that had caused scores of cases of poisoning among printers in New York City. Rather than submit a secret report to management at the completion of the study, the division's director, Leonard Greenburg, explained the situation at a union meeting. Greenburg also conferred with employers, their insurance carriers, and the manufacturer of the toxic ink. This intervention forced the substitution of an innocuous product for the deleterious one. New York remained a place where state labor officials broadly construed their mission to spread warning information.[32]

Just as the PHS extolled the virtues of the Connecticut system, the DLS, run by migrants from Albany, promoted the New York model. Indeed, this worker-friendly program received the enthusiastic endorsement of that federal agency, which historians David Rosner and Gerald Markowitz aptly characterized as openly partisan. The DLS saw itself serving labor in the same manner that the officials of the Department of Commerce served commercial interests or, as we will see in chapter 3, the Department of Agriculture served farm owners. In 1939, the division published a detailed description of the system operating in New York State. Jean Flexner's pamphlet, *The Work of an Industrial Division in a State Department of Labor*, defended this orientation in the face of the dramatic rise of the health agency–based plans. Flexner observed that the NYDoL had its own medical staff whose duties included not only connecting reported illnesses to their causes by visiting workplaces but also sharing discoveries with workers, their doctors, and their unions.[33]

Beyond its promotion of a particular strategy at the state level, the DLS on its own account promoted greater transparency regarding occupational disease. Consistent with its interest in treating workers not merely as wards of the state but as active participants in maintaining their own well-being, Zimmer's office offered another sharp contrast with its bureaucratic rivals. Beginning in 1935, the DLS put out a number of short pamphlets on important hazards that at least pointed toward a right-to-know perspective. To be sure, the first few pamphlets in the series did not supplement their main message about the necessity of engineering controls with any mention of the advisability of warning workers or involving them in the disease prevention process. Beginning with the publications appearing in 1937, however, the division struck a more activist note. Language encouraging employers to warn their employees about hazards like methyl alcohol and carbon tetrachloride and encouraging endangered workers to share their observations with their peers and to engage in collective self-protection became standard. The National Silicosis Conference of 1936–1937, sponsored by the DLS, brought forth formal recommendations that management take responsibility for instructing employees about silica hazards and how to avoid them. These recommendations harnessed not only the growing authority of the national government but also the endorsements of committees composed of prominent public and private experts, which conferred a measure of additional legitimacy on the concept of greater workplace transparency. In this fluid and turbulent political context, even modest attempts to activate workers helped to stimulate a sense of entitlement that pointed the way toward the subsequent dawning of a deeper consciousness of rights.[34]

State-level labor administrators and their allies struggled to limit, if not reverse, the dominance attained by their rivals in the health bureaucracies. Besides their relative lack of resources compared to the federally endowed health organizations, the labor departments resented the way that they were kept in the dark about investigations and were otherwise the victims of a lack of cooperation. As the 1930s came to a close, supporters of the labor-friendly approach waged two battles in the legislative realm. The first of these seized on the Roosevelt administration's efforts to forge a comprehensive national health program, which had been revived at the National Health Conference of 1938. In addition to the primary interest in a government health insurance plan, deliberations at that event did reach the issue of the allocation of funds for occupational health. The conference's Technical Committee recommended that all states develop industrial hygiene programs under the control of health departments, in part to meet the need to expand education on occupational disease.[35]

When reform proponents advanced their proposal the following year, the stage was set for another jurisdictional battle on which one object of contention was the distribution of information to workers. Because the National Health Bill only called for vague forms of cooperation between labor and health officials, skeptics testified in Senate hearings in support of an amendment that would secure funding for state-level labor departments. Matthew Woll of the American Federation of Labor worried about the withholding of facts about hazards needed by compensation applicants and defended the New York system of integrating investigative and compensation functions. Leonard Greenburg spelled out the mechanics of New York's procedure in contested cases: "When a man makes a claim for compensation for an occupational disease we get a record of his claim and our medical expert goes to the factory where he works, he sees the process at which the man was engaged, he takes samples of the material to which the man was exposed, and he brings it back to the chemical laboratory for analysis, and he writes a report based on the medical findings, and the chemist writes a report on the material analyzed, and they go into the compensation folder as evidence." Mary McGorkey, chair of the Health Committee of the New York section of the Congress of Industrial Organizations, applauded the work of Greenburg's team and maintained that the next challenge for the labor movement was educating its membership. Defenders of the health department model held that labor department programs suffered from crippling liabilities. C. P. McCord of the Michigan Department of Health alluded to their "disagreeable" associations with issues like strikes. (McCord did not share with the senators the fact that two years earlier Michigan had passed a law that hid from public view the findings of state investigations of occupational disease, except where the health commissioner deemed it advisable to divulge information to employers.) Morris Fishbein of the American Medical Association dismissed the successful experience of New York State as an exceptional one that could not be replicated elsewhere. Thomas Parran, New York's health commissioner, not only trivialized his own state's industrial-hygiene program as a fluke of history but pointed admiringly to the system invented in neighboring Connecticut. Invoking his twenty-two years in the

NYDoL, Verne Zimmer responded to this provocation by criticizing the inability of Connecticut's public experts to convey information helpful to victims of occupational disease seeking benefits. Zimmer contended that the educational duties undertaken by government authorities should extend to encouraging the "part to be played by workers in preventing occupational disease." Defenders of the now-embattled New York alternative won no congressional concessions from this altercation.[36]

In the second assault on public health monopoly control over funds, James Murray, a liberal Democratic senator from Montana, sponsored a bill—drafted by the DLS and one for which it attempted to mobilize union support—that would allow state labor bureaus to obtain financing from Washington. On the eve of hearings on this proposal, Frances Perkins did her best to set the terms of debate. In her view, "The major need at present is not one of additional medical research but a wider use of existing knowledge about these health hazards. This can be promoted by extended distribution of non-technical information to workers and management," as well as by regulations that imposed well-known engineering controls. She criticized the Connecticut policy of withholding assistance from compensation claimants and denounced the actions of health officials elsewhere. Perkins was especially appalled that, in Illinois and Pennsylvania, health department physicians had served as expert witnesses for employers' insurance carriers to oppose occupational disease claims. For its part, the PHS prepared for the hearings by lining up witnesses from Connecticut.[37]

The Senate hearings held in May 1940 generally ranged over familiar ground. Supporters of Murray's proposition contended that wider availability of information gathered by the state for workers seeking much-needed public benefits was only fair. Opponents attacked the bill as a wasteful duplication of effort while insisting that state health departments cooperated with their labor department colleagues and offered appropriate technical assistance to the compensation system. Albert Gray, still the director of Connecticut's Bureau of Occupational Disease, blandly assured senators that "in most States cooperation between industrial hygiene units and compensation bodies is excellent." The bill, which lacked President Roosevelt's endorsement, died quietly. Although skirmishing on this issue continued for a decade thereafter, this moment marked the end of any viable chance of limiting the control held by health authorities at the state and federal levels.[38]

Having effectively consolidated its authority over occupational disease as a societal issue, the PHS and its allies pressed forward in propounding an enlarged conception of their domain. Confined by industrial hygiene and long oriented toward nonoccupational disorders, in the 1940s the PHS increasingly described its mission in terms of the more capacious concept of industrial health. The emergency conditions of World War II were propitious for focusing on ailments like influenza or the common cold. Maladies of that sort caused considerable absenteeism, impeding productivity in vital defense industries. Thus, state health departments took up nonoccupational problems of adult health more frequently. In 1940, Ohio converted its Bureau of Occupational Disease into an Adult Hygiene Division. Broader horizons meant additional attention to noninfectious chronic conditions like cancer and cardiovascular disorders while continuing to deal with familiar infections like tuberculosis and sexually transmitted diseases. With inevitable limits on staffing and other resources, this expansionist move left occupational disease further down the lengthened agenda of the public health bureaucracy and of the health-care providers under its influence. As Carey McCord, then an adviser to Chrysler Corporation, told the Institutes of Wartime Industrial Health in 1942, "All physicians have been brought closer to industrial health through the realization that work injuries and occupational diseases make up only a minor portion of the health conservation problems of industry." Educating workers about occupational health hazards, especially those with long latency periods, became an even lower priority. The PHS promoted joint labor-management committees, which proliferated during the war, as a key instrument for delivering health messages to workers. Under the preferred division of responsibilities, management committee members would teach employees about the occupational hazards they faced, and labor representatives would cover risks emanating from outside the working environment. In 1944, PHS health educator Elna Perkins advised that "labor unions will be expected to assume their share of the responsibility for education of their members on health matters." To Elna Perkins, this meant that "unions should promote health education that will help individual members to improve their own hygienic habits of living and to take advantage of health services available." In a 1946 editorial in its monthly newsletter, the PHS Division of Industrial Hygiene promoted "the modern concept of industrial hygiene." Using data flawed by under-reporting and under-recognition, the federal health agency maintained that "for every day lost to industrial diseases and accidents, fifteen are lost as a result of ordinary adult illnesses." The editorial went on to encourage company doctors to "give workers advice on nonoccupational illnesses." As unions in the postwar years began to press more forcefully for employer-funded hospital and medical benefits, an emphasis on educating employees on health-promoting behavior had a clear money-saving value for management. Assigning company physicians an educational role also served to placate the medical establishment's unease about competition from that source in the lucrative delivery of clinical services. The new industrial health paradigm renovated and reinforced the old victim-blaming strategy.[39]

The bureaucratic battles over occupational disease that played out over almost four decades had come to a decisive resolution by midcentury. Programs located in state and federal labor agencies had been subordinated or eliminated by their adversaries in health officialdom, led by the PHS. A postwar reactionary wave inflicted severe budget cuts on the DLS and the dismantling of its educational program. It is impossible to gauge with any precision the number of opportunities for enlightening workers about their health hazards that were lost as a result of the triumph of secrecy over transparency. But the crucial nexus weakened, if not severed, was that between government authorities and a resurgent labor movement. With union membership in the United States quintupling between the early 1930s and the late 1940s, there was definitely potential leverage for making gains against unhealthful working conditions. But a wider and deeper awareness among the union rank and file of its peril was an essential precondition for progress. Health officers preoccupied with research and with maintaining cordial relations with those who owned and managed their research sites could not deliver the necessary warnings. As Rosner and Markowitz have demonstrated, the DLS worked in close alignment with organized labor and supported state-level agencies with the same orientation.[40]

Some sense of the opportunities lost comes from the exceptional experience of federal intervention in the rayon industry. In 1937, the Textile Workers Organizing Committee, an affiliate of the insurgent Committee for Industrial Organization (which a year later renamed itself the Congress of Industrial Organizations), sought the assistance of the Division of Labor Standards on the carbon disulphide (or carbon bisulphide, but today known more commonly as carbon disulfide) and hydrogen sulphide hazards sickening workers in the burgeoning viscose rayon industry. The DLS enlisted the services of Alice Hamilton, in what would be her final major assignment as a federal consultant. Hamilton was all too willing to address a threat that management had obscured under what she termed "a mantle of almost complete secrecy." After helping the Pennsylvania Department of Labor and Industry design a survey assessing the problem among the state's approximately ten thousand rayon workers, Hamilton led a national study involving thirteen plants in ten states. Her 1940 report on this project brought to light pervasive acute and chronic intoxication from carbon disulphide as well as widespread adverse effects of hydrogen sulphide exposure. She made clear that she had written this document to be understandable to union representatives and other laypeople. Rather than await the results of this investigation, the DLS offered a new entry in its health and safety pamphlet series in 1937. The DLS pamphlet urged that a worker suspecting that he or she was being poisoned by this substance "talk the matter over with his fellow workers and with the management," as well as to notify the state labor department about the situation. The guidance to employers whose worksites harbored this toxic chemical contained this suggestion: "Inform all employees about the possible danger of carbon bisulphide poisoning, and the measures for their protection." In this case as in others at this juncture, federal agents promoted activism based on transparency. The DLS's Clara Beyer announced in 1937 that, in response to "tremendous interest" from workers, her agency had distributed 150,000 copies of each of its hazard pamphlets. Union branches were requesting them in batches of five hundred. This information dissemination strategy departed radically from that employed by their counterparts in health agencies, which concentrated on reaching employers and physicians. If it had become the norm, the Labor Department alternative methods might well have substantially benefited unionizing workers, particularly in the manufacturing sector. Instead, the dominant trickle-down approach fostered by health officials depended on employers accepting responsibility to create knowledge that might expose them to lawsuits or compensation demands.[41]

3

THE PATH OF SELF-CORRECTION

> Speaking of danger emblems, there seems to be a growing sentiment towards the elimination of the negative and the substitution of the positive, and for that reason I believe that the term "caution emblem" will eventually meet with more general approval than "danger emblem."
>
> —W. L. Chandler, 1916

> An effort has been made to avoid the term "Poison." . . . It has been suggested rather that the wording "Caution" be used[,] followed by the most obvious reason for caution.
>
> —A. G. Granch, 1944

As A. G. Granch, a physician with Union Carbide, made clear, the prediction of W. L. Chandler, an executive at the automaker Dodge Manufacturing, proved to be an accurate one. Employers' abiding interest in only limited, often euphemistic disclosure of unpleasant facts about occupational health hazards dominated the discourse of information dissemination in the quarter century after World War II. Protection of self-interest often required warning messages in order to curb liability in the judicial and legislative arenas. At the center of a regime of self-regulation were the warning labels generated by the Manufacturing Chemists' Association (MCA). The readiness of public health officials to authorize and to defer to such a private plan helped to elevate the MCA apparatus to hegemonic status. Private capture of public authority stood out as the hallmark of policy development throughout this interval.

The placid, corporate-dominated midcentury period did, however, witness some counterhegemonic stirrings. With countless workplaces awash in a flood of novel toxic synthetic chemicals, the drive to ignore, deny, or minimize risks encountered the skepticism and even hostility of a small cohort of critics. These dissenters wanted messages that were more readily comprehended by workers and that warned of the full range of adverse effects of exposures. To a significant extent, these critics began to cast their concerns and demands in terms of a right to know about hazards.

Even before the middle of the twentieth century, employers who exposed their subordinates to health risks faced mounting hazards themselves, but these hazards were in the political realm—from judicial decisions, legislative enactments, and administrative regulations carrying the force of law. David Egilman and Susanna Bohme observed incisively that "most warnings have not been instituted because of abstract ethical duty, but because of the constraints of statutory and common law." Since the turn of the twentieth century, established doctrine in the field then known as the law of master-servant relations imposed a duty to warn endangered subordinates of the less-than-obvious risks surrounding them on the job. As one overview of tort law put it in 1895, "The master may be bound to give to his employee all the information he may possess with regard to the danger of the employment, whether arising from the nature of the occupation or from extraneous causes." In the era before workers' compensation, advising workers of hazards, especially upon hiring, served to absolve the employer of responsibility for subsequent injury or illness. Indeed, the principle of assumption of known risk stood as a sturdy common-law defense for businesses sued for damages. In addition, beginning in the Progressive Era, some farsighted capitalists encouraged disclosure of workplace problems in the interest not only of escaping liability but also of promoting harmony across class lines.[1]

Producers and users of dangerous substances also had to deal with government labeling and other warning requirements. In almost all cases, the early statutes aimed primarily at protecting consumers outside the workplace or at reassuring consumers that the product they were purchasing actually contained the ingredients needed while appending a bit of warning information, albeit incidentally. Nonetheless, some legislation also served to alert at-risk workers. In 1910, Congress passed legislation to protect purchasers against misbranded or adulterated insecticides. This law provided only that all products containing arsenic be labeled as such, without any insistence on either characterizing that element as a dangerous toxin or offering any precautionary guidance on its proper handling. Throughout the early twentieth century, the states were the main arena of reform. In 1905, the legislatures in Minnesota and Massachusetts enacted measures that mandated the labeling of the industrial solvent methyl alcohol. Both these precedent-setting laws prescribed that the containers carry the word "poison" in sizable letters. A number of other states followed these examples. One proponent of workplace reform seized on the well-established, widely prevalent, state-level policy on drugs. In 1912, the Cornell medical professor W. Gilman Thompson offered this suggestion to the American Chemical Society: "I see no reason why there should not be warning labels attached to the containers of paints, varnish and volatile chemical irritants of all kinds, just as we now have compulsory labeling of the contents of all containers of dangerous drugs." The American Chemical Society took this message to heart, at least up to a point. Charles Baskerville, the organization's representative in the deliberations of the New York Factory Investigating Commission, recommended that the state impose a duty to label methyl alcohol. The legislature, failed, however, to put through any such requirement, which left the state's Division of Industrial Hygiene frustrated as it viewed the crusade to protect consumers outside the work setting. The industrial hygienists complained in 1917 that "little information has been given in popular form to those who are obliged to work with material containing wood alcohol of the dangers from inhaling its vapors or when the liquid comes in contact with the skin." The division proposed that all containers bear a label that described the substance as a poison and that bore the traditional warning symbol of the skull and crossbones. This recommendation went unheeded by decision makers. Despite this setback and other shortcomings, the Progressive Era did witness a significant start toward creating a duty to warn about workplace health hazards with the use of labels.[2]

The threat of federal intervention precipitated a thorough privatization campaign. In 1927, Congress passed the Federal Caustic Poison Act, which required that containers of acids and other caustic substances sold for household use carry a label featuring the word "poison." Because that law exempted industrial containers, the Workers' Health Bureau called for federal legislation requiring placement of similar warning messages on dangerous chemicals present in workplaces. Although that agitation bore no fruit, five years later Senator Hiram Bingham of Connecticut revived the issue with the introduction of a bill to expand labeling requirements, albeit still for household chemicals only. Despite its circumscribed nature, this proposal triggered a strong preemptive move by concerned industrialists. The MCA advised Bingham and his colleagues that it was engaged in discussions with the Surgeon General on a voluntarist label plan. Bingham obligingly indicated that he would prefer this method of solving the problem and ended his legislative effort. But the resumption of reform at the state level added to anxiety in business circles on this matter. In 1933, Massachusetts made mandatory the labeling of benzene receptacles with the message "Beware of Poisonous Fumes."[3]

In 1934, the US Public Health Service (PHS) and the MCA formed the Chemical Products Agreements Committee. In short order, this joint body produced warning messages for containers, available through the MCA, for eight types of substances, including benzene and carbon tetrachloride. The label for carbon disulfide advised that this was a highly volatile material and that it was a poison. The trade association also published manuals to guide the dissemination of information among producers, shippers, and users of hazardous chemicals. With the threat of congressional action gone, however, the Chemical Products Agreements Committee became passive after its initial burst of activity. In 1941, Surgeon General Thomas Parran moved to appoint a replacement member after determining that the committee was "not functioning at the present time." Parran's attempt to revitalize the group accomplished nothing. As of early 1944, the PHS-MCA operation still had reached only a total of eight agreements, covering nearly the same list of chemicals for which it had set requirements a decade earlier. Nonetheless, at that time, Warren Watson, an MCA committee member, told the committee chair, "There is no question . . . that adequate labeling plays a vital and important part as a safety device and that the use of precautionary labels and literature should be extended for hazardous products."[4]

For the chemical industries, the extension of labeling work became a matter to be taken into their own hands, not advanced through a partnership with federal officials. The lawsuits that involved substances not under the workers' compensation system catalyzed a determination to institutionalize more systematically the industrialists' own method of warning. In introducing a plan to collect data on member companies' experience with chemical "accidents" in 1939, the secretary of the MCA stated that "the marked upward trend of liability suits since 1930 needs no emphasis." The association later frankly explained the impetus for taking the initiative: "There was always the shadow of litigation that faces any producer as the result of real or fancied injury by a product. Chemical manufacturers had already seen the possible alternative of federal and state legislation which might or might not be wisely framed. MCA chose the path of self-correction." A system dominated by private parties had been the aim of the association since at least 1936. Shortly after its Conference on Liability Suits in April 1944, the association created the Committee on Labels and Precautionary Information. This small committee of corporate medical experts and other staff professionals would play a critical role in determining the extent and nature of hazard information dissemination for the subsequent quarter century.[5]

The MCA immediately expanded its preexisting program. In mid-1945, the MCA published a manual, *Product Caution Labels* (Manual L-2), comprised of sixty-seven entries for its affiliates and others in the field. The entries followed a format delineated in a companion publication, "A Guide for the Preparation of Warning Labels for Hazardous Chemicals" (Manual L-1), which was made public in *Chemical and Engineering News*. Implying the need to forestall government intervention, these manuals set forth a broad managerial obligation: "The education of employees regarding chemical hazards is, and must remain, the direct responsibility of their employers." The guidance in Manual L-1 spelled out a label's necessary components—the chemical (not trade) name, a signal word, a statement of the hazard, appropriate precautionary measures, and instructions for dealing with incidents. The three signal words expressed the degree of severity of the hazard—"danger" for the most severe, "warning" for the less severe, and "caution" for the least severe.[6]

The guide's treatment of general principles set out to frame issues in the most innocuous terms possible. The MCA criticized what it perceived as "indiscriminate use" of the problematic word "poison." The association proffered a narrow definition: "The commonly accepted meaning of 'Poison' refers to single dose oral toxicity." The section of the MCA guide devoted to defining terms offered the concession that "there is no definition adequate for all cases" but then referred readers to the aforementioned general principle. Under this definition, when the route of entry was either inhalation or percutaneous absorption, there was no poisoning. Similarly, when numerous doses of the intoxicant experienced over time caused a delayed response, there was no poisoning. This analysis offered no citations to the scientific literature or even passing reference to one toxicologist's acceptance of that interpretation of the concept. The readily available scholarship by Alice Hamilton, which synthesized a wealth of substantial findings, was premised on a wider sense of the legitimate types of chemical toxins and their range of actions in the human body. The opening sentence of the first chapter of Hamilton's 1925 overview, *Industrial Poisons in the United* States, makes this plain: "Industrial poisoning is typically chronic, the acute forms are relatively rare." Her subsequent work and that of other experts who used various methods of investigation proceeded from the same assumption regarding the scope of the field of industrial toxicology. Instead of validation by scientific authority, the trade association invoked the notion of a "commonly accepted meaning," without any substantiation of how widely shared this understanding of the concept was in the United States at the time. The association considered the word "poison" to be toxic.[7]

Much the same constricted perspective governed the designation of carcinogens. The inaugural edition of *Product Caution Labels* acknowledged the existence of one carcinogenic substance, beta naphthylamine, well known to attack the bladder. For chromates and bichromates of sodium and potassium, the recommended signal word was "warning," followed by the hazard description "harmful dust," advice to "avoid prolonged and repeated breathing or skin contact," and first aid procedures. This weak warning came eight years after two reviews of the literature appearing in the highly regarded *Journal of Industrial Hygiene and Toxicology* recognized chromates as a cause of lung cancer. It came three years after Wilhelm Hueper, a pioneering researcher who specialized in occupational and environmental carcinogenesis and who later directed the environmental cancer program at the National Cancer Institute, dismissed attempts to continue to deny carcinogenicity: "This optimistic outlook was destroyed definitely in recent years by the demonstration of an excessive incidence of pulmonary malignancy among workers of several German chromate factories." Hueper hastened to add, "The workers should be informed of the dangers to which they are exposed and of the significance of the prophylactic measures taken." In a follow-up article in the *Journal of the American Medical Association* in 1946, Hueper published a list of fourteen recommendations for the control of occupational cancer. This item stood at the top of his list: "Plant management officials, industrial workers and members of the medical profession must be made increasingly aware of the fact that numerous agents of our new industrial environment possess carcinogenic properties." This was guidance for which the chemical manufacturers had little use. The MCA's reticence on this score fit within a prevailing pattern across US culture of treating cancer as unmentionably terrifying.[8]

Notwithstanding its limitations, from its inception the MCA venture into the daunting, largely uncharted territory of chemical labeling did mark an important advance in the dissemination of hazard information. Manufacturers, shippers, and end-use handlers of dangerous substances received warnings where previously none had appeared. Widespread availability of labels that gave chemical names rather than meaningless or misleading trade names represented significant progress in sharing knowledge. With the implementation of the manufacturers' system, fewer containers carried unhelpful identities such as "LT-54F" or "Electric Motor Cleaner." At minimum, the MCA apparatus of a compendium of recommended labels and the concomitant guidance material, combined into Manual L-1 that originally held only the latter, served to orient employers of at-risk workers to the existence and importance of underappreciated risks, if only from the perspective of potential legal liability.[9]

The Manufacturing Chemists' Association strove to establish its labeling system as the national authority on the subject. As of 1946, it gained additional credibility by loosening its poison definition to cover doses taken by inhalation. Three years later, the association's interpretation of this term also encompassed toxins absorbed through the skin. By that time, the MCA's ambitions were reflected in a declaration of interest in expanding the distribution of facts about hazards: "Precautionary information should, so far as practicable, reach every person using, handling, or storing chemicals." The implicit commitment was that the MCA labeling program, supplemented by its catalog of Chemical Safety Data Sheets for managers and staff, would be the vehicle for reaching this lofty goal.[10]

The association's campaign to attain and maintain authoritative status involved regularly updating its Manual L-1, which reached a seventh edition in

1970. But even this final version of the publication perpetuated the corporate author's reluctance to acknowledge cancer threats. Beyond the concession it had made more than two decades earlier for beta naphthylamine, the Labels and Precautionary Information Committee was only prepared to identify the carcinogenic nature of one more substance, benzidine. The chromates still did not receive such recognition in this important reference work. Nor did bischloromethyl ether, another chemical known to chemical management to cause cancer. The precautionary principle was thus only cautiously applied in this regard.[11]

The MCA program marginalized further the cooperative arrangement devised with the Surgeon General in 1934. The role of the PHS became that of placing its stamp of approval on labels devised by its trade association partner and otherwise promoting the manufacturers' warnings. In 1949, the Labels and Precautionary Information Committee learned that the PHS wanted to discontinue their joint program and to formally endorse the chemical manufacturers' system. This was, of course, welcome news to industrial interests. However, the PHS feared that such a move would show an embarrassing lack of interest in a significant public health problem. In 1952, the PHS leadership finessed this potential difficulty by replacing the old joint Chemical Products Agreements Committee with a its own Chemical Products Labeling Committee. The purpose of this new entity was merely to advise the MCA, particularly in promoting uniform practices for household products. Such a transfer of authority served to confer additional legitimacy on the self-regulatory regime. The accommodating deference of federal authorities marked perhaps the greatest triumph of the midcentury drive for private control.[12]

The PHS retreat left the privatizers with ongoing challenges. Government action at the state level posed a constant menace to the chemical producers. In spelling out its future plans regarding the shape of public policy in 1949, the MCA Labels and Precautionary Information Committee made clear that its action would be "limited *primarily* to promoting labeling that will limit the need for legislative regulation on the subject, or that will serve to encourage revision of outmoded legislation." One of the first chores undertaken by the Labels and Precautionary Information Committee was the drafting of a model state bill. The association's Legal Advisory Committee tracked state judicial and legislative developments and refined their model proposal. As of 1952, that is, at a time when most states still had no labeling laws, the organization's stance was defensive in refusing to initiate legislative action. Only when other parties introduced legislation not in accord with its guidelines did the MCA enter the political arena to advocate for its prescription, in pursuit of uniformity across state lines and other principles.[13]

As the administrative capacity of states grew, the promulgation of regulations received more attention. When California regulators issued labeling orders for

114 substances in 1946, the Labels and Precautionary Information Committee reviewed them with care. To their relief, they found that the state had followed MCA recommendations "practically word for word." Nonetheless, within two years, the committee felt the need to propose a public relations campaign "to combat unreasonable demands" from state regulatory bodies. Another preemptive gambit was to influence the drafting of regulations. In 1950, an MCA representative met with the Illinois Industrial Commission on its pending rules and won their acceptance of the principles in the association's Manual L-1. That regulations in California, Illinois, and elsewhere were being designed by the respective state's labor officials placed them in need of closer scrutiny. Tracking the impending revision of the California rules in 1953, the Labels and Precautionary Information Committee found that state prepared to follow its prescriptions without deviation. Among other things, this meant dropping the requirement for benzene containers to display the unpleasant skull-and-crossbones image. The proliferation of varying rules, like that of varying statutory requirements, intensified the interest of the chemical producers in standardization. In 1950, the MCA decided to write a model label regulation "to avoid confusion of conflicting regulations." This was plainly the same reactive approach as the association adopted regarding legislative affairs.[14]

The quest for statutory and regulatory uniformity and minimal intervention necessitated the recruitment of a network of supporters in critical positions. Chemical industry agents pressed their case with a number of organizations in the hope of gaining support or at least neutralizing opposition. After the International Association of Governmental Labor Officials created a labeling subcommittee, Sanford Hill of du Pont appeared at its 1953 annual meeting to offer insights from the MCA's decade of experience. Hill described the association's system and noted that California's Department of Industrial Relations had used it in its regulatory scheme, as had Illinois, Oregon, and Rhode Island. "Uniformity is of major importance when regulations of this type are drafted," he contended, leaving no doubt that adherence to the manufacturers' model was the best means to that end. Hill gave the labor officials copies of the manufacturers' label manual and assured them, "You will find that it covers your needs." The labor group responded by resolving to rely on the MCA-influenced Illinois regulations, supplemented by the guidance of Manual L-1 itself, in constructing their codes. Hill became a member of the labeling subcommittee of this association and delivered its report at the 1955 convention. He singled out for praise the recent law enacted in Massachusetts, which forced the Department of Labor and Industries to share regulatory control with the Department of Public Health. Hill also took the opportunity to reiterate the priority of attaining uniform requirements. A more enlightened perspective regarding the growth of public policy for a new, complex phenomenon developing under uncertain circumstances would have been to promote varied state innovations in order to find by experimentation an optimal approach or a number of better approaches. Under that alternative route, a uniform pattern might eventually coalesce as experience demonstrated the superiority of one state's method. That an employee of a private corporation became directly involved in making policy for a group of state officials indicates unmistakably the extent to which public sector leadership was prepared to acquiesce to outside interests during this period.[15]

Industrial hygienists working for state and, to a lesser extent, local and federal agencies were another constituency that the MCA sought to influence. The 1952 meeting of the American Conference of Governmental Industrial Hygienists (ACGIH) declared its support for labels on harmful substances and pledged to work with the MCA. When the ACGIH attempted to determine how many substances should be subject to warnings, however, it found itself divided between those willing to accept the MCA list and those seeking a longer one. A division of opinion also existed over whether to follow without deviation the guidance in the MCA manual. Because several states had already taken action based on the industry's plan, its preemptive role exerted a shaping force. Sanford Hill defended his association's well-established system at the industrial hygienists' 1955 conference. Hill attacked deployment of any wider poison definition and reiterated the imperative for uniformity. He also offered the blithe prediction that "precautionary statements listing do's and don'ts should gradually become unnecessary" on labels. When the ACGIH leaned away from the MCA's pinched notion of a poison and otherwise proceeded with devising recommendations at variance with the wishes of industry, the association complained repeatedly. In that regard, the MCA represented only the tip of the spear among industry critics. When the ACGIH sent a draft of its own proposed label guide to a number of trade associations in 1957, they received a torrent of criticism. The following year, Hervey Elkins, a member of the hygienists' labeling committee, told his colleagues, "The protests varied from specific criticisms of various portions of the Guide to the blunt suggestion that we retire from the area and leave the handling of labeling to people who knew something about it." Elkins, a veteran administrator with the Massachusetts Department of Labor and Industries, objected to the MCA's preoccupation with acute toxicity and concomitant refusal to identify toxic substances yielding chronic effects as poisons. He also insisted on the need to provide labeling for more chemical mixtures, unintimidated by assertions about possible violations of trade secrets. Thomas Nale, medical director at Union Carbide, followed Elkins's presentation with a full-throated defense of the MCA principles. Nale criticized the ACGIH label committee for failing to have any members from industry, oblivious to the fact that this was an organization composed of government professionals. At their next gathering, the industrial hygienists were undeterred and approved a "Guide to Rules and Regulations for the Labeling of Hazardous Materials" that defined poisons as including "any substance or mixture of substances with cumulative toxic effects that may prove slowly fatal on [sic—or] permanently disabling." The proposed code provided no exemptions or special treatment for trade secrets. The hegemony of the privatizers was less than absolute. Nonetheless, publishing this guide and having it adopted by state lawmakers were two different matters. The ACGIH functioned as a repository of technical expertise, not as a political advocacy group, and retreated from the labeling battlefield after 1959. The organization disbanded its label committee in 1966.[16]

Warding off deep federal intervention represented another front in the contest between public and private forces. The fact that the 1949 edition of Manual L-1 incorporated a sizable section devoted to agricultural chemicals—then commonly known as economic poisons—offered another indicator of the manufacturing chemists' determination to oversee the distribution of hazard information across the spectrum of chemical industries. The timing of this extension of the MCA's scope of attention was telling. Two years earlier, Congress had passed the Federal Insecticide, Fungicide, and Rodenticide Act (FIFRA), superseding a 1910 federal statute designed to prevent consumer fraud, not worker illness. The earlier law had required only that containers of insecticides with arsenic as an ingredient bear a label attesting to its presence, with no obligation either to declare the poisonous nature of that element or to provide any precautionary message. In contrast, FIFRA covered a wide range of pesticides and prescribed several standard label provisions. The act required that highly toxic substances have a label that included the word "poison" in red letters, the skull-and-crossbones symbol, and antidote information. It required that a label be "in such terms as to render it likely to be read and understood by the ordinary individual" but set forth no circumstances under which a label had to be understandable to those who did not read English. FIFRA also outlawed false or misleading claims about the safety of products. In their endeavors to meet these new obligations and to contain the impact of the 1947 statute, industry interest groups had the advantage of dealing with the US Department of Agriculture (USDA). The USDA epitomized the captive public agency, dominated by those it was supposed to regulate. Labor activist Marion Moses viewed the midcentury USDA as "the federal agency most hostile toward farmworkers and most resistant to any changes in policy that would ameliorate their harsh working conditions."[17]

For the MCA, the market segment devoted to agricultural products presented both promise and peril in the quarter century after World War II. With food and fiber production increasing on ever-larger farms as Americans consumed more food and clothing throughout a prolonged phase of prosperity, demand soared for synthetic chemicals that killed unwanted fauna and flora. Newly formulated organophosphate and organochlorine pesticides and other inventions to eradicate pests and weeds were generally greeted as wonders of progress. But even amid the chorus of acclaim, some apprehension and criticism of health hazards arose, especially for risks to livestock downwind from poisons and homeowners who might misuse products in their yards or gardens. Little early dissent focused on the precarious plight of farmworkers, who were subject to far greater exposure. In this context, framing the issues and manipulating the policy and practice of the USDA regarding warning labels took on great importance.[18]

The chemical producers wasted no time in pursuing their interests with the FIFRA administrators. Both the implementation of this law and the possibility that it could function as an entering wedge for further federal intervention mobilized both the MCA and the National Agricultural Chemicals Association (NACA), a trade group whose membership overlapped with that of the MCA. The MCA's Labels and Precautionary Information Committee had formed a pesticide subcommittee in 1945. The regulations generated to implement the law offered no significant challenges to industry's conception of proper labeling. The USDA granted the trade association's request for an exemption from labeling rules for its inventory of products that did not meet the new federal standards. The USDA's Pesticide Registration Division readily approved both manufacturers' preexisting warning labels, with little or no modification, and their newly drafted ones. In the view of the historian Pete Daniel, the lax approval procedures during the 1950s and 1960s amounted to "government-industry collusion" at the expense of the public welfare.[19]

With a national regulatory mandate, the USDA held the power to do a great deal to advance the manufacturers' objective of standardization. Both the USDA and the agrichemical industry reached out to state regulators to support their drive for uniformity. The plan to create a single nationwide labeling system could obviously be undermined if states exercised their right to impose different requirements. Here again, the demand for simplicity overrode any consideration that encouragement of varied state-level initiatives might lead to discovery of beneficial innovations in communicating hazard information and thereby preventing additional disease, disability, and death. In 1948, Albert Heagy, the secretary of the Association of Economic Poison Control Officials (AEPCO), the national organization of state regulators, reported that the USDA was soliciting the opinions of state officials on the proper labeling of insecticides. Heagy signaled a readiness to assist the incipient federal campaign to surmount the prevailing lack of standardization. "Collaborative study and effort are necessary," he told his assembled colleagues, "to attain our objective of uniformity in legislation, regulation and enforcement of laws controlling economic poisons." The published volumes of the association's proceedings for 1948 and for many subsequent years carried both its Proposed Uniform State Economic Poisons Bill and its Proposed Regulatory Principles. The bill encouraged state agricultural administrators to adhere to the standards set by the USDA, which in turn was following the MCA principles. One principle was to require the conspicuous use of the word "poison" accompanied by the skull and crossbones for materials deemed highly toxic to humans. In enumerating criteria for what constituted a high level of toxicity, however, the guidelines opened a loophole by allowing exemptions for substances deemed "not in fact highly toxic to man," without indicating how officials were to determine such innocuity.[20]

Standard practices of the AEPCO and its successor after 1954, the Association of American Pesticide Control Officials (AAPCO), facilitated close correspondence between their positions and those of the pesticide makers. The state officials' group always invited representatives of agrichemical firms to participate in their deliberations. At the 1949 AEPCO sessions, thirty-five industry men joined fifty-two state officials and twenty USDA staff members. At that meeting, the association's Executive Committee formally invited industrialists to take part in the discussions of its State Relations Committee. The Executive Committee also thanked du Pont's Sanford Hill for his presentation on the MCA guide. The roster of speakers at annual conferences regularly included experts from both the chemical associations and individual firms. When the MCA attorney John Conner addressed the 1951 meeting, he reinforced the familiar central theme. "I know," Conner declared, "that I speak for the entire chemical industry when I state that the activities of this Association in support of the development of uniform legislative and enforcement policies have our enthusiastic and wholehearted support." Conner also advised against hasty, unnecessary legislative action. (The attorney's presentation gave no glimpse of his current project of coauthoring a *Manual of Chemical Products Liability*, which compiled scores of recent pesticide liability cases.) The government agents ingesting a steady diet of self-interested messages gave no evidence of any qualms about possible undue influence from outside parties legally subject to their oversight.[21]

The success of the tight partnership of private and public pesticide parties was immediate and obvious. In 1953, Walter Murphy, editor of the *Journal of Agricultural and Food Chemistry*, praised recent accomplishments: "The LAPI [Labels and Precautionary Information] Committee worked in cooperation with state authorities and has been quite effective in encouraging the development of regulations which correspond closely with its system. Special attention has been given to encouragement of uniformity among the laws of our states." Recognizing which partner drove this process, Murphy singled out the MCA for congratulations for its contributions. Two years later, the AAPCO president Floyd Roberts reiterated the priority of invariability in legislation and regulation. Roberts noted, somewhat euphemistically, that reaching this goal involved having "due regard for the voice of industry" and called attention to his Executive Committee's recent meeting with industry representatives. "The informal manner and the fact that that meeting is strictly off the record are conducive to a free discussion of any disturbing matters," he maintained. That this committee would be holding similar conversations with farmworkers or other workers endangered by toxic agricultural chemicals was unimaginable. Roberts announced that most of his association's members currently accepted the proposed basic principles and definitions, that is, the ideas of the MCA. In the agricultural regulatory arena, private forces enjoyed hegemony.[22]

Poisonings in the household setting, especially those victimizing children, drew the medical profession into the political realm in ways that were more challenging to those producing pesticides and other chemical products. The campaign of the American Medical Association (AMA) for federal legislation to further control a range of toxic substances presented the MCA, the NACA, and their colleagues with an advocacy group not so tractable as state and federal agricultural officials. (Unlike civil servants, physicians were not looking for better-paying jobs with chemical firms.) The AMA initially supported only a voluntary system of hazard controls. Bernard Conley, secretary of its Committee on Pesticides, promoted voluntarism, with additional educational work by manufacturers, at the 1950 AEPCO conference. But by 1958, the medical association saw the necessity of a more potent remedy and drafted a bill that would grant wide federal authority over labeling rules. In announcing the rationale for this move, Conley characterized the current state and federal regulations as "sketchy, nonuniform, and generally inadequate." He also pointed out, "There are no federal laws for the precautionary labeling of industrial chemicals." At a conference of the National Association of Sanitarians in July 1958, Conley pointed out that "ninety percent of the states have no laws for industrial chemicals and both morbidity and mortality statistics provide ample evidence of the harm from overexposure to work chemicals." On this occasion, having noted the fatal poisonings of preschool children, he also argued for the value of warning images, such as the traditional skull and crossbones. In his view, these devices surmounted any "language barrier by reason of age, education or foreign birth." Thus, the AMA's plan sought to extend regulations beyond household products to those used in the nonagricultural workplace and called for the use of easily comprehended symbols.[23]

The best defense was renewed offense. The manufacturers and their supporters had long been advocates of education, but as a voluntary matter under private auspices. Based on the fallacious premise that labeling alone constituted a sufficient risk management strategy, the industry made a panacea of proper reading of labels and compliance with their guidance. From this angle, poisonings resulted almost invariably from the negligence of users. Victim blaming was a long-held tendency in economic poison circles. In 1948, the trade journal *Agricultural Chemicals* made this exculpatory pleading: "The manufacturing industry is helpless when it comes to careless applications. Labels mean nothing if they are not read and heeded; yet, the manufacturer is too often criticized for the misdeeds of persons who misuse his products." Seven years later, the MCA unveiled a Read the Label program. On occasion, proponents of this strategy did venture to suggest additional obligations for education and training. In 1954, Wayland Hayes, Jr., a senior toxicologist in the PHS, offered this advice to western cotton planters: "Greater importance needs to be given to the importance of careful reading of labels. The labels, which are subject to State and Federal control, are the product of careful thought. Accidents with pesticides which do not involve a violation of the instructions and precautions on the label are extremely rare. However, the mere reading of labels is not enough. Each agricultural laborer must be made to understand the reason for precautions." Given the prevailing inattention to such considerations during this period, Hayes went on to warn quite strikingly, "Proper training may present very real difficulty when laborers are illiterate or when there is a language barrier between them and their supervisors. However, adequate training is a moral responsibility of the employer and the foremen." At the 1958 meeting of the state pesticide regulators, L. S. Hitchner, executive secretary of the NACA, urged greater attention to education of those exposed to chemical hazards "in order to minimize the need for legislation and regulation." Hitchner also voiced fears of reformist legislators eager for publicity.[24]

With the AMA's abandonment of voluntarism, the manufacturers found themselves confronting formidable opponents. The doctors entered the political arena not only organized in the prestigious and powerful AMA but also as righteous caregivers who had to rely on inadequate information as they dealt firsthand with poisoned patients. Accounts of fatal intoxications of children amounted to a public relations nightmare for the industrial chemists. Well-publicized incidents involving pesticide residues in grocery products amplified public uneasiness, adding to the industrialists' discomfort. In these circumstances, it became necessary to accommodate the advocates of reform. The MCA and its besieged fellows set their defensive perimeter at the boundaries of the worksite. The duty to offer additional protection to the general public was undeniable. But somehow the workers whose risks were usually far greater had to be disregarded.[25]

On being apprised of the AMA's intentions, the MCA's Labels and Precautionary Information Committee held an emergency meeting to devise a response. In ensuing discussions with organized medicine during mid-1958, industry officials stressed their objection to the inclusion of chemicals used outside the home environment. At one encounter involving about one hundred industry representatives at which "critical remarks came hot and heavy," the Chemical Specialties Manufacturers Association told the AMA Committee on Toxicology that any federal legislation should be limited to household products and that the definition of a toxic substance should be narrower than that offered by the AMA. With support from the MCA, the specialty manufacturers promoted their own alternative bill. By January 1959, the industry proposal had gained the backing of the American Petroleum Institute and the National Paint, Varnish and Lacquer Association. The united trade associations hastened to distribute copies of their bill to sympathetic members of Congress. If nothing else, the chemical producers' machinations from the outset clarified that uniformity was not their paramount principle after all. Federal legislation could standardize labeling and other related informational issues on a national basis, superseding a welter of state laws and rules. But that goal disappeared under the threat that federal standards would reach into the workplace.[26]

Despite the failure of its initial round of discussions, the chemical interests continued to try to persuade the AMA to change course. However, not one member of the AMA Committee on Toxicology accepted the invitation to attend a session of the Industrial Hygiene Foundation in October 1958 devoted to the topic of label legislation. They missed a presentation there by J. T. Fuess of the chemicals division of Eastman Kodak, a member of the MCA Labels and Precautionary Information Committee, that damned the purported excesses of the AMA formulation. Fuess contended that no regulation of workplace substances was needed because "the safety record of chemicals in industry is excellent." He explained this by the claim that industrial chemicals were handled by "a relatively few experienced operators." This critique received a warm reception from the corporate crowd that dominated the foundation. For the medical men who had bypassed this opportunity, Fuess's paper was published in the medical association's own industrial health journal in March 1959. Meanwhile, his Eastman colleague J. H. Sterner carried the message to his fellow members of the AMA Board of Trustees. The densely networked business interests had no shortage of ways to engage in outreach to dissuade their opponents.[27]

The introduction of rival bills led to brief congressional hearings in 1959 and 1960. Lawmakers gave formal consideration only to the industry bill, granting one day of hearings in each chamber. At the Senate session in August 1959, the Chemical Specialty Manufacturers Association took the lead in defending its plan. The MCA's expert, Nicholas Walker, reviewed his organization's lengthy history of contributions in the field. Regarding the exemption of workplace materials from the pending proposal, Walker observed, "A fifty-five-gallon drum would generally be used by an experienced workman in a plant, while a small household product might be used by a housewife who would be quite unfamiliar with the hazards involved." American Federation of Labor and Congress of Industrial Organizations (AFL-CIO) witness George Brown endorsed the AMA bill. Brown disagreed with Walker on workers' knowledge of hazards, given the lack of proper labeling. The labor federation official told the senators that treating industrial and nonindustrial substances by the same standards would achieve uniformity across many types of products, effectively turning the manufacturers' preoccupation with that principle against them.[28]

At the hearings in the House of Representatives seven months later, the chemical industry's perspective prevailed, notwithstanding further difficulties in maintaining a consistent stance on uniformity. MCA witness Chester French contended that federal involvement in labeling workplace substances would constitute an intrusion into an aspect of employer-employee relations traditionally left to the states. But French gave no assurance that the fifty states would all handle this problem in the same manner. The most important turn of events in this session was the AMA's formal concession of defeat. The principal sponsor of their bill, Representative Thomas Curtis, testified that the industry's proposal now satisfied him. The medical association's O. Benwood Hunter, Jr., also endorsed the manufacturers' measure but did propose some amendments to it. These included mandating the placement of warning symbols on containers of the most dangerous substances. Hunter praised the "simple and striking" images devised by the International Labour Organization (ILO) and specifically promoted the widely recognized skull and crossbones. While conceding the exemption of the manufacturing sector from the scope of regulation, the AMA did recommend that containers in other workplaces carry labels. In contrast, the labor movement's George Brown continued to hold out for applying the label requirement to all places of employment. Brown expressed particular concern for employees in nonunion settings. In his view, the unorganized masses of US workers had a "right to know the hazards they face handling and working with dangerous substances and they need to know it promptly and simply. An effective labeling law whose coverage included America's workers would safeguard that right." At this moment, such a somewhat precocious claim of entitlement fell on deaf ears.[29]

After this cursory review, Congress passed the Federal Hazardous Substances Labeling Act on July 12, 1960. The range of substances put under regulation was confined to household products, leaving all but domestic service workers unprotected. The category of highly toxic substances requiring the signal word "poison" was narrowly drawn by reliance on acute effects. The legislation imposed no requirement for the display of warning symbols. The underlying premise that the attachment of labels to containers constituted a sufficient preventive strategy was further ratified in national policy. The chemical manufacturers had another victory.[30]

A scattering of dissidents pressed against the limitations of the privatized midcentury regime. Individuals from within both the public and private sectors voiced discontent that ranged from mild unease to bitter outrage at the secrecy that prevailed. In a few cases, these people came forth from unexpected institutional locations. Dissident activity often involved inchoate attempts to articulate a worker's right to knowledge that extended beyond the opportunity to read an MCA label. Even within the mainstream institutions that comprised or acquiesced to the privately controlled system, a significant contingent of individuals in positions of responsibility took a relatively expansive stance on the distribution of health hazard information. Some even joined those asserting a right of workers to know the facts regarding their risks of occupational disease.

Individuals in corporate management occasionally espoused interest in making their subordinates aware of workplace health risks. To be sure, the main thrust of educational activity in the 1950s and 1960s remained the nonoccupational risk factors of employees' lifestyle choices. Yet the communication programs of some companies also delivered warnings about health threats on the job. In 1956, Raymond Murray, the medical director of Sperry Gyroscope Company, told attendees at the Industrial Hygiene Foundation annual meeting that employees deserved "frank and honest answers" about hazards. "All of the unpleasantries associated with inadequate or false information, with its necessary poor personal relations, can be dissipated in an hour's lecture," Murray assured, perhaps too optimistically. At the Union Carbide plant in Institute, West Virginia, the medical director, Richard Sexton, along with other managers, gave out written materials and led group discussions on the hazards of hydrogen cyanide and ethylene oxide; workers displayed "intense interest" in the topics. From Sexton's standpoint, "all chemical plant employees should be made aware of the injury potential of all chemicals and should be apprised of the appropriate first-aid measures." After reviewing how little the AMA had done to promote workers' education, he presented the case study of his program at the 1959 meeting of the American Academy of Occupational Medicine as one practical, replicable way for his colleagues to move forward. Sexton and others in the management ranks saw the plant nurse as a key figure in increasing the flow of information. Some in the business community clearly expected management to be forthright about sharing the knowledge it held.[31]

Professionals across the field shared that expectation, at least in the immediate postwar years. In 1946, the ACGIH imagined the creation of a network of "health stewards" who would warn and educate rank-and-file workers. "There should be no particular objection to such a program," argued the conference's Committee on Industrial Hygiene Education, "since the trend in management is to inform workers of the potential hazards of their occupation and, thereby, enlist their assistance in safeguarding against these hazards." When the government hygienists revisited the issue in 1955, its Committee on Worker Health Information retreated from the bottom-up approach, maintaining that "the most important channel for transmitting industrial health information to the worker is *from plant management.*" Four years later, that committee expressed disappointment regarding the ability of joint labor-management worksite health committees to foster educational activity. The industrial hygienists had found that management commonly opposed the establishment and empowerment of such bodies. They had learned that openness toward transferring information had tight limits.[32]

Beyond their hopes that employers would voluntarily support or take steps to spread knowledge, the government industrial hygienists promoted transparency in public policy. The ACGIH put forth a model state industrial hygiene regulatory code in 1948. The document offered an unequivocal endorsement of the right to know: "Every employer shall inform his employees regarding the hazards to which they are exposed, the methods which have been taken for the prevention and control of such hazards, and the proper methods for utilizing such control measures." However, the clause establishing this new right was embedded in a much larger formulation that led to its entanglement in the ongoing jurisdictional dispute between health and labor authorities. Because the hygienists' plan called for regulatory control of occupational disease by state health departments, it incurred the wrath of the International Association of Governmental Labor Officials. Opposition from an organization predisposed to favor the enlargement of workers' rights diminished whatever chances of realization this democratic proposal possessed. No state adopted the ACGIH proposition, another indication that the midcentury quest for uniform policies was a circumscribed one.[33]

One academic scientist strove conscientiously to help demystify the composition of mysteriously named hazardous pesticides for farmworkers and other users. "I am continually being plagued with letters asking 'What is Super-Bugoo-12?'" lamented the Penn State professor Donald Frear in 1947. Frear's discomfort with the widespread confusion caused by the proliferation of trade-name products led him to approach the Agricultural Insecticide and Fungicide Association (forerunner of the National Agricultural Chemical Association) about their interest in producing a reference work that would identify the actual chemical ingredients in products on the market. Rebuffed by that trade association, Frear took it upon himself to compile a trade-name index. In a declaration that illuminated his motivation for this project, he offered the industry this unsolicited, and unheeded, piece of advice in 1948: "I feel rather strongly about the indiscriminate use of new and untried materials by the general public. I believe that the insecticide and fungicide manufacturers should be responsible for keeping the new materials completely out of the hands of the using public until all of the factors concerning these materials are known rather completely." Charles Smith, a pesticide trade association representative, defended the recent additions to their product lines as "not highly toxic" and told Frear that his proposal would stifle progress. Amid the ongoing flood of innovative formulations, the agricultural chemist kept up the difficult task of updating his *Pesticide Handbook* through numerous editions.[34]

The industrious Frear found time to undertake other chores to promote wider understanding. Beginning in 1949, he assisted the AMA's campaign to warn the public about pesticide hazards. The following year, he published *Newer Pesticides*, an overview that covered dichlorodiphenyltrichloroethane (DDT), parathion, and other products. "It is our feeling," he told the AMA's Bernard Conley in explaining the booklet's aim, "that the average user of the newer materials used for pest control purposes is not fully informed on the potential hazards of these materials."[35]

Probably the foremost midcentury advocate for a transparent approach to occupational health information was physician Herbert Abrams. In 1947, Abrams became head of the Bureau of Adult Health in the California Department of Public Health. Much to his advantage, amicable relations prevailed between that state's Department of Industrial Relations and its Department of Public Health. No law blocked state agents from providing health-related information to workers and their representatives. Abrams made the most of this hospitable environment by adopting democratically inclusive and participatory methods. An exceptional willingness to work closely with the labor movement was the most obvious manifestation of his class-bridging and race-bridging orientation.[36]

Abrams came to California at a moment of ferment in progressive public health circles. Traditional principles of state responsibility for protecting the well-being of the citizenry had always carried an admixture of paternalism. Since the 1930s, a rights-claiming perspective had begun to challenge that attitude and its underlying premise of noblesse oblige. Ascendant concepts of human rights were reframing questions related to improving the health of

Americans. Abrams introduced his bureau's mission to the California medical profession by quoting from Milton Rosenau's classic *Preventive Medicine and Hygiene*: "Industrial Hygiene is one of the most important topics in preventive medicine and hygiene, as it deals with the health, the welfare, and the human rights of the vast majority of the adult population." Because this invocation of human rights came from a standard textbook by a much-respected Harvard professor, no leftist ideologue, it served to legitimate a disruptive mission of expanding workers' rights.[37]

The pesticides in California's enormous agricultural sector occupied much of Abrams's attention as he began his service as a state official. Because those substances were among the few workplace chemicals subject to systematic labeling regulation, that focus provided him with a fortuitous orientation toward right-to-know issues. In 1949, Abrams pressed for reform of FIFRA to the ACGIH, calling for "a labeling law by which all economic poisons are clearly labeled according to their content and amount of each ingredient." This meant identification of the actual chemical ingredients comprising a pesticide, not merely provision of a sometimes-meaningless trade name, as mandated by the federal statute. Recognizing the limited value of placing labels on containers, Abrams also encouraged the industrial hygienists to "disseminate appropriate educational material for farmers and . . . the employees engaged in handling and manufacturing economic poisons." The following year, he pointed out that the regulations issued by the California Department of Agriculture required that labels name all active ingredients and indicate protective measures. He underscored this observation by urging that "workmen in actual contact with hazardous chemicals should be made aware of the dangers of improper handling, and should be kept informed of effective control methods." Very early in his tenure with the Department of Public Health, Abrams became a member of the AMA Committee on Pesticides. In that capacity, he was able to inform the AMA of poisoning cases in his state. In the 1950s, California was one of few jurisdictions that kept any systematic records on pesticide intoxication.[38]

In attempting to prevent occupational disease in California farming, Abrams and his colleagues in the state government had to rely heavily on their own difficult-to-enforce rules. At far-flung rural worksites where no labor unions stood watch on a daily basis, this guaranteed frustration. The situation increased Abrams's appreciation of the potential value of unions as partners in enforcing rights. At the American Public Health Association meeting in 1951, Abrams described a recent experience in which an unidentified union at a lead smelter had requested state assistance to deal with lead poisoning. One issue there was the employer's refusal to divulge the results of periodic employee medical testing. Abrams reported that when state industrial hygienists conducted environmental monitoring in the smelter, there was "as full participation by the company and union as any agency could hope for." A union representative accompanied the hygienist; the union was informed of the air-sampling results. In arranging the medical phase of the study, Abrams and his team negotiated these concessions from management: "The fundamental right of each employee to decide to what medical personnel his findings should be made available was established and safeguarded from the outset." His Bureau of Adult Health's general policy required that "identical reports of findings are delivered both to management and to the union" in those instances in which the union had requested a study. As previously noted, the information gathered elsewhere by state inspectors and investigators very often remained inaccessible to workers and their unions, even though workers as taxpayers financed state-level labor and health agencies. In the context of widespread solicitude for the privileges of industry, the Abrams method stood out as exceptional, if not unique.[39]

This method of sharing information soon faced a test. Since the 1920s, the Johns Manville Products Corporation had mined and processed diatomaceous earth, a substance used as a filtering medium and in other commercial applications, in Lompoc, California. In 1932, Robert Legge and Esther Rosencrantz published their discovery that the mineral extracted and refined at this site had caused silicosis among a sizable share of the largely Latinx workforce. Despite this warning of the existence of a serious risk of dust disease, Johns Manville refused to let an investigator from the state health department enter its facilities in 1940. When granted access four years later, the state found numerous poorly controlled, dust-generating operations. Subsequent attempts to mount a follow-up study in Lompoc were thwarted by the company and its allies at Metropolitan Life Insurance Company, as was an attempt to publish an additional medical report on pneumoconiosis cases there. Company doctors who examined dust-exposed workers failed to inform their patients of pneumoconiosis diagnoses. Given this legacy of obstruction, the Johns Manville plant in Santa Barbara County presented a setting very unpromising for any sort of democratic intervention.[40]

Creative maneuvering overcame corporate opposition. Late in 1951, Abrams encouraged Robert Goe, an editor of the state tuberculosis association's magazine, to explore the situation confronting the six hundred workers in Lompoc. Goe's investigation dug up more than one hundred workers' compensation cases related to the dust hazard. The article he published in January 1952, entitled "Death by Dust," offered graphic details of autopsy findings and other facts revealed in compensation proceedings. This exposé also indicted the damming up of information: "Industry has not, as far as can be determined, carried on a realistic program to educate the employee to accept effective disease prevention measures or to acquaint him with the hazards." Goe's call for further medical research and employee education functioned as a work order for Abrams. His bureau immediately began planning a survey of the Lompoc facilities.[41]

Deepening controversy at the plant also served to draw Abrams and his colleagues further into this matter. On March 17, 1952, Local 146 of the International Chemical Workers Union (ICWU) began a work stoppage against Johns Manville. The primary issue in contention was a performance pay system that gave workers a perverse incentive to refuse to wear respirators that diminished their productivity. The union sought the elimination of this unhealthful compensation scheme and held out for over seven months to that end. In the midst of the dispute, Abrams released the results of a study on the thirty-two workers' compensation cases he had located and on the numerous instances in which Johns Manville workers had been hospitalized with work-related respiratory conditions. Local 146 leader John Rodrigues noted that, despite their awareness of the dust hazard and its ill effects, "the company representatives insisted that their physicians informed them that the dust in this occupation is no more hazardous than the dust raised by the farmer in the fields." Although its eventual settlement left the speedup system in place, the dispute underscored the need for an improved flow of information to at-risk employees.[42]

The battle in southern California prompted ICWU leaders to increase their organization's capacity to protect members' health interests. When Abrams left California to set up a clinic for the Building Service Employees Union in Chicago later in 1952, he agreed to become a consultant for the ICWU. From this seemingly marginal position, he gave the union a wealth of guidance and made the right to know a cardinal principle of the union's position on occupational health. Reflecting on the Lompoc experience in the ICWU newspaper, Abrams drew out this lesson: "In motivating employees for health, first of all is the necessity of informing workers of the facts. Have the workers know what they are doing and know the potential hazards of the job and know how to protect themselves and fellow employees against these hazards." He maintained that in the aftermath of the strike, Johns Manville management had adopted a better attitude and was cooperating with Local 146 in a new joint health and safety committee. This consultancy placed Abrams within a very small group of occupational health professionals employed by the labor movement. As late as 1973, the US labor movement employed only one full-time physician and three industrial hygienists.[43]

Based on the ICWU's experience in California, Abrams advised his medical colleagues not to assume that workers had little or nothing to contribute to the systematic recognition and control of workplace hazards. "We are prone to conclude quickly that the worker is unintelligent," he contended in the *AMA*

Archives of Industrial Hygiene and Occupational Medicine, "and the destructive germ of cynicism begins to replace a healthy constructive approach." The conflict in Lompoc had, in his view, brought about a transformation there. Abrams concluded his analysis of the design of a successful workplace health program with an endorsement of the inclusive, bottom-up approach: "Finally, and perhaps most important, give working people an opportunity to participate in the health program. No amount of exhortation and pontification from above about safety will do the job as well as just permitting the working man to help himself and his fellows." Abrams closed his appeal with a concrete proposal for the creation of jointly controlled workplace committees whose functions would extend to soliciting workers' ideas for eradicating hazards. He made this message more palatable to employers and their lieutenants in the health professions by adopting the rhetorical framing and institutional devices of the state-of-the-art human relations paradigm. Abrams's proposition seized upon growing managerial anxiety over employee motivation, a newfound preoccupation with the value of communication, and the recent introduction of modest participative initiatives like suggestion boxes.[44]

In 1953, Abrams took on the work-related diseases afflicting ICWU members employed in mining and processing phosphates in central Florida. Just as the diatomaceous earth workforce had included a sizable contingent of Latinos, the miserable toil of extracting phosphorus ore and refining it into phosphates for agricultural fertilizer and other commercial uses had long been left to African American men. In the early twentieth century, this unhealthful work had often fallen to victims of the convict labor system. Abrams determined that the Florida phosphate workers underwent exposure not only to toxic phosphorus but also to the uranium interspersed with the phosphorus deposits and to fluorides in gaseous and particulate forms. In October 1954, ICWU Local 38 leader Harvey Baker told Abrams that if management denied him access to their plants on his upcoming visit, that denial would serve a useful heuristic purpose. Such a move would, in his opinion, lead to "the membership better realizing there must be something to hide if the company would not permit your entry." When Abrams visited Florida, employers did keep him off their property. Nonetheless, his off-site conversations with members of the phosphate locals confirmed the gravity of the situation.[45]

With both the ICWU and Florida State Board of Health lacking the resources to sponsor a large-scale study, the only way to gain additional information was to turn to the PHS. The federal officials agreed to work in partnership with Florida authorities on a modest preliminary investigation. In the fall of 1956, they met with the management of the central Florida phosphate firms to plan a hazard-monitoring study of their approximately four thousand employees.

In this section of the conservative South, the union was excluded from these deliberations. Abrams's attempts to connect the PHS crew with the relevant local unions also yielded no role for labor in the conduct of the measurements of air pollution beginning in October 1957. Several months later, a preliminary report of the very high levels of fluorides, silica, and so-called nuisance dusts detected went only to management. A conference held to discuss these findings also excluded labor representatives. On August 19, 1958, ICWU president Walter Mitchell complained to Henry Doyle, the acting chief of the PHS Occupational Health Program, calling it "surprising to have a preliminary survey [report] submitted to the companies without giving the union access at the same time." Making his point more emphatically, Mitchell told Doyle that "union representatives of the workers concerned have every right to be involved in all phases of the survey, including any discussions of the preliminary report." At this juncture, however, participation in this investigation had become a moot point. The federal and state officials' recommendation for a larger follow-up study was never implemented, despite Abrams's persistent efforts to induce the PHS to perform a more systematic assessment. Although the specific reasons for a failure to follow through on this problem are unclear, it was not the general inclination of the federal agency during this period to pursue questions of work-related cancer aggressively. In the view of Wilhelm Hueper, the occupational cancer specialist at the National Cancer Institute, the PHS feared retaliation in the form of reduced funding if it antagonized politically potent business interests. Hueper alleged that the agency feared denial of other research opportunities. "I heard a member of the former Division of Industrial Hygiene," he recalled, "making the statement that this organization must maintain 'harmonious' relations with industrial management so as to retain opportunities to work in fields other than occupational cancer, which represented a sensitive subject in public relations."[46]

Instigating this evaluation of working conditions did produce some positive outcomes for the phosphate workers. The union put on a four-day educational conference in February 1959 at its hall in Mulberry, Florida, at which state and federal public health officials discussed their findings. One session, moderated by Abrams, was open to the public and served to convey the intertwined threats to phosphate workers and to the surrounding community. This event drew a good deal of media attention and helped mobilize broader support for reduction of the pollution of both the workplace and ambient environment. The added leverage from agricultural interests whose crops and livestock were injured by the phosphate processors' emissions significantly strengthened the ICWU's position in demanding hazard controls. In mid-1960, Local 613 struck International Minerals and Chemicals Corporation to protest managerial failure to abate hazards of fluoride dusts and mists. This pressure caused the firm to invest in hazard control technologies, as did other companies in the phosphates belt.[47]

In his capacity as the ICWU's medical consultant, Herbert Abrams struggled to meet mounting demands for information, training, and guidance on a long and ever-lengthening list of hazards, mostly mysterious synthetic chemicals. Commencing in March 1953, Abrams wrote a column for the union's monthly newspaper, *The International Chemical Worker*. The right of workers to a fuller understanding of the manifold health risks facing them became a strong underlying theme in these journal contributions. At the union's 1953 convention, two delegates described to Abrams how their employer had recently dealt with a cluster of bladder cancer cases at a Monsanto Chemical Company plant in St. Louis. Management examined over fifty employees and sent six to a surgeon it had retained, who operated on them. Recounting this episode in his newspaper column, Abrams described himself as "shocked to learn that although the operations were performed several months ago, these men were not aware of the findings of the operation or the prognosis of their disease. In discussions with these and other workers, it was apparent that many persons are not aware of their rights to medical information." (The Monsanto situation undoubtedly took on greater urgency for Abrams because it resonated with his experience in California. His examination of workers' compensation claims records for Lompoc employees had found that a physician retained by Johns Manville had failed to inform at least one man of his diagnosis of diatomaceous earth pneumoconiosis.) To enlighten his readership regarding a physician's or surgeon's primary obligation, he cited the ethical code of the AMA. The code required that medical professionals ensure that patients and their families have the knowledge of the patient's condition that would serve their interests. Advancing the right to know meant creating awareness of basic moral standards, a necessary task at a time when management sometimes held extreme prerogatives over the control of even life-or-death medical knowledge. After their setbacks to the insurgent labor movement in the 1930s and early 1940s, American employers were certainly reasserting their right to manage. In this context, Herbert Abrams and the ICWU could only try to resist aggression.[48]

The necessity of ready access to important facts was a recurrent message in the articles in the *International Chemical Worker* that discussed recognition and control of chemical hazards. Abrams saw warning labels as one potentially valuable informational resource, although they were no panacea. His endorsement of the AMA's labeling bill advised that, under the patchwork of state protections, "many thousands of hazardous chemicals today come under no regulatory laws." Beyond advocating for labeling, Abrams pressed the point that disease prevention depended critically on systematically educating and training workers at risk. His August 1954 column contended that "unless the worker himself knows what he is doing and handling and how to protect himself, all other measures will fail." In his view, plant-level committees should play the primary role in delivering the needed facts.[49]

Abrams took on a variety of other chores related to the right to know. He helped train health and safety committees and other local union leaders. He wrote pamphlets and other educational literature for the ICWU to distribute. In at least one instance that involved the Monsanto facility in St. Louis that had hid its cancer cases, he pressed management to go along with the formation of a joint health and safety committee, in part to improve communications. He made the most of his regular participation in the organization's annual conventions. For the 1954 event, he arranged for the National Cancer Institute to set up an exhibit on occupational carcinogens and to distribute a large supply of Wilhelm Hueper's booklet surveying that problem. At the 1955 convention, the doctor assured chemical workers of their competence to intervene: "You have a store of knowledge, believe it or not, that many of the physicians don't have." He went on to argue that such competence entailed responsibility. This responsibility meant forcing employers to divulge information not usually made available.[50]

In the following decade, the Chemical Workers found ways to shift some occupational health responsibilities off their medical consultant's shoulders. In 1960, the ICWU expanded its research operation into a Department of Research, Education, and Health and Safety. The designated functions of the department very much centered on the pursuit of right-to-know matters like dispensing of hazard information and training of workplace committees. Throughout the 1960s, Abrams continued to assist the union, contributing his regular columns and serving as a liaison with public health agencies. His 1962 guidance for rank-and-file members started with utilizing the local health and safety committee and then, if necessary, requesting a state investigation. The presumption of a right to government information came through in Abrams's advice to ask that state agents "provide the union as well as management with a copy of their findings and recommendations."[51]

At the same time, in his primary assignment as medical director of the Union Health Service in Chicago from 1952 to 1966, Abrams found openings to promote a right-to-know orientation among the janitors and other building services workers he served. His frequent articles in a local Building Service Employees International Union newspaper warned of the hazards of toxic cleaning products and other chemicals. He also used that forum to urge the formation of workplace health and safety committees, rally support for stricter labeling requirements, and argue for the extension of union health education activities to encompass recognition and control of occupational health hazards. Despite resource constraints, Abrams engaged in significant outreach and advocacy to help raise awareness and mobilize collective action on occupational health matters among these low-income service workers, largely African Americans and recent Polish immigrants.[52]

Throughout the course of his varied endeavors, Abrams maintained a perspective that envisioned rank-and-file workers as mainly responsible for their own self-protection and capable of providing it. Rooted in the progressive ideals of social medicine, his conception of a workers' right to gain and use knowledge about workplace hazards helped to point the way to the subsequent movement for rights. He also saw workers and unions as deserving of a partnership role with employers and the state in preventing occupational disease.

The activities of Herbert Abrams and of a relatively small number of other like-minded individuals throw into relief the limitations of the predominant system in midcentury US employment relations and public policy. The Manufacturing Chemists' Association and other employer interests managed to dominate the making of informational policy and practice over the quarter century that preceded the passage of the Occupational Safety and Health Act in 1970 despite their advocacy of quite limited protections in the face of increasing risks. The industrialists' capture of their supposed regulators meant a continued dearth of critically lifesaving information for endangered workers. Despite the triumph of a system whose main goal was avoidance of legal liability, the resistance to corporate hegemony from progressive bureaucrats in state and federal agencies and from the labor movement did represent a not-insignificant countervailing force. This resistance only foreshadowed the intensifying conflict between top-down and bottom-up approaches in the years to come.

4
A MATTER OF INCREASINGLY PUBLIC RECORD

Workers' right to know is law.

—Local 1557, United Steelworkers of America, 1971

Twenty-one years before the United Steelworkers (USW) local in Clairton, Pennsylvania, made this triumphant declaration, Frank Burke, the union's safety director, participated in the annual meeting of the American Conference of Governmental Industrial Hygienists (ACGIH). A presentation by any labor official at the ACGIH meeting was quite an unusual phenomenon at that time. Besides the membership of hygienists employed by state government and other public agencies, the association always hosted a sizable contingent of corporate representatives. Vastly outnumbered but unintimidated, Burke announced that he would speak from "bitter experience." After conceding that "labor is far behind management and government in the field of industrial health," he contended that "labor has a right to participate in industrial hygiene programs." The refusal of state agents to divulge their findings particularly troubled Burke. "There have been far too many instances," he observed, "when union people made complaints to State health departments about conditions in particular plants, and then when the industrial hygiene people proceeded to make their investigations, the reports of those investigations were given only to plant management." He insisted that "the workers are the people exposed to these hazards, and they have a right to know exactly the outcome of a complaint to their own government." This assertion of workers' rights sounded a note seldom heard in the discourse of occupational health professionals during that period.[1]

Burke's angry presentation did not spark any reconsideration of policies within the ACGIH, however. The organization had been over this ground before and was not prepared to return to a controversial topic. In 1944, the conference discussed sharing the results of its work with the workers and unions affected. Opinion was divided. On one side, some expressed fears that expanded access to their findings would lead to entanglement in lawsuits or workers' compensation cases. Not unexpectedly, J. J. Bloomfield, the Public Health Service's (PHS) chief liaison with the ACGIH, warned that reports in the hands of a union "might be used in a manner not conducive to further cordial relations between the official agency and management." Manfred Bowditch of the Massachusetts Department of Labor and Industries, that is, not a representative of a health department, worried that divulging data to unions would result in management withholding needed information in the future. On the other side, a few participants in this debate maintained that transparency would promote employee cooperation in hazard control programs. "I really can't understand what harm would come from exposing the results of an inspection to a responsible organization," argued Irma West of the California Department of Public Health. "I can see a great good accomplished in the development of trust." Herbert Walworth, chief industrial hygienist at the Tennessee Department of Public Health, concurred. "As soon as the plant study is under way," Walworth claimed, "opportunities for education are presented. The long accepted policy that industrial hygienists should not discuss the plant study with employees is not practical. If a worker is interested enough to inquire as to what the industrial hygiene study is about, he should be shown the courtesy of a concise and uninvolved explanation. Certainly the uninformed worker will not have any great desire to cooperate in your or the plant's efforts for maintaining a better working environment." Despite a decade of indoctrination by the PHS on the dangers of distributing facts about health hazards and despite the strong influence of corporate players in this organization, cracks appeared in the façade of official opacity. Note that some dissent emanated from within health departments and that some officials in labor agencies did not uphold the value of transparency. Nonetheless, the dominant orientation continued to be that of maintaining secrecy.[2]

Legal barriers also blocked action on the nondisclosures criticized not only by the USW in 1950 but also by the United Auto Workers (UAW) several years later. Numerous states had statutes on the books in the 1950s and 1960s denying public access to or use of investigatory findings. Less than a year after Herbert Walworth announced a receptivity to explaining his work with employees, his state passed a law that kept his office's findings out of lawsuits and compensation proceedings. In 1967, one state even took the commitment to keep secrets one step further. Texas made it a crime for a state employee to divulge information that could be construed as a business secret. As local health departments became more involved in examining workplace hazards, the PHS counseled them to avoid providing detailed data to anyone other than management. In 1959, the PHS engineer Charles Yaffe counseled local health officers that "if there is any question about the release of certain information, it should be cleared with the proper company officials." As a legitimate exception to the general guidance to sequester specific investigatory determinations, Yaffe gave the example of a study of sodium fluoride at Republic Steel Corporation. "When our findings were made available, absolving sodium fluoride of any toxic effect," he reported, "the union printed and distributed the report." The episode of the disclosure of exonerative information underscored that the primary consideration remained solicitude for the employer's interests. Conversely, the handling of this affair also might suggest that whenever government officials refused to come forth with information, they were concealing a hazard. Obviously, the underlying principle was not preservation of confidentiality but rather the preservation of amicable relations with management.[3]

Despite these obstacles, the years after 1950 witnessed a series of labor challenges to the prevailing policies and practices and to the values that underlay them. These challenges drew strength from a more favorable context, particularly with regard to promoting the availability of information from government agencies. The historical sociologist Thomas Schudson observed that "the term 'right to know' did not appear in any Supreme Court opinions or even in popular rhetoric until 1945." Schudson's luminous study of the emergence of that right after 1945 captures a transformation in government openness about its own activities. Beginning with the passage of the Administrative Practices Act of 1946 and culminating in the passage of the Freedom of Information Act in 1966, Congress gave Americans much-enhanced access to documents held in federal offices. A number of states enacted public records legislation during this period. Pennsylvania put in place an open records law in 1957. Although the statutes harbored exemptions and restrictions related to confidentiality, they constituted a profound shift in orientation. These reforms altered the expectations that citizens had about their entitlement to information that they themselves, with their tax dollars, had created. Beyond expanding the range of observable government materials, the larger movement for transparency extended to new requirements for improved product labeling to better inform consumers. Mandated warning messages began to appear on cigarette packages in 1966. Despite the changing tenor of public policy, the supposed imperative to protect trade secrets would continue to obstruct union-led campaigns for transparency.[4]

The budding environmental movement contributed to a growing sense of entitlement to scientific and business information. Activist scientists like the ecologist Barry Commoner advocated democratization of access to information as a matter of societal and global survival. More than anything else, the publication in 1962 of Rachel Carson's best-selling *Silent Spring*, with its demands for hazard disclosure, reframed the discourse on toxic chemicals. Carson drew on this declaration by the French biologist and philosopher Jean Rostand: "'The obligation to endure gives us the right to know.'" Not quoted in Carson's book but illustrative of the subversive thinking occurring at the time was Rostand's call for wider participation in decision making: "The time is clearly coming when the man in the street will have his say with regard to the great social, national, international, and moral issues latterly raised by certain applications of science." Coming from scientists who might have maintained an elitist, technocratic stance, such encouragement of lay engagement with complex, often abstruse issues signaled a fresh empowering perspective.[5]

Carson's revelations placed the right to know about toxic chemicals on the national policy agenda. In a book that revealed numerous accounts of workplace intoxication, her contention that "we have subjected enormous numbers of people to contact with . . . poisons, without their consent and often without their knowledge" helped shape the federal inquiries into pesticides that she precipitated. A presidential advisory committee decried the paucity of studies of occupational pesticide exposure and the lack of knowledge about pesticides among physicians. The committee's report in May 1963 called for "initiation of a broad educational program delineating the hazards of both recommended use and misuse of pesticides." This document helped shape the terms of debate for Senate hearings two months later. At those hearings, chemical manufacturers, agricultural employers, and their allies in the US Department of Agriculture (USDA) and elsewhere in government mounted a spirited defense of both the innocuity of pesticides and the sufficiency of their current labeling. Lawmakers devoted little scrutiny to endangered workers, compared with that fixed on household users. Nonetheless, the deficits in hazard awareness found among at-risk fieldworkers did surface as a matter of concern for some witnesses. In the view of the Cornell entomologist Edward Smith, "Specific attention should be directed to the education of personnel employed as agricultural workers." Less worried about the home gardener than some others, Smith maintained that, because of transitory relationships, "the most difficult problem is that of educating the help the farmer employs." Although these deliberations yielded no breakthrough in policy formation regarding rights, they did bring to the surface the need to enhance awareness of chemical agents of occupational disease, an important preliminary step.[6]

The difficulties of unlocking evidence about hazards held by health administrators dominated one of the first systematic initiatives mounted by organized labor in the postwar period. Beginning in the early 1950s, the United Mine Workers of America (UMW) and its Welfare and Retirement Fund pressed the

PHS to conduct a prevalence study of coal workers' pneumoconiosis, a chronic disease they believed to be rampant among active and retired union members. Rebuffed by that agency, the unionists turned to the Pennsylvania Department of Health, which was receptive to this proposition. However, the department encountered opposition from employers. In 1957, a representative of the Bureau of Industrial Hygiene learned that those in charge of the mining operations at US Steel "had the attitude that it would be much better to leave sleeping dogs lie than to stir up matters." According to Leslie Falk, the UMW fund's administrator in Pittsburgh who was at the center of this affair, the faltering coal industry feared that mass screening of miners and apprising them of their condition would generate countless compensation claims, which would bankrupt many firms. The coal operators grudgingly agreed to participate after the attorney general's office provided the assurance that Pennsylvania law prohibited disclosure of diagnoses in such inquiries. In 1958 and 1959, in conjunction with the state's Department of Mines and Mineral Industries, the Department of Health proceeded to examine about eighteen thousand current and former mine workers, who were not notified of their diagnoses. The project discovered widespread dust-induced respiratory disease, especially in the anthracite fields.[7]

The state adopted a different approach with the wealth of data they gathered on underground dust concentrations during this project. In the aftermath of the revelations of the extent of disease and its causation, the Pennsylvania Department of Mines and Mineral Industries embarked upon an ongoing dust-monitoring program. In 1961, the department's Roger Howell told his colleagues in the Mine Inspectors' Institute of America that "all dusts, whether they contain silica or not, are harmful, and this is particularly true in the mining industry." Howell informed his fellow inspectors that the practice now in Pennsylvania was to give the UMW a copy of reports on the hazard. Three years later at the Governor's Conference on Pneumoconiosis, Gordon Smith, the deputy secretary of the mining department, defended what had become established policy: "This spread of information makes possible further study and interpretation of collected data, along with contributing to the general knowledge of the situation." Such a departure represented a promising breakthrough, one that contrasted strikingly with the stance of their counterparts in the health department.[8]

Although the Pennsylvania coal workers' project did not produce any breach in the Department of Health's ironclad policy, that study did serve the strategic purposes of the UMW. Under the pressure generated by fresh and compelling evidence of the magnitude of this disorder, the PHS finally acceded to the union request to perform a national prevalence study. Beginning in 1963, federal epidemiologists ran a major investigation across several bituminous mining regions that confirmed the pattern discovered in Pennsylvania. The federal agency refused to share diagnostic findings of pneumoconiosis with the thousands of workers examined. The PHS rationalized nondisclosure by expressing its fear that, "if release of information were permitted, the study would immediately become a compensation study." The union thus won the validation of the extent of the pneumoconiosis plague that it had sought for many years, but at the price of the withholding of valuable information that might well have substantiated valid claims made in workers' compensation cases or lawsuits. Even that limitation was surmounted to a significant extent, however, by the increase in general awareness of occupational disease in the coalfields that flowed from the state and federal fieldwork. The elevated rates of compensation claims in Pennsylvania so infuriated coal operators there that they instigated the removal of Jan Lieben, the head of the occupational health unit in the health department. In a sense, prior to his ouster Lieben inhabited the worst of both worlds. His disclosures of general information antagonized mine owners; his (and his colleagues' and his successor's) repeated refusals to deliver specific data on working conditions exasperated labor.[9]

Lieben's dismissal came despite his willingness to comply with his department's nondisclosure position. With regard to his knowledge of the risks associated with beryllium, this compliance went to great lengths. In 1962, he refused to testify in a product liability suit against the Beryllium Corporation unless ordered to by his superior. In this case, he was asked to testify only about work that had appeared in published form. But once again, the presumed need to maintain cordial relations with management precluded any expert testimony. After Lieben apprised C. Earl Albrecht, the deputy secretary of health, of his expectation of future involvement with the company, Albrecht replied, "It is my advice that you should not appear even in support of your paper, since your work in the Department of Health must continue with all parties concerned." The "parties concerned" apparently did not include the victims of beryllium-related disease and their representatives. The desire to accommodate Beryllium Corporation management took other forms as well. In 1965, Marlin Brennan of the UMW asked Lieben to investigate conditions at this firm's plant in Hazleton, Pennsylvania, by making a surprise visit. Brennan complained that "in the past when inspections were made, the Company was completely prepared" and had cleaned up prior to the state agents' arrival. When the Oil, Chemical and Atomic Workers replaced the UMW as the Hazleton workers' bargaining agent at the end of the decade, it met similar obstruction. That union's request for a copy of a state hazard survey received the standard response about the imperative of protecting possible trade secrets. The behavior of the Pennsylvania health officials regarding the beryllium hazard belied claims of impartiality to the extent that solicitude for employers undercut their ability to identify and evaluate hazards.[10]

The dissatisfaction of the USW with the secretive and biased ways of the Pennsylvania Department of Health mounted over the course of the 1960s. In 1966, Frank Burke asked the state industrial hygienist Haven Williams for the results of the state's monitoring of manganese dust at the Johnstown, Pennsylvania, plant of Bethlehem Steel Corporation. He was told that he would have to get the report from the company. Burke exploded: "I do not intend asking Bethlehem Steel for a copy of your survey. I do not work for Bethlehem Steel, and neither do you." Williams responded that he was following settled policy in order to protect possible Bethlehem trade secrets, without suggesting that there were any such secrets at stake in this situation. When Burke appealed to Williams's boss, E. J. Baier, he received the same vague invocation of the sanctity of trade secrets. Burke's other attempts to extract information from senior administrators in the Department of Health received curt denials that claimed, without substantiation, that long experience had shown that their stance was objective and acceptable to labor organizations. These bland assurances did nothing to placate the determined unionist.[11]

A more protracted and much more consequential contest over access to hazard data began in the late 1960s involving the USW locals that represented Pennsylvania coke oven workers. Coke ovens cook coal to remove impurities and thereby convert it into a more efficient fuel for smelting iron ore. This process has the unfortunate side effect of liberating numerous cancer-causing chemicals that attack the lungs and kidneys of workers who load and unload the ovens and perform other tasks around the coking apparatus. Because coke-making jobs were insufferably hot, dirty, and otherwise unpleasant, they had for decades been largely reserved for African American and Latino men. Among the several branches of the union that became immersed in this controversy, the leading role was taken by USW Local 1557, composed of employees at the Clairton Works of US Steel, near Pittsburgh, Pennsylvania. At that time, this facility, which processed about thirty thousand tons of coal per day, was the largest coke producer in the world.[12]

The initial attempt by USW Local 1557 to gain a better understanding of the risks associated with the gases and dusts around the Clairton ovens brought familiar frustrations. In October 1967, Frank Rudman, the chair of the local's safety committee, asked the Department of Labor and Industry to look into the conditions at the coke batteries. That department referred the matter to the Department of Health, which conferred at once with US Steel management. Neither Rudman nor any other union representative was invited to this meeting. The parties arranged for a preliminary survey of the coke plant, which the state conducted on November 1. At this event, in which no union officials participated, the Department of Health took no measurements of the concentrations of coal tar pitch volatiles, benzene, or any other health hazard. Instead, the two industrial hygienists assigned to this project contented themselves with observing that the workers present were wearing respirators and accepting managerial assurances that coke workers were always provided with the personal protective equipment. W. C. Mawhinney, one of the state technical experts involved, concluded that "no bona fide hazard to health" existed at the site. Perhaps unaware of feasible engineering controls of emissions by use of closed systems, Mawhinney fatalistically dismissed the "condition of general air pollution" in this working environment as inevitable but inconsequential because of the use of respirators. His confidence in the efficacy of respirators did not rest on any data gathered on the substances comprising the emissions that would have confirmed the suitability of this particular type of respiratory protection. It apparently did not rest on any assessment of the fit, maintenance, or daily availability of the protective devices. D. A. Tyler, the other professional staff member involved, sent US Steel a minimal report that recommended continued use of respiratory protection. He gave the company an extra copy of this document for its possible discretionary delivery to the union. In this instance, perhaps because of its exonerative nature, US Steel transmitted the copy to the union.[13]

Notwithstanding its seeming disinclination to engage seriously with the issue of coke oven emissions at Clairton, the Pennsylvania Department of Health undertook a comprehensive study of the problem. The department's hygienists measured coal tar pitch volatile levels in all twelve coke oven plants in the state between 1966 and 1969. Beginning on April 30, 1969, representatives of the Division of Occupational Health, accompanied by managers but no unionists, spent three days monitoring the air around the hundreds of ovens operating in Clairton. The concentrations of respirable pitch volatiles in this facility exceeded the recommended threshold limit value (TLV), that is, the standard devised by the ACGIH for permissible exposure (a weak, unprotective limit), for thirty-six of the thirty-nine samples. Fifteen samples came in at ten or more times the TLV, including one that registered fifty-two times the limit value. In its report to plant superintendent James Plasterer on June 13, the division's director conveyed nothing like alarm. E. J. Baier told Plasterer only that "results indicate that exposures may exceed the threshold limit value." Baier did advise a number of remedial steps, including to "investigate methods to alter equipment and/or operating procedures." His recommendations did not extend to having management warn or educate the at-risk workforce. Baier sent no report to Local 1557. A month earlier, he had appeared at the ACGIH annual meeting and pleaded with his colleagues to make their profession more "people oriented" by focusing on parameters such as the numbers of people at risk and being protected from hazards, not the number of evaluations conducted. This professed interest in reorientation unfortunately did not extend to sharing information with the four thousand at-risk workers in Clairton.[14]

US Steel management did not see fit to give Local 1557 a copy of this damning information. The union's inquiry into this subject at the monthly joint safety committee meeting received a vague, deflective response. Management conceded only that "some exposures may exceed" the state limits on safe exposure. On June 20, 1969, James Plasterer sent a reassuring letter to all employees. The works superintendent declared that the recent state survey had determined that no employee who wore this respirator was in danger, even though the state had done nothing to assess the efficacy of that protective equipment. Plasterer advised that "each person working in such areas owes it to himself and his family to make absolutely certain to use the respirator provided." This placing of responsibility entirely on the exposed employees ignored engineering and administrative controls for oven emissions, which the state had urged the firm to consider. The senior manager's letter did not acknowledge the difficulties of wearing cumbersome respiratory equipment for workers whose lung function was already impaired. It also failed to identify what was at stake for those exposed in terms of adverse health effects.[15]

If Plasterer sought to lay to rest anxieties raised by the presence of government investigators, he did not achieve that objective. Instead, he had the opposite effect. The Department of Health rejected Local 1557 President Daniel Hannan's request for a copy of the report itself and, as usual, told him to ask the company for it. This incensed Hannan, who, along with his safety committee, had been instrumental in prompting the study. In Hannan's view, Plasterer's letter had "managed to distort the truth and give a slanted version of these results." Whereas the militant local president refused to ask US Steel for the report, his safety leader Frank Rudman did. The company denied Rudman's request.[16]

Hannan took the matter to his state senator, Edward Zemprelli. He reminded Zemprelli that discontent with the high-handed stance of health administrators had previously led him to encourage the senator to sponsor corrective legislation. "Nothing has been done," Hannan complained, "and our members are becoming disturbed." He told the legislator that "the people that you represent should have the same considerations as industry" regarding knowledge of state-produced information. The exasperated unionist also expressed indignation at the unilateral ability of managers to accompany and guide government inspectors. Zemprelli professed his shock and anger at the situation and promised to address the issue of impounded information. Hannan used his regular column in the next issue of the local's newsletter to lambaste the "lack of cooperation that we receive from State agencies that we are asked to support with our tax dollars." His article was accompanied by a copy of the much-sought-after hazard-monitoring report, with its specific details of the astronomical levels of coal tar pitch volatiles at numerous locations around the ovens. The USW's state legislative committee had gotten a friendly political leader, Herbert Fineman, Speaker of the House of Representatives, to force the Department of Health to hand over the document. Fineman, who also chaired the Appropriations Committee, was simply in a position to threaten bureaucrats dependent on legislative funding.[17]

The coke workers' demands for changes, both in their immediate working conditions and in the state law governing the distribution of information, took on added urgency as the stakes in human health became clearer. A growing body of evidence indicated the carcinogenicity of oven emissions. In 1955, drawing on British research over the past two decades, Wilhelm Hueper called attention to the elevated rates of respiratory system cancer among coke workers. In 1960, an expert consultant supporting the workers' compensation claim of the dependents of the deceased Clairton coking worker William Scott described the toxic substances he inhaled for many years as "accepted . . . industrial carcinogens." Those without the standard credentials of professional expertise contributed equally compelling insights. Daniel Hannan (whose formal education ended with graduation from high school) pointed to workplace cancer hazards in the union newsletter in 1967 and numerous times thereafter. He used his testimony in hearings in the House of Representatives in 1969 to apprise federal lawmakers of "the terrible working conditions in the coke plants of America." "I am deeply concerned," he told the congressional panel, "about the documented evidence in our possession showing some members of our local union are and have been suffering from lung cancer, silicosis, pneumoconiosis, pulmonary fibrosis, emphysema, and other occupational diseases." This accumulation of troubling facts resonated with daily observations of coworkers in failing health and their frequent attendance at funerals. In December 1969, the Clairton health and safety activist Howard Holmes reflected on the recent funeral of Jeff Craig, who spent twenty-three years around the coal-baking apparatus: "It's not surprising when an employee on the batteries becomes ill or develops an ailment such as arthritis, emphysema, heart trouble or even lung cancer." For rank-and-file workers, especially the African Americans like Holmes who disproportionately got the worst assignments, it was common knowledge that extreme exposure to contaminated air wrecked one's health. Some coke workers turned down promotions to jobs on the tops of the ovens, where the pollution was most severe. Taken together, this stream of evidence pointed to the existence of serious problems.[18]

More systematic exploration confirmed the danger posed by the dusts and gases emitted by the ovens. In the late 1960s, William Lloyd, a doctoral student at the University of Pittsburgh, undertook epidemiological analysis of the cancer mortality rates in the coking workforce. The research by Lloyd and his colleagues yielded a series of articles in the *Journal of Occupational Medicine*, the first of which appeared in June 1969. These articles painted a grim portrait. For those employed in close proximity to the ovens, deaths from respiratory system cancer occurred at almost three times the rate expected across the steel workforce as a whole. Among men who worked five years or more atop the ovens, the vast majority of whom were black, the mortality rate observed was ten times that expected. Daniel Hannan was one of those who saw Lloyd's publications as an important breakthrough in winning general recognition of the widespread hazards and their ill effects.[19]

On the political front, the USW knew that its members could not just rely on the sort of pressure tactic that had succeeded in gaining the release of the Clairton monitoring data. After the Division of Occupational Health evaluated the air quality at the ovens of the Aliquippa Works of the Jones and Laughlin Steel Corporation later in 1969, USW Local 1211 was thwarted in its attempt to see the survey findings. In reaction, maneuvering to amend the state's Right to Know Act intensified. In September 1969, Democrats in the Pennsylvania Senate introduced a proposal to close a loophole in the 1957 law. The problematic provision declared that "the term 'public records' shall not mean any report, communication or other paper, the publication of which would disclose the institution, progress or result of an investigation undertaken by an agency . . . or which would operate to the prejudice or impairment of a person's reputation or personal security." This section of the statute gave state health administrators all the authorization they needed for the secrecy that facilitated the maintenance of amicable relations with business firms and associations. Conservative forces in the Senate kept the reform bill from coming to a vote. This move prompted an angry letter to all senators from the USW's chief Pennsylvania political operative, Julius Uehlein. The Steelworkers leader told the senators that passage of this measure would help address the problem that "ignorance of mass proportion dominates the whole field of occupational health and safety." Speaking on behalf of the quarter million members of the largest union in the state, Uehlein took a militant yet moderate position: "The United Steelworkers believe in free enterprise. We do not believe, however, that free enterprise has a divine right to exploit workers to the point of death." He underscored the modest objective of the bill under consideration, placing it in the context of the minimal policing of working conditions. "The ratio of game wardens as compared with state safety inspectors is astronomical," Uehlein maintained. "However, if

Senate Bill 1072 was enacted the workers would at least be in a position to know whether or not the company is complying with results of the investigation."[20]

The union and its allies kept up the pressure. After their failure in the upper chamber, the proponents of the right to know shifted their attention to the Pennsylvania House of Representatives. A bill introduced into that body in June 1970 passed within a month and made it through the Senate a few months later. Republican governor Raymond Shafer vetoed the measure just before leaving office. In the next legislative session, Shafer's successor, Democrat Milton Shapp, approved the reintroduced proposal in June 1971 and declared himself "delighted" to do so. This amendment to the 1957 statute changed the definition of accessible public records to encompass "reports filed by agencies pertaining to safety and health in industrial plants." The newsletter of the Clairton coke workers, whose troubles had catalyzed the reform campaign, triumphantly announced that their "right to know is the law."[21]

In Clairton and other coke-making sites, the USW made profitable use of their newfound trove of information and their right to obtain more of it. The hazard evaluation data collected by the state aided disabled coke oven workers in winning workers' compensation benefits. In the 1974 round of contract negotiations, the union pressed for implementation of closed systems and other forms of engineering controls, relegating burdensome and often ineffective respirators to a marginal role. The agreement reached at Clairton brought a breakthrough provision for employee access to their company medical records. Armed with data on the severity of the risks they faced and motivated by resentment over the long denial of access to that data, the USW also mobilized a campaign for a strong federal regulatory standard for oven emissions, as will be discussed in chapter 5.[22]

The rancor that characterized the US Steel-USW conflict paled in comparison to the dispute between California grape growers and their adversaries—the National Farm Workers Association and the Agricultural Workers Organizing Committee, groups which, in August 1966, merged to form the United Farm Workers Organizing Committee (UFWOC). (Seven years later, the organizing committee became the United Farm Workers of America.) Whereas the coke oven emissions case involved a long-established union dealing with an oligopolistic corporation within the context of settled relations, the embryonic farmworkers' group posed their demands regarding pesticides against agricultural firms in the context of an organizing drive in a sharply competitive industry. The collision occurred in the midst of a crucial battle in that drive, the strike of grape workers around Delano in the San Joaquin Valley of central California that began in September 1965. This was a marathon contest that raged for almost five years, extended far beyond the Delano area, and drew widespread national attention and support from diverse conscientious supporters. Throughout this struggle, the workers' organization lacked most of the traditional sources of strength that a union could command. They had to maneuver with great creativity to find leverage against powerful adversaries.[23]

Unhealthful conditions in the vineyards became a big issue in the union-building project in central California. Awareness of the threat of pesticide intoxication had risen across the state and, to a lesser extent, beyond it by the mid-1960s. In 1935, Robert Legge, a professor of public health at the University of California, Berkeley, identified some salient threats. Legge advocated cautioning all those at risk throughout the nation: "Every state board of health, workmen's compensation commission, state and agricultural college, farm advisory board, etc., should use its offices and bulletins to spread information concerning the methods by which the occupational hazards of the agriculturist may be decreased." Government officials contributed to elevating the visibility of the chemical threat and conferring legitimacy on it. During his relatively brief tenure as head of the Bureau of Adult Health in the California Department of Public Health, Herbert Abrams illuminated the growing menace. Public health officials continued to pursue this matter after his departure. Physician Irma West led the effort to protect the state's agricultural workforce of roughly a quarter million. At a session of the American Medical Association Congress on Occupational Health in 1963, she noted the exceptionally high rates of occupational disease among California's farmworkers and identified heat stress and pesticides as the leading hazards facing them. Explaining the need for special oversight of this group, she maintained that "agricultural workers, because of migrant status, seasonal work, language barriers, substandard education, marginal health, and poor hygiene, are the least able to protect themselves against occupational hazards." Her department had begun to tabulate and publish statewide statistics on fatal and nonfatal intoxication of workers in the 1950s. Of course, this data collection system captured only a fraction of the total number of cases of illness. In 1963, West relied on this source to advise a US Senate subcommittee that, in 1961, more than five hundred of her state's farmworkers (more than one-third of whom had Spanish surnames) had suffered chemical poisoning. Two years later, on the eve of the Delano strike, she observed that "employers were often either uninformed themselves or reluctant to provide adequate occupational safety information because they did not want to alarm workers." By that time, the Department of Public Health was calling for bilingual labels on pesticide containers. The bureaucratic activism of Abrams and West contrasted with the role played by their colleagues in the California Department of Agriculture. Robert Rollins, chief of the Division of Chemistry in that department, considered agricultural chemicals to be exceptionally heavily regulated. In a 1963 article in the

American Journal of Public Health, Rollins stated his belief that existing labeling requirements had taken care of this problem. He contended, without any corroborating evidence, that aspirin killed more people than did all pesticides. In the same vein, a gubernatorial committee three years earlier dismissed California's increasing rates of pesticide-induced occupational illness as simply the result of carelessness. This whitewashing body addressed the carelessness issue by concluding, "There appears to be some need for public information concerning the lack of a significant public health problem, and a supportive educational program to emphasize the proper use of these substances." The advocacy work of West and her colleagues in opposition to powerful entrenched forces helped to confer legitimacy on the health claims of farm workers and made the curt dismissal of such claims impossible.[24]

Rachel Carson's best-selling *Silent Spring* prepared the ground for consumer receptivity to the union's nationwide boycott of all California table grapes, launched in 1967. Grocery shoppers' fears of toxic pesticide residues became another weapon of the weak in this struggle. In the recruitment campaign to win and retain the support of grape workers themselves, the organizing committee raised the pesticide issue as a matter of health and respect. A community-organizing approach led it to run a service center that delivered various forms of assistance to union members in need. Her experience working at the center gave Jessica Govea firsthand experience dealing with the victims of poisoning. When Govea transferred to the UFWOC legal office in 1968, she advised the attorney Jerry Cohen of the frequency and severity of this problem. The savvy lawyer took up this matter as both important in its own right and something that might well garner public sympathy for the workers' cause.[25]

On August 22, 1968, Cohen visited Sheldon Morley, the county agricultural commissioner, to review records of pesticide use in his possession. Morley not only denied Cohen access to these public records but immediately obtained a temporary restraining order. The rationale for the order was that the pesticide formulations constituted trade secrets. A subsequent judicial decision upheld the legality of the order. Negotiations with both grape growers and pesticide providers over access also failed. The UFWOC was stymied in gathering publicly held information on hazardous conditions endured by its members.[26]

The secondary benefits of this withholding of facts offset the disadvantages of the ignorance perpetuated by this legal setback. The UFWOC president Cesar Chavez and other union leaders and activists pounced on this obstruction, demanding to know what the employers and their subservient public agent had to hide. As the Chavez biographer Miriam Pawel noted, "Boycotters relied on Chavez and the Delano crew for a steady stream of fresh outrages to generate consumer support" so that, in this case, "the growers handed him a perfect issue for the boycott." Beyond the opportunity to publicize the possible risks for the grape-eating public, criticism of the pesticide coverup became itself another component of the boycott campaign. From the perspective of Robert van den Bosch, a biologist at the University of California, Berkeley, who testified for the union in its challenge to the restraining order, the denial of access to the pesticide spraying records constituted "one of the most shocking acts of collusion between public officials and a vested interest of which I am aware."[27]

Besides its outreach to sympathizers, the UFWOC used this episode to focus and activate rank-and-file members and recruit new members. The union-affiliated newspaper *El Malcriado* passed along Cohen's contention that he sought hazard information for future bargaining over contractual health protections. The newspaper reported on a court hearing on the request to see the impounded documents under the headline "What Are They Hiding?" and relayed Commissioner Morley's claim that he had never heard of any cases of workers injured by pesticides. The cover of the January 15, 1969, issue of *El Malcriado* displayed the image of a grotesque spider-like creature whose head was a human skull, surrounded by three detached skulls, over the caption "Economic Poisons: A Threat to Workers and Consumers." The drawing was credited to the early-twentieth-century Mexican illustrator Jose Guadalupe Posada. The imagery thus not only conveyed in easy-to-grasp, dramatic terms the lethal peril of pesticides but also connected the farmworkers' struggle to previous progressive movements for social change in their homeland. In the same vein, Cesar Chavez avoided the use of arcane, incomprehensible medical terminology and instead described the diffuse syndrome of headaches, nausea, muscle weakness, and other symptoms that often resulted from chronic exposure simply as "walking death."[28]

The union leadership shrewdly raised the priority of pesticide poisoning in its bargaining strategy. The growers' refusal in early 1969 to enter into negotiations limited solely to this issue brought them further negative publicity. *El Malcriado* advised its readers that the only way to get proper training in pesticide use was to win a union contract that required it. These agreements authorized the union's safety committee to use its bilingual capability to instruct those tasked with handling dangerous chemicals. As the UFWOC leader Dolores Huerta told a US Senate subcommittee in April 1969, "Many of the workers that apply the pesticides don't speak English and they do not know what they are doing." Later that year, in an appearance before a different Senate panel, Cesar Chavez praised the recent signing of an agreement with one vineyard that gave the union access to company pesticide records. Jerry Cohen contrasted that situation with the one prevailing in Delano workplaces: "We don't see any [warning] signs at all. We have no way of knowing whether or not there should be signs because we don't have access to the records indicating what the growers have used." Cohen also gave the lawmakers a glimpse of the state of knowledge of one widely used toxic substance when he pointed out that "about seventy percent of the workers we have talked to don't even know what parathion is." This set of hearings also heard a witness from the California Department of Agriculture defend the unavailability of records based on their trade secrets and a San Joaquin Valley physician's rejoinder. Dr. Lee Mizrahi told the Subcommittee on Migratory Labor, "It is totally wrong that one man's trade secret or payroll size should preclude another man's appropriate and/or emergency medical care." During 1969 and 1970, the union gained a series of grape contracts that established health and safety committees with the right to be informed on all pesticide-related matters and to examine all relevant records. The unionization drive in the grape industry culminated in July 1970, when the twenty-six growers in the Delano area finally came to terms with the UFWOC. That agreement followed precedent in granting the union committee broad rights to know about pesticide use, as well as imposing outright bans on the deployment of a number of highly dangerous formulations. These hard-won employer concessions represented monumental breakthroughs for this group of poor workers of color.[29]

By the end of the 1960s, Washington, DC, had become the main venue for criticism of asymmetrical access to hazard information as demands grew for comprehensive reform of occupational safety and health. By that time, government at the state and local levels had had more than a century to demonstrate that they could adequately safeguard the nation's workers from work-related injury and illness. A 1968 review concluded that the occupational health programs in about half the states carried out "token activity" or only responded to requests for assistance and took no initiative. Another analysis found a "general pattern of neglect" in understaffed state offices. The performances were especially poor regarding emerging epidemics of often insidious, chronic, work-induced disease. Irving Selikoff, the nation's foremost authority on asbestos-related disorders, came to this dismal conclusion: "It might be better to dissolve the meager industrial hygiene divisions in most states than to have them continue as ineffectual shells." The states, with a few exceptions, had failed in their duty of public protection. Pressure mounted for legislation that gave the federal government primary responsibility for protecting workers.[30]

This sad state of affairs plainly implied an indictment of the deficient vision of the designer and promoter of this system. Nonetheless, the PHS responded to the unavoidable evidence of its sorry performance of its institution-building project by seeking a mandate for a larger leadership role in occupational health. The agency justified its 1965 proposal for expanded powers and resources in part on the basis of experience disseminating informational materials, but the reforms it sought to lead made no significant commitment to expanding workers' rights to know. In any case, as Nicholas Ashford observed in his postmortem on the midcentury regime, the service's self-aggrandizing plan died quietly, "unnoticed by Congress and the public."[31]

Opponents of the status quo vigorously attacked the lack of transparency in the state-run system. The refusal of public officials to share findings with workers and their organizations came in for repeated criticism. In Senate committee hearings on reform legislation commencing in November 1969, union officials delivered a chorus of complaints. Thomas Boyle, a representative of the International Chemical Workers, described the typical procedure of state agents investigating illness in a workplace. Boyle contended that investigators gave advance warning that enabled the company to alter conditions and generally kept their findings and prescriptions secret from the workers affected. The USW legislative director John Sheehan made the same critique and demanded that reforms require the granting of workers' access to state and federal inspection reports.[32]

When the Senate conducted field hearings in early 1970, local and district unionists underscored and elaborated on the complaints and demands made by top-level leaders. After the UAW local at Climax Molybdenum in Langeloth, Pennsylvania, brought in a state official to study the toxic fumes, their request for a copy of his report was rejected. A USW district safety and health coordinator insisted that workplace union representatives had a right to know what government investigators found regarding hazards. The Clairton local USW president Daniel Hannan reviewed his difficulty learning about measurements of coke oven emissions. Hannan told the senators, "We receive almost no cooperation from the State safety and health inspectors of the Pennsylvania Department of Health." His comrade George Cope of the USW branch representing coke workers at the Jones and Laughlin Hazelwood plant in Pittsburgh discussed receiving the same noncooperation in his attempts to understand the emissions situation.[33]

The activist attorney Ralph Nader joined the unionists in advocating a robust right to know in his appearance before the Senate panel. Nader assailed a provision in the Nixon administration's bill that prohibited the use of government investigatory findings in civil lawsuits for damages and barred public employees from testifying in such cases. To Nader, these restrictions would add "another weight to the privileged scales so heavily tipped toward industry and commerce." As evidence of how the scales were currently rigged, he cited both the California pesticide situation and the long-standing policy of opacity maintained by US Department of Labor inspectors who policed federal contractors, under the terms of the Walsh-Healey Act. He denounced the administration proposal as a whole as "a giant loophole, a sham."[34]

At the same time, labor witnesses presented the House Select Subcommittee on Labor with a thorough indictment of the inequitable failings of the current system. The USW secretary-treasurer Walter Burke, citing the experience of his Clairton local, among others, called for the amendment of his organization's favored proposal to require "full disclosure of an inspector's report." Daniel Hannan followed up with a characteristically blistering denunciation of the prevailing secrecy and called out the names of former Clairton coworkers suffering from industrial disease and "living on borrowed time." (US Steel was sufficiently impressed by Hannan's performance to transfer him immediately to a location where he would be less likely to cause them trouble in the coke plant.) Paul Jennings, president of the International Union of Electrical Workers, echoed Walter Burke's suggestion that legislation mandate that unions receive copies of inspection reports. Jennings also underscored his USW colleague's criticism of federal enforcement of the Walsh-Healey Act. Although his union had had its share of impossibilities getting information from noncooperative government agencies, Anthony Mazzocchi of the Oil, Chemical and Atomic Workers focused his fire on uncooperative managers. His survey of 130 locals determined that management at more than two-thirds of the plants that conducted employee medical tests refused to divulge any findings. According to Mazzocchi, "Most companies have rung down a curtain of secrecy. They deny to workers an opportunity to improve their own lives, individually or through their union."[35]

Agricultural interests sought to exempt pesticides from regulation, arguing that the existing system of state regulation and federal labeling standards had created sufficient protection. The agricultural sector had long received special treatment regarding worker protections. Influential racist political forces had seen to it that coverage under the National Labor Relations Act, the Social Security Act, and other sources of social protection like workers' compensation was denied to farmworkers. Such protection was deemed inappropriate for a workforce that contained such a large nonwhite component. Besides this larger historical context, the regulatory system created by the Federal Insecticide, Fungicide, and Rodenticide Act (FIFRA) and anchored by the USDA had been in place for more than two decades and reinforced an expectation of separatism. At the House subcommittee session in San Francisco in November 1969, Matt Triggs of the American Farm Bureau Federation urged the exclusion of pesticides from the scope of any legislation. Triggs touted the "effective approach" of the status quo and praised federally approved labels as keys to this effectiveness, without supplying any supporting evidence for his assertion. A chart he submitted on laws governing ground application of agricultural chemicals showed that sixteen states had no legislation at all. Administrators in the California Department of Agriculture presented their state's program as exemplary. Their state required the posting of signs warning laborers to stay out of newly treated fields but did not require any training for pesticide-exposed workers. A California state witness held that the presence of labels on containers rendered training unnecessary.[36]

Of course, the UFWOC did not share the agricultural establishment's enthusiasm for the prevailing system. The organizing committee opposed any exclusionary privileges for pesticides and disputed claims about the availability of information. Jerry Cohen maintained that worker knowledge about chemicals was crucial and recounted his experience dealing with the Kern County agricultural commissioner. Dolores Huerta controverted a California Department of Agriculture official's claim that his agency ran pesticide-training workshops for workers. Instead, she held that hazard and hazard control information reached fieldworkers only when union health and safety committees conveyed it to them. Drawing on the experience of the Delano conflict, Cohen and Huerta described recent cases in which grape workers became ill after exposure to chemicals about which they had received no oral or posted warnings. After offering her own review of the withholding of information by Kern County, Huerta urged Congress to view assertions about trade secrets with skepticism. Thomas Milby, chief of the occupational health unit in the California Department of Public Health, shared this viewpoint. Milby maintained that growers could game the system by adding a little fertilizer to their economic poisons and call the mixture a secret formula. "The use of toxic chemicals, far from being shrouded in greater secrecy, should be a matter of increasingly public record, with everyone concerned—growers, commercial applicators, foremen, workers, physicians—being as fully informed as possible," he argued. "Due process and protections for employers are, of course, necessary," Milby acknowledged, "but so are protections for workers, including the right of access to pertinent information." Any aura of critical necessity surrounding business secrets did not mystify some of those most aware of the human costs of maintaining that secrecy.[37]

The Occupational Safety and Health Act of 1970 (which did not exclude pesticides from the scope of regulation) established new rights for workers to understand their status regarding hazards and their effects. The statute's policy declaration made clear that its aims encompassed "providing for research, information, education, and training." The federal Occupational Safety and Health Administration (OSHA) and the state programs that could continue to exercise authority if they met federal standards pursued those aims in the course of carrying out two core functions—creating safety and health standards and enforcing those standards. Regarding the former, the law mandated that all its standards "prescribe the use of labels or other appropriate warnings as are necessary to insure that employees are apprised of all hazards to which they are exposed, relevant symptoms and appropriate emergency treatment, and proper conditions and precautions of safe use or exposure." If it had done nothing else to expand workers' rights to know about their risks on the job, this provision of the Occupational Safety and Health Act would have marked substantial progress toward workplace transparency in the United States. For standards that called for periodic monitoring of specific hazards, the law authorized employees or their unions both to observe the hazard evaluation process and to see the records thereof. When that monitoring detected unhealthful exposures, that is, those exceeding the regulatory limit, management had a duty to promptly notify affected employees not only of that hazardous exposure but also of what corrective action was being taken. The law also charged the Department of Labor with the task of developing regulations to force employers to maintain records of their hazard-monitoring activity, with access to the stored records guaranteed for workers and their representatives. These new entitlements departed dramatically from the prior system of voluntary labeling and withholding of investigatory findings.[38]

In the enforcement realm as well, the 1970 act set forth opportunities for workers' enlightenment. Employees won the right to have a representative accompany government agents during their inspections. When an OSHA inspection found violations of the law or its regulations and issued a citation to the employer, it had to "describe with particularity the nature of the violation." The law required that a copy of the citation "shall be prominently posted . . . at or near each place a violation referred to in the citation occurred."[39]

The act established the National Institute for Occupational Safety and Health (NIOSH), within the complex of the National Institutes of Health (NIH), to provide scientific guidance to OSHA in its promulgation of specific standards and in shaping its regulatory agenda. To explore problematic situations that might shed light on previously unknown or underrecognized risks, NIOSH was authorized to administer a health hazard evaluation program. Unions gained the right to request the hazard evaluations. NIOSH had to submit its findings "both to employers and affected employees as soon as possible." This marked a dramatic departure from and implicit renunciation of the long-standing secretive policies and practices for the assessments done by state health investigators, in other words, the behavior that Frank Burke, Daniel Hannan, and others in the labor movement found so objectionable. When the institute conducted research involving medical examinations, the employees examined could have their results furnished to their own physician. The statute obligated NIOSH to publish within six months and to update at least annually "a list of all known toxic substances by generic family or other useful grouping, and the concentrations at which such toxicity is known to occur." Besides these particular circumstances in which facts had to be shared, the law imposed a general requirement that information obtained by NIOSH had to be disseminated not only to employers but also to workers and their organizations. Although this institute lay outside the more hospitable Department of Labor, thus perpetuating the old jurisdictional boundaries within the field, it received marching orders that compelled transfer of critical information to those at risk.[40]

Taken together, the provisions of this long-overdue federal takeover of occupational safety and health represented an unprecedented embrace of transparency regarding information about health hazards. By liberating previously hidden types of information for use by workers, the law demonstrated an unprecedented national commitment to extending workplace democracy, albeit one with a number of remaining limitations. However, those limitations would immediately come under an intensifying attack by forces both inside and outside the government.

5
NO NEED TO ALARM EMPLOYEES

> We believe that the employer has the responsibility to inform his employees about the substances they work with and that every employee has the right to know how his job may affect his health.
>
> —John Finklea, 1976

The Occupational Safety and Health Act opened new channels through which to pursue a wider right to know about workplace health risks. A number of unions representing workers in the manufacturing sector had fought hard to secure passage of this landmark legislation. Those organizations and their allies naturally sought to explore the possibilities presented by the system of federal protections. Their interest was heightened by decades of frustration in seeking redress from state-level officials and their patrons and advisers in the Public Health Service (PHS). Testing the willingness and ability of the Occupational Safety and Health Administration (OSHA) and its partner the National Institute for Occupational Safety and Health (NIOSH) to safeguard the workforce became one of the most important initiatives for partisans of a wider right to know about hazards of occupational disease after 1970. In this exploratory process, the proponents of legally guaranteed informational rights enjoyed widespread, authoritative support for the principle of transparency. John Finklea declared his commitment to the right to know while serving as a senior official in the conservative administration of President Gerald Ford testifying before a congressional committee in his capacity as the head of NIOSH. Yet translating acceptance of an abstruse principle into concrete national policy and administrative practice proved difficult. Advocates of an expansive interpretation of workers' entitlement to lifesaving information met obdurate opposition at every turn. As a result, the record of advances toward more complete access to facts about hazards in the early years under the new federalized system was very mixed.

A clearer awareness of the magnitude of the problem lent a sense of urgency to the quest for transparency after 1970. However limited, the evidence available at the time pointed to an immense and growing threat of occupational disease. In the mid-1970s, NIOSH estimated that about 25 million workers could be exposed to at least one of the approximately eight thousand chemical substances and physical agents that it had already identified in its National Occupational Hazards Survey. This survey found that almost three-fourths of hazard exposures involved trade-name products and that neither employees nor their employers knew the chemical composition of 90 percent of those products. The fact that American workers had come to view improvements in their precarious working conditions as a top priority further encouraged their representatives to venture into the forbidding territory of bureaucratic regulatory processes.[1]

Revelations about the carcinogenic potential of numerous substances previously considered innocuous intensified worries. By the second half of the twentieth century, cancer trailed only cardiovascular disorders as a cause of death in the United States. When the National Cancer Act of 1971 declared a "war on cancer," the legislation reflected the depth and breadth of public fear of this mysterious category of disease. But victory over cancer seemed to remain forever over the horizon, which only deepened that prevalent fear. In 1976, NIOSH's Joseph Wagoner used the two-hundredth anniversary of the first discovery of a work-induced cancer (scrotal tumors among English boys who cleaned chimneys) to reflect on the current scene. "Today," Wagoner observed, "the problems of occupational carcinogenesis are greater, more visible yet more subtle, and more pervasive than they were in the past." The ever-expanding roster of confirmed or suspected etiological agents found in the workplace included both familiar old substances like asbestos and unfamiliar recent formulations like dibromochloropropane. Wagoner commented insightfully on both categories of hazards. He reported that eighty years after aromatic amines were proven to cause bladder cancer and several nations had banned them, "thousands of American workers were literally sloshing in them." He also found especially worrisome the estimates that most of the hundreds of new chemicals entering the workplace had had no prior testing of their potential to cause malignancies. A 1977 assertion by the United Steelworkers (USW) of a general right of workers to know about occupational hazards focused on carcinogens, citing recent revelations about vinyl chloride, kepone, and bischloromethyl ether. The USW found these revelations not only disturbing but infuriating as well. The union pledged that for employers who "just don't give a damn" about their workers, "It's our job to make them give a damn." There was plainly a growing recognition that this emerging public health crisis warranted both drastic federal intervention and determined union representation.[2]

Against this backdrop, endangered workers and their unions sought to take advantage of the tools now available to them under federal law in order to gain useful information. Of course, more complete knowledge of the perils of the job was sought not as a matter of enlightenment but as a necessary resource for preventive interventions. Unions and individual employees filed complaints that led to OSHA inspections. Both participation in the inspections themselves and inspectors' posting of citations that enumerated violations served to illuminate unhealthful conditions. Labor organizations initiated NIOSH Health Hazard Evaluations (HHEs) that often brought to light evidence of health risks. When fresh evidence led NIOSH to issue a hazard alert about a substance, the Oil, Chemical and Atomic Workers sent copies to the locals whose members were exposed to it.[3]

Beyond the responsibilities imposed in its foundational statute, OSHA from its inception had other chances to dispense hazard information to workers. These were not opportunities that the agency seized initially. Most early-phase educational work targeted employers, not employees. The emphasis of the Office of Training and Education on worker carelessness failed to address the larger challenges before it. One critique of this victim blaming derided the way that the educational unit had "squandered its funds on childish radio commercials" that revisited the tired trope. Another indication of misplaced focus was the inordinate attention devoted to workplace injuries, at the expense of the larger, little-understood phenomenon of occupational disease.[4]

An infusion of funds from the National Cancer Institute gave OSHA the resources to tackle one critical set of issues more constructively. To develop principles for reaching those facing carcinogens, the partners turned to the National Research Council for guidance. The council formed the Committee on Public Information in the Prevention of Occupational Cancer. This committee's symposium in December 1976 aimed to "assure mobilization of the best information on occupational cancer education." The meeting gave various parties their chance to define the issue. Protecting workers from frightening messages, not granting them rights to information, preoccupied some participants. If carcinogens could be euphemistically termed as only suspected agents of dread disease (pending further, perhaps endless research), then apprising workers of possible risk was a mistake. Robert Eckardt of the Exxon Corporation argued against needlessly scaring the workforce. Benjamin Van Duuren, professor of medicine at New York University, also counseled caution: "Until this [experimental] data is evaluated I do not see any reason why the worker should be scared stiff or why they should be told that they are dealing with a potential carcinogen." In contrast, the Episcopal theologian Joseph Fletcher saw possible anxiety as a small price to pay. From Fletcher's viewpoint, "dangerous knowledge is never half as dangerous as dangerous ignorance." Andrea Hricko of the Labor Occupational Health Project at the University of California, Berkeley, held that workers, former workers, and the surviving family members of deceased workers were entitled to know everything that management knew. Hricko deplored reliance on trade secrets claims as "most reprehensible" and "unconscionable." To David Wegman of the Harvard School of Public Health, "The idea of frightening workers by frankly informing them is absurd." Undoubtedly drawing on his experience with rank-and-file worker activists in Massachusetts, Wegman maintained that "we continually underestimate the ability of workers to know or understand about cancer, about their bodies, about science."[5]

Beyond debating what substantive messages were appropriate, the conferees considered the proper design of an educational program. Paul Kotin, a physician and senior executive at the Johns Manville Corporation, a leading manufacturer of asbestos products, appeared to be more interested in designating the best messenger than in tailoring the message. Conceding the workers' right to know, Kotin sought to place company doctors at the center of any system of transferring cancer knowledge. Citing the attempted cover-up of the asbestos catastrophe at Johns Manville, Andrea Hricko told the federal officials that corporate self-regulation had had its chance. Speech communication expert Herbert Simons criticized the top-down approach that dominated health education and confessed that "people in my field do not know a lot about bottom-up approaches." But based on his familiarity with the effective confrontational information-gathering methods of the Philadelphia Area Project on Occupational Safety and Health, this Temple University professor explained that "one of the premises of a bottom-up approach is that education and action go hand in hand." Simons challenged OSHA to produce publications that promoted worker activism and to "experiment with bottom-up programs." In the discussion of Simons's presentation, Paul Cornely, a professor of preventive medicine at Howard University, expressed disappointment with the absence of worker participation in the symposium. Cornely considered it "a pity that we are talking among ourselves." Indeed, only one member of the endangered working class appeared on the program at this meeting. Richard Marco, an autoworker from the Chicago area who made clear that he had no college degree, offered the practical suggestion to enclose educational materials in employee pay envelopes, to underscore the risk involved in earning a living. Marco called on federal officials to advise workers about how to request a hazard evaluation from

NIOSH. Delivered in the waning days of the Ford presidency, these provocations in all probability helped to reorient educational policy for the incoming administration of President Jimmy Carter. The subsequent report of the Committee on Public Information in the Prevention of Occupational Cancer to OSHA proceeded from the premises of the right to know and the duty to inform. The committee dismissed the notion that workers could not handle the disturbing facts about the risks they encountered. Although hardly a strong declaration of support for subaltern empowerment, the group did urge that information "be sufficient to permit the worker to assist, to the limit of his capability, in monitoring and improving the environment of his workplace."[6]

OSHA standard setting held out great potential for expanding knowledge rights, which in turn meant that it would become a major site of conflict over those potential rights. Upon assuming authority, OSHA confronted the immense task of regulating innumerable chemical, physical, and biological threats to workers' health. As an expedient first step, the agency chose in May 1971 to adopt the preexisting standards established by the American Conference of Governmental Industrial Hygienists (ACGIH). These skeletal regulations set exposure limits (often of a weak nature) but did not impose on employers labeling or other disclosure requirements for toxic chemicals. Adoption of the ACGIH rules did carry with it, however, an obligation to post warning signs for exposures associated with both ionizing and nonionizing radiation. In addition, containers holding materials that emitted ionizing radiation had to display a warning label. But these were exceptions to the prevalent pattern of obliviousness for the approximately four hundred chemical substances covered in this blanket interim regulation. In belated acknowledgment of its inadequacy, OSHA and NIOSH announced in 1974 the Standards Completion Program whose objectives encompassed the addition of information distillation sections to the chemical standards. The following year, perhaps in response to prodding from reform advocates, NIOSH officials insisted that they did plan to move ahead to supplement the interim standards with mandatory warning messages for employees. Despite this assurance, in the end, the Standards Completion Program stalled and did nothing to alter the rules regarding access to hazard information.[7]

As OSHA and NIOSH set out to make rules on workplace health risks, they grappled with another legacy of the preceding era of corporate control besides the ACGIH standards. After endeavoring for almost three decades to minimize the disclosure of information and to establish themselves as the national authority in that area, the chemical industries were not prepared to step aside for a freshly commissioned team of Washington bureaucrats. The Manufacturing Chemists' Association (MCA) recognized the threatening ramifications of a federal takeover for control of the dissemination of facts about hazards. As the association's Task Group on OSHA Regulations put together recommendations for the government in 1972, its Labels and Precautionary Information Committee stressed the need for adherence to the guidance in their manual. G. Robert Sido, the chair of the labeling committee, delineated this aim for the MCA board of directors on January 9, 1973: "The committee objective now is to see to it that Manual L-1 is recognized and used as the labeling pattern or working document by the Department of Labor (DOL), the National Institute of [sic] Occupational Safety and Health (NIOSH), and other involved standards-making associations such as the American Society for Testing and Materials." Sido told the board that "to insure Manual L-1 influences OSHA label regulations," he had nominated one of his predecessors, C. Boyd Shaffer of American Cyanamid Company, for a place on a proposed OSHA Advisory Committee on Labeling and Hazardous Materials. (And Shaffer would play an active role in pressing industrial interests within that advisory body, as we shall see.) A month later, Frank Mackison, a NIOSH guest at an MCA labeling committee meeting, received a blast of criticism for his institute's failure to involve the chemical association sufficiently in constructing a labeling system. The committee got no reassurance from Mackison's statement that the top consideration for NIOSH in its warnings was the well-being of workers, not the erection of an effective defense against lawsuits for work-related disease. Because Mackison's superior, Charles Powell, had previously delivered a similar message to MCA's Occupational Health Committee, the priorities at the national institute could not have been clearer, or less welcome. The new federal agency had, in a sense, affixed a stark warning label on itself that alerted the chemical producers to a political hazard. Further frustration for MCA stemmed from NIOSH officials' failure to consult with it when they solicited commentary on a draft of their labeling scheme in early 1973. Despite this setback, the association continued maneuvering to gain a larger role in shaping informational policymaking.[8]

The NIOSH apparatus for devising a model warning framework did not accommodate formally the MCA. However, corporate presence therein was hardly nonexistent. The institute's roster of ten review consultants had five corporate representatives and no labor representatives. Although the members of the MCA Labels and Precautionary Information Committee from Shell Chemical Company and Olin Corporation did not gain review positions, both had coworkers on the panel. Nonetheless, producer influence was now circumscribed. The NIOSH recommendations for a hazard identification system sent to OSHA in December 1974 demonstrated that MCA hegemony had ended. The proposal for an identification system made plain that federal decision makers had considered and rejected existing models, an obvious dismissal of the long-standing MCA program. Of particular importance, the ingrained practice of trivializing chronic outcomes of hazard exposure came in for unprecedented criticism. "It is essential," NIOSH declared, "that delayed or chronic health effects must be given the same attention as are immediate or acute problems." A fresh perspective was beginning to take hold under federal auspices.[9]

When the battlefield for creating an overarching design for warning workers shifted from NIOSH to OSHA, the struggle over transparency continued unabated. NIOSH envisioned a system comprised of three components—symbols, labels, and material safety datasheets. Another noteworthy indication of the shifting of forces underway was the insistence of the labor and government representatives on the OSHA Advisory Committee on Hazardous Materials Labeling on supplementing those components with requirements for employee education. Despite employer resistance, the committee decided to advocate inclusion of educational and training activities never advocated under the MCA regime. Their report of June 6, 1975, proposed a "total systems approach" because "the most sophisticated use of hazard placarding and labeling may not accomplish the desired objectives unless coupled with an effective program of employee education and training." They recommended that new employees receive training prior to their first job assignment and that additional training occur at least yearly, with topics to include hazards of chronic exposure.[10]

The OSHA advisory body attempted to find symbols that would unmistakably and instantly apprise workers of a hazard to their health. In this exercise, the advisers acknowledged the significant number of hazard-exposed, non-English-speaking laborers who could comprehend an image placed on a label on a container but who might not grasp other types of warnings. The committee benefited from the recent belated willingness of the MCA to accept the value of pictorial warnings, after two decades of opposition to the set of images published by the International Labour Organization (ILO), an affiliate of the United Nations. Nonetheless, the Standard Oil representative held out against adoption of any such symbol, contending that the mere presence of a label on a container constituted sufficient warning. After much debate, the committee offered a qualified endorsement of the preexisting Department of Transportation symbols that were based on the UN system. As the best symbol to alert illiterate and non-English-speaking workers of highly or extremely toxic substances, the committee supported use of the widely recognized traditional skull and crossbones, an image used in the UN system.[11]

With C. Boyd Shaffer chairing the labeling subcommittee, it was predictable that the OSHA Advisory Committee on Hazardous Materials Labeling sought continued use of some basic elements of the MCA scheme. Without settling on the particular circumstances under which the terms would be applied, the committee accepted the three conventional signal words—"caution," "warning," and "danger"—and the possible application of the term "poison." The extent to which the committee ended up supporting perpetuation of the MCA labeling methods, along with other concerns, led the four union members to file a formal dissent with the Secretary of Labor. The dissenters criticized the proposed warning labels for failing to require that components be listed by chemical name. They also objected to the difficulties that those not literate in English would encounter in understanding warning messages on these labels. For carcinogenic hazards, the group put forward the euphemistic phrase "suspected cancer agent" because they were unable to acknowledge the existence of confirmed workplace carcinogens. In line with the MCA template, the advisers also called for mandatory hazard descriptions, precautionary measures, and first aid steps. Taken as a whole, the advisory committee guidance reflected the fraught, fluid, and laborious nature of the regulatory process as it pertained to setting general rules.[12]

Nothing came of this advice. OSHA continued slowly to study varied perspectives on a general plan for hazard communication. More than a year and a half after receiving the advisory committee report, the agency gave notice formally soliciting further input on this subject. One measure of the broadening horizons was the request for comments on "appropriate training requirements and other means of informing the employees." But this reopening of the topic, with OSHA under the more hospitable authority of the newly inaugurated Carter administration, proved to be a false dawn. Pressure from the Health Research Group and other progressive advocates could not overcome business resistance to any substantial reform. A belated proposal to establish systematic informational requirements for all health standards offered during the final week of the Carter presidency was stymied by the Ronald Reagan administration's imposition of a moratorium on all new regulations.[13]

Unable to devise a sweeping regulation for information disclosure, OSHA moved forward throughout the 1970s with the promulgation of specific standards for which right-to-know factors often came into play. Asbestos presented a critical early test case for willingness to warn workers exposed to a highly dangerous hazard. In anticipation of the conflict to come over numerous facets of federal rulemaking on this substance, the industry in 1970 created the Asbestos Information Association. As Gerald Markowitz and David Rosner have shown, this group crafted and carried out a wide-ranging, strenuous public relations campaign to minimize the risks of this hazard. The association had its work cut out for it. By the 1970s, asbestos was well on its way to killing hundreds of thousands of American workers. By that time, its ability to cause cancer of the lungs and other organs was well established. Yet in neither of its first two regulatory actions—inclusion of asbestos under the consensus standards adopted in May 1971 and issuance of an emergency temporary standard seven months later—did OSHA mandate any hazard notification. In the latter instance, that oversight ignored a request by the American Federation of Labor and Congress of Industrial Organizations (AFL-CIO) for just such a provision.[14]

Because the temporary standard had to expire in six months, OSHA was under pressure to move quickly. In January 1972, it published a notice of a proposed permanent standard. This draft remained silent on the question of labeling containers but offered text for warning signs for work areas with hazardous conditions. The proposed language went so far as to broach the subject of carcinogenicity: "Asbestos dust may cause asbestosis, a severe lung disease, and is implicated in the development of certain cancers." Further guaranteeing conflict, the proposal would give employees' own physicians the right to see the results of their required medical examinations.[15]

OSHA's Advisory Committee on Asbestos Dust took up these controversial disclosure-related issues in February 1972. The proposals and positions of the employers' side consistently demonstrated a determination to cut off as many opportunities for employee enlightenment as possible. But in this setting, unlike in similar discussions held by the MCA, the deliberative body of five had only one employer member, along with one union leader and three government officials.

The absence of any provision in OSHA's proposed standard for the affixing of warning labels on containers caused employers no difficulty. The NIOSH criteria document had urged the affixing of labels with the stark warning that dust inhalation "may cause asbestosis, pleural or peritoneal mesothelioma, or lung cancer." The Textile Workers Union offered language for a strongly worded label that would not only alert workers to a cancer hazard but also call attention to the need for adequate ventilation (a management responsibility). When it became clear that majority sentiment within the advisory committee favored a requirement for labeling of containers, Isaac Weaver of Raybestos-Manhattan suggested that use of the weakest signal word, "caution," would suffice. Weaver saw this term as helpfully fixing responsibility on the endangered employee: "I recommend caution because I feel that that denotes action on the part of the person. It is up to the individual to do something to avoid exposure." He advocated glossing over the possible risk of cancer: "In small print, I propose the words inhalation of asbestos over long periods of time may be harmful." Fellow committee member Jack Baliff of the New York Division of Industrial Hygiene called this "an excellent label for management, but not for labor." Baliff preferred branding asbestos dust dangerous, not merely worthy of caution. He also supported identifying the dust as cancer-causing. Weaver held his ground and predicted dire consequences for application of the more severe term: "I think if you put 'danger' on there, they'll get guys so scared they won't even open the bag or container. And I don't think that's necessary. It will have an adverse effect on sale and use of asbestos-containing products above and beyond the actual hazards." As a senior manager at a firm that relied substantially on sales of asbestos-containing brake shoes and clutch plates, Weaver knew well the stakes in this contest.[16]

Much the same dispute played out over the phrasing of warning signs. Isaac Weaver called for the placement of signs only in locations where asbestos contamination was known to exceed the limit for permissible exposure, a proposition that took no account of the variability of hazardous conditions and the frequent lack of definitive, up-to-the-minute data on those conditions. Like other attempts to limit knowledge, that proposal met considerable resistance. Here, too, the industry member's preference for the more innocuous signal of "caution," rather than "danger" and for exclusion of any references to cancer encountered stern opposition.[17]

On February 25, 1972, the advisory committee presented its decisions to the Department of Labor. The committee concluded that both the warning sign and the container label carry the signal word "danger." It urged language in the hazard statement that included the wording "may cause asbestosis and cancer." On the thorny matter of the availability of medical records, both Isaac Weaver of Raybestos-Manhattan and Andrew Haas of the Asbestos Workers dissented from the majority judgment to allow access to the physicians of the workers examined. Haas doubted that records of procedures conducted by company doctors and retained in the employer's custody could be prevented from being used to the detriment of employees. Acceding to a request from the Textile Workers Union, the committee advised that employees have the right to see the findings of the mandatory air-monitoring exercises that determined the extent to which they were at risk. This set of decisions brought no comfort to the employer side. Weaver sent an angry letter to George Guenther, the assistant secretary of labor in charge of OSHA. In his view, the failure to allow testimony from industry experts had rendered the committee proceedings "patently biased." This purported impropriety meant that "the recommendations of the committee are totally invalid and must be disqualified from consideration in the proposed rulemaking."[18]

When OSHA held open public hearings on its proposed standard in March 1972, both capital and labor, as well as their allies, took full advantage of their opportunities to plead their cases. Advocates of strong protection showed no inclination to fall back in the face of the asbestos industry's fierce and often defiant opposition. One witness on the first day of hearings argued that workers should have more than just access to their medical examination records. Sidney Wolfe, director of the Naderite Health Research Group, maintained that "access to these records should be controlled by workers, not management, lest they be arbitrarily used to fire or demote workers because they show evidence of disease." Anthony Mazzocchi of the Oil, Chemical and Atomic Workers believed that the proposed examination provision "truly allows the fox to guard the chickens" because of the tendency of management-paid practitioners to fail to recognize cases of occupational disease. Mazzocchi agreed with Wolfe's diagnosis but not his prescription. He favored allowing workers to select their own examining physician and have the records stored with NIOSH. Witnesses for corporate medicine recoiled at the notion of allowing employees to select their medical examiners. Norbert Roberts, president of the Industrial Medical Association, feared the likelihood that employees would choose less competent examiners. Roberts joined his colleague Lain Tetrick of the American Iron and Steel Institute in declaring practitioners in their specialty to be objective experts dedicated to the welfare of their patients. He denounced as deplorable any use of findings to weed out potential litigants or compensation claimants. In the view of these leaders of occupational medicine, employer-retained healthcare providers had to control both the administration of examinations and the records created in order to fulfill their professional responsibilities.[19]

Discussion of signage appropriate for asbestos work areas found industry representatives mounting a diversified attack. Their primary objective was to avoid any association between their products and cancer. One stratagem, one so well characterized in the title of David Michaels's book *Doubt Is Their Product*, was to portray a causal link to the dread diseases as premature. In support of his contention that there was "no need to alarm employees with inflammatory and suggestive signs," Bruce Phillips of Certain-Teed Products Corporation counseled patience. He offered no refutation of the accumulation of damning scientific evidence of carcinogenicity. On the advisability of posting signs only when a permissible limit was being exceeded and then with a message that left out any mention of cancer, Phillips offered this rationale: "Before using such scare tactics in the workplace, we feel much more should be known about the relationship between cancer and asbestos than is known at present." Another gambit was to plead for exemptions for products in which asbestos fibers were bound up so tightly as to not become airborne and were thus rendered harmless. Charles Neumann of Kentile Floors asserted that his firm's products were innocuous due to the encapsulation of mineral fibers. This argument, which held a kernel of truth, failed to address the probability of the release of dust when products were sawed, sanded, or otherwise treated in ways that liberated the immobilized material. On the labor relations front,

Neumann worried that frightening signage could "only result in employment discouragement, excessive demands, difficult attitudes and lowering of morale." From this vantage point, the best alternative was for signs that urged caution rather than warning of danger and that were devoid of references to cancer or, better still, any disease.[20]

Industry witnesses took perhaps an even more adamant stance with regard to labeling. Besides reiterating the main objections offered against strongly worded signs, corporate officials envisioned dire consequences when labeled packages scared away previously ignorant customers. Matthew Swetonic, an employee of the Johns Manville Corporation representing the Asbestos Information Association, predicted that a label that cited asbestosis and cancer "would surely spell the demise of a number of major product lines of the industry." Swetonic advised that adoption of the labeling requirement put forward by the OSHA advisory committee would "result in the unnecessary loss of millions of dollars in sales each year" and cause "large-scale unemployment." His Johns Manville colleague Fred Pundsack elaborated on this future scenario of unwarranted fear and havoc, with the elimination of thousands of jobs, that would result from "unnecessarily frightening and alarming" labels. For their part, unionists endorsed the stronger language under consideration. George Perkel of the Textile Workers Union testified that many asbestos-exposed workers resented not having been advised of their peril. Sheldon Samuels of the AFL-CIO Industrial Union Department urged OSHA to order placement of the well-understood skull-and-crossbones emblem on containers.[21]

The asbestos standard brought forth by the Nixon administration on June 7, 1972 (i.e., in the early stages of the incumbent's reelection campaign), gave the industry the relief it sought on characterization of the severity of the hazard. OSHA leadership decided that "words such as 'danger' and 'cancer' are unwarrantedly alarming." Neither the prescribed signs nor labels warned of any risk of cancer. Instead, signs had to state "Breathing Asbestos May Be Hazardous to Your Health," and labels had to warn that "Breathing Asbestos Dust May Cause Serious Bodily Harm." Label specifications called for the term "caution," not "danger," and did not include any requirement to display the easy-to-grasp skull-and-crossbones symbol. This permanent standard imposed no obligations on employers to offer any training on the nature of the hazard or the means of controlling it. However, the agency did allow employees access to records of the monitoring of their dust exposure. When hazard monitoring determined that workers had been subjected to dust levels above the permissible limit, the regulation required the employer to provide written notification to those affected within five days of such a finding. It permitted the employee's personal physician to see their medical records. However, OSHA refused to have medical findings withheld from employers. The standard's authors offered this reassurance: "There is no intention to allow employers to abuse medical information obtained pursuant to the Act, to the detriment of employees. Therefore, the administration of the medical records requirement will be closely watched." In its protest petition, organized labor focused on the deficiency of the warning terminology, which it held "grossly understates the true nature of the threat." The petitioners contended that the alarming quality of the proposed terms only had bearing if that characterization of the hazard was inaccurate, something the industrial agents had failed to prove. On the opposing side, the Asbestos Study Committee of the Friction Materials Standards Institute, chaired by Isaac Weaver, rejoiced that OSHA had selected "caution," the "least sensational" of the signal words.[22]

Despite its manifest shortcomings, the 1972 asbestos standard did advance transparency significantly. The rights of access to hazard and medical information represented new entitlements of some importance. Because this was the first original health standard developed by the infant agency, these breakthroughs set precedents for subsequent rulemaking. Although the final standard fell short of requiring that management educate or train dust-exposed subordinates, forceful argumentation on that issue helped to lengthen the agenda for future deliberations. When OSHA revisited this standard three years later, one item in its proposed plan for revision was the addition of an educational component.[23]

Subsequent early OSHA regulatory activity with right-to-know dimensions witnessed conflict along the same lines as the initial engagement over asbestos. Any acknowledgment of carcinogenicity remained a flash point for the industries involved. On May 3, 1973, OSHA responded to a petition by the Health Research Group and the Oil, Chemical and Atomic Workers by setting an emergency temporary standard for fourteen carcinogens deemed to pose "a grave danger to employees." Employers had to display signs warning of a "cancer-producing agent" wherever these substances were present. Containers of contaminated clothing, equipment, and materials had to be marked with this label: "Danger/Contaminated with Cancer-Producing Agent." In the face of heavy industry criticism, the agency altered the warnings by changing "cancer-producing agent" to the more ambiguous "cancer-suspect agent" for all fourteen substances. Despite the recommendation of the Standards Advisory Committee for a stronger description of the hazard, the permanent standard published on January 29, 1974, retained the softer language for all fourteen substances, including even those few recognized by the MCA and other chemical organizations to be carcinogenic for humans. The final standard did heed the advisory committee's recommendation, however, for requiring an extensive employee-training component. Education and training provisions of this sort reflected recognition of the need to close the gap between information and the right to know.[24]

OSHA grappled with the challenge of reaching workers who could not comprehend messages written in the English language. In the agricultural sector, a diverse workforce composed in large part of non-English-speaking international migrants encountered a host of toxic pesticides whose risks they often did not understand. OSHA inherited not just a daunting substantive problem but also a regulatory mess. For more than two decades, the US Department of Agriculture (USDA) had done little to require warning signs and labels that surmounted communication barriers. A 1969 congressional investigation found that agricultural regulators had often approved pesticide labels with confusing and contradictory warnings. University of Illinois consultants subsequently retained to evaluate labels confirmed these failings. Their study of 349 items concluded that the typical pesticide label was difficult to read, suitable only for those with at least ten years of formal education. Under pressure to intervene from both farmworkers' groups and the Nixon White House, OSHA entered this territory with an emergency temporary standard covering organophosphate formulations. The emergency standard called for the posting of signs at the entrances to farm fields and at locations where workers assembled for instructions from management. The signs were to be composed "in the English language and any other language which may be necessary to communicate the warning." The regulation also aimed to protect illiterate workers: "Where an employer has reason to believe that any employee is unable to read, he shall give the employee oral warning." Congressional backlash against this measure led first to its suspension and then to the ceding of authority over these hazards to the rival Environmental Protection Agency (EPA). The EPA rules finalized a year later dropped the requirement for signage at work locations and gave employers the option of either displaying signs at assembly points or giving oral warnings. These rules did retain the obligation to communicate in languages other than English, wherever deemed necessary.[25]

Further OSHA attempts to expand the use of non-English and nonverbal messages led to varied forms of frustration. NIOSH criteria documents prodded the labor agency to prescribe bilingual warnings. The institute's 1973 recommendations regarding inorganic mercury called for signs "printed in English and in the predominant primary language of non-English-speaking workers, if any." OSHA did not see fit to overhaul the mercury standard to impose this protection. In early 1974, NIOSH wanted identical text for safeguarding the health of workers exposed to carcinogenic inorganic arsenic. OSHA did not follow this recommendation in the proposed standard it put forward the following year, and the final standard promulgated three years later carried no such provision. The NIOSH 1974 guidance for benzene, which causes leukemia, repeated the bilingual signage requirement but also gave managers the alternative of seeing that workers at risk were "otherwise trained and informed of the hazardous areas." When OSHA issued its permanent standard four years later, the plans for bilingual signs or delivery of information comprehensible to those unable to read signs in English had vanished. The 1975 criteria document that addressed hexavalent chromium put forward the same language as for benzene. OSHA did not produce a final standard on this carcinogen until 2006. Beyond undertaking these exercises in futility, regulators appear to have given little if any serious thought to requiring pictorial warnings, in particular the widely comprehended skull and crossbones, a simple device for apprising those without English language proficiency. For several reasons, the most important of which was the strenuous resistance of the ever-more-powerful business community, federal administrators made little headway toward effectively alerting those workers who were in an especially precarious plight due to language impediments.[26]

As the standard-setting contests of the 1970s unfolded, usually slowly and often unsuccessfully, the configuration of contestants remained nearly the same. Organized labor brought its team of top union officials and legal, medical, and technical advisers to meet their counterparts from the employer side, with federal administrators and scientists generally in a mediating role. As had been the case during the previous period under the ACGIH, rulemaking on occupational diseases under OSHA was a cloistered, technocratic affair. But much as it did in other realms of the American administrative state at this time in response to pressure for a measure of participatory democracy, the established pattern for regulating risks of occupational disease changed dramatically with the transactions that led to the standard for coke oven emissions. In this case, the USW pursued an innovative participative approach. This represented quite a departure not only for federal bureaucrats but also for the USW, which was by the 1970s among the more staid labor organizations, accustomed to a legalistic and bureaucratic style of operation. Leading the storming of the elitist regulatory ramparts was Clairton's chief activist, Daniel Hannan. High school graduate Hannan debated aggressively in the Standards Advisory Committee sessions and, more important, orchestrated the large-scale participation of rank-and-file coke workers in the public hearings. He helped to arrange for regular attendance at the Washington hearings of sizable delegations from the Baltimore, Maryland, Sparrows Point plant of Bethlehem Steel and for the testimony of more than forty workers and disabled former workers.[27]

The primary right-to-know concern illuminated by oven workers was nondisclosure of medical and industrial hygiene findings. The inaccessibility of employee medical records emerged early in the standard-setting process as a condition unacceptable to the USW. Experience with management refusal to share diagnostic findings and falsification of records had engendered suspicion and resentment. The union's critique of the NIOSH criteria document in mid-1973 pointed to the need to make all such records open to employees themselves, without the requirement for a request from their physician. The union also demanded to see employee exposure data. On March 4, 1975, USW official James Smith gave the OSHA Standards Advisory Committee this assessment of prevailing attitudes on diagnostic revelations: "In all of our discussions with coke plant workmen, we have yet to find one who sincerely believes that his employer will furnish him with the truth on such a matter unless the employer is compelled to do so." The standard that OSHA proposed in July 1975 granted employee access to the findings of both medical examinations and emissions monitoring mandated by its rule. The USW protested the proposal's failure to allow access to those company emissions records not legally required.[28]

At OSHA's hearings on its proposal in December 1975, rank-and-file veterans of the coke ovens apprised the government of some realities of asymmetrical class conflict over crucial medical information. The panel members from the Inland Steel coke works in East Chicago, Indiana, maintained that they didn't know the results of their company-administered medical examinations. Witness Bobby Tompkins explained that his request to see his doctor's report was rejected; Inland management assured him that "everything is ok." Wayne Robinson, who chaired the workers' compensation committee of the Clairton local, described disabled workers "literally dragging themselves to the gate in the morning" to try to work. Robinson denounced the tendency of the company's doctor to advise those he examined that they had emphysema rather than a compensable, work-induced respiratory disorder. In response, his committee arranged for an independent medical consultant to evaluate workers with breathing difficulties and then assisted in the filing of numerous compensation claims in cases where a diagnosis of lung cancer or pneumoconiosis justified them. Roosevelt Johns, retired from Republic Steel due to disability, testified that his employer's examination had yielded no advice to him about his lung cancer. In addition to his grave medical situation, Johns revealed that he was currently struggling to keep from losing his home. The militant activist Eugene Pughsley, another Republic coking worker, presented quantitative data supporting his contention that "very seldom does a man live to retire." He recounted the experience of a longtime coworker whose impairment had reduced him to taking a lower-paid janitorial job. That man learned nothing from his employer's medical examinations about the cancer that would take his life; the cancer was only belatedly disclosed to him by his personal physician. (In a previous interaction with federal authorities, the audacious Pughsley told NIOSH staff that they should be forced to write their criteria document while sitting atop a coke oven.). At the Gary Works of US Steel, management apparently dispensed medical facts selectively. According to Willie Chapman, after the annual evaluations that included chest X-rays, only benign results were conveyed. "I don't know of anyone that they've given the bad news," reported Chapman. "They give the reading if it's good." This policy undoubtedly helped limit workers' compensation outlays for the corporate giant, as it did for others in the industry. Four men from Sparrows Point bore witness to their employer's refusal to share knowledge. Nolie Wilson only learned of his troubling X-ray findings when he fortuitously overheard Bethlehem Steel's examining physician discussing them with a colleague. An unmistakable pattern of nondisclosure emerged from this body of workers' testimony.[29]

Beyond their revelations about secrecy regarding health effects, worker witnesses also enlightened OSHA on inadequacies in the distribution of facts about respiratory hazards. The Bethlehem panel complained that company training failed to cover the carcinogenicity of the emissions in which so many of them were enveloped on the job. As Louis Buchanan of the Johnstown, Pennsylvania, operation put it, "They never tell us nothing about cancer." Their comrades from Inland and US Steel concurred.[30]

The standard published ten months later responded to the strong indictment laid out by the USW's members. Citing the evidence that those examined were currently denied diagnostic information, OSHA required that employees given mandatory periodic examinations receive written copies of the physician's opinions. Similarly, at-risk workers gained the right to see emissions-monitoring measurements. The obligatory warning signs where oven emissions were present had to declare a cancer hazard. Mandatory training programs had to discuss the nature of the hazard. Even demanding critic Daniel Hannan deemed the standard "not that bad." In large part the product of the activism of rank-and-file African American workers, this was the first OSHA standard whose primary beneficiaries were workers of color.[31]

Despite the eventual success in the coke oven emissions case and a number of other advances in protection, the manifold difficulties of combat on the federal regulatory battlefield had become painfully apparent as the 1970s wore on. Larry Ahern of the International Chemical Workers expressed the disappointment felt within the labor movement: "In 1970, we thought we were in heaven. We finally had a law which guaranteed a healthy and a safe working environment. That is what Congress said then, but here we are in 1977, and we find ourselves still trying to secure the names of the substances that the people work with." The frustrations of the convoluted bureaucratic process of standard setting, coupled with many other difficulties of dependence upon the federal regulatory system—too few enforcement officers, weak penalties, the structural flaw of allowing states to choose to administer their own programs—sent many occupational health activists in search of more aggressive strategic alternatives.[32]

6

NEW WORKER-ORIENTED COUNTER-INSTITUTIONS

> **Workers are being stabbed in the back without a chance even to know what they work with. Without this basic knowledge, workers cannot participate in the vital decisions of whether or not to accept or continue employment, or whether or not to seek union or governmental action against an employer.**
>
> —Peter Greene, Sidney Wolfe, and Andrew Maguire, 1976

In their petition to the Occupational Safety and Health Administration (OSHA) to set a general right-to-know standard, Peter Greene, Sidney Wolfe, and Andrew Maguire not only dramatized the meaning of toxic ignorance but also shed some light on the remedial options available to endangered workers. Beneath the surface of their request to OSHA lay an upsurge in grassroots frustration and anger and various attempts to channel that discontent into systematic, innovative organizing. The underlying premise of the petition was that workers were not hapless victims or potential victims of toxic ignorance. By the mid-1970s, rank-and-file workers and their professional allies were fashioning novel organizational weapons to battle against both corporate and government bureaucracies. For the most part, these were what the organizer Daniel Berman characterized as "new worker-oriented counter-institutions." These institutions became the main structural components of a viable social movement. Whereas Maguire was a member of the US House of Representatives whose district in New Jersey had a large number of constituents who were exposed to ill-explained hazards, Greene and Wolfe both represented the Health Research Group, created by Ralph Nader in 1971. The petitioners were soon joined by the Philadelphia Area Project on Occupational Safety and Health (PhilaPOSH), an activist outfit born in 1975. After 1970, a national movement, not a handful of isolated individual advocates, led the fight for access to information about workplace hazards. At the center of the complex of counter-institutions was a network of local and state committees, coalitions, or projects on occupational safety and health, commonly known as the COSH groups. These organizations represented some of the earliest, perhaps the very earliest, of what are currently known as "alt-labor" formations. Like the worker centers that came later, these versatile movement organizations crafted a repertoire that combined service provision with political advocacy.[1]

The prevailing atmosphere in the United States at the beginning of the 1970s promoted the birth and growth of movement experiments. The seminal influences of the African American freedom struggles, the surging wave of protests against the war in Vietnam, and the rise of the New Left had generated a proliferation of progressive initiatives for social and political change. The situation epitomized what the social scientist Sidney Tarrow has defined as a "cycle of contention": "a phase of heightened conflict across the social system, with rapid diffusion of collective action from more mobilized to less mobilized sectors, a rapid pace of innovation in the forms of contention employed, the creation of new transformed collection action frames, a combination of organized and unorganized participation, and sequences of intensified information flow and interaction between challengers and authorities." The ferment and the inclination to address social problems through militant activism helped to give birth to this occupational health movement. Besides the general forces operating at this moment, the ascendant environmental movement, activism among physicians and other health professionals, militant self-organization among rank-and-file workers, and the protest movement of coal miners afflicted by dust-induced respiratory disease especially gave impetus to the right-to-know challengers.[2]

By the end of the 1960s, the embryonic right-to-know movement already had its dominant framing principle, one well established in liberal and radical circles. Since the 1930s, progressive claims on the state and social order had been cast as petitions for political and social rights. In adopting this familiar stance, those seeking to establish an entitlement to knowledge about the risks they faced on the job drew added leverage and resonance from the growing demands for health-related rights, expressed in calls for universal access to health services, in calls for the availability of reproductive health services, and in other proposals as well. This would prove to be a useful ideological resource in shaping the discourse on this matter.[3]

As this movement was coming together, perhaps the most critical determinant of its viability was whether activists could forge cooperative relations among rank-and-file workers, union officials, and health professionals, including medical students and others in advanced professional training. In a moment that recalled the conscientious middle-class reform campaigns of the Progressive Era, the 1970s witnessed a rethinking of the potential for those in the professional strata of society with scientific and other types of conventional expertise to ally with and assist the working class. The class-bridging process encountered difficulties, but in numerous instances ended in a functional division of labor and mutual appreciation. The COSH groups were the organizational inventions that embodied that coalitional success. In not only their class-bridging capability but also their emphasis on educating workers at risk, these organizations followed in the footsteps of the pioneering, if short-lived, Workers' Health Bureau of the 1920s. From the outset of their involvement, the COSH challengers insisted that rights to knowledge be linked to rights to act on that knowledge.[4]

As the letter by Greene, Wolfe, and Maguire plainly indicates in its demand for a formal rule from the national government, the emergent right-to-know movement reflected both a frustration with and a determination to continue to operate along the established pathways of the administrative state. The movement represented a synthesis of conventional legalistic, top-down actions and less conventional bottom-up disruptions. As such, it pursued a blended strategy that persevered in seeking reform within the technocratic strictures of the regulatory system forged by the Occupational Safety and Health Act. Hence, the developments of the 1970s simultaneously unfolded in hearing rooms in Washington, DC, and in workplaces and union halls across the nation.[5]

To a great extent, the search for creative alternatives to heavy reliance on the federal bureaucracy was led by the Oil, Chemical and Atomic Workers International Union (OCAW), whose members confronted a huge and ever-expanding array of toxic substances. Like the United Farm Workers Organizing Committee (UFWOC) and its successor, the United Farm Workers of America, OCAW embraced a social movement style of militant action on occupational health and safety that departed from the dominant conservative orientation of mainstream organized labor. To be sure, like the United Steelworkers (USW) and other engaged labor organizations, OCAW adopted a blended approach that combined conventional navigation of bureaucratic channels with more adventurous forms of advocacy.[6]

The key figure driving the OCAW's efforts was its legislative director, Anthony Mazzocchi. Mazzocchi arranged for Ralph Nader to address the union's convention in August 1967. In his characteristically unsparing manner, Nader condemned not only government and corporate inaction but also that of the labor movement. He saw unions like OCAW as "uniquely positioned" to make progress in this important area. Nader provoked the convention to vote to launch a health and safety program that would have political, collective bargaining, and educational components. This decision gave Mazzocchi the mandate he wanted, one that allowed him to fight to extend workers' right to know and to act on knowledge gained.[7]

On the political front, OCAW pursued change related to the wider dissemination of occupational health information from a number of angles. Demands for strong enforcement of government regulations, however inadequate, formed one part of the organization's repertoire. In the late 1960s, the union had already used the meager leverage available against federal contractors subject to US Department of Labor (DoL) oversight under the Walsh-Healey Act. Because inspectors divulged their findings only to the employer, OCAW attempted (without success) to dislodge this information through the Freedom of Information Act. In the same vein, Mazzocchi decried the refusal of state officials in possession of facts regarding health risks to disclose what they knew. The union pressed for the passage of the Occupational Safety and Health Act. At congressional hearings in 1969, Mazzocchi gave voice to the concerns of at-risk workers by entering into the record scores of their verbatim statements on the hazards they faced and the obstructions they routinely encountered in learning about them. Beginning at once when the act went into effect in 1971, this union worked for its fullest implementation. The first citation ever issued by OSHA following a workplace inspection came at an Allied Chemical plant in West Virginia where workers had OCAW representation to deal with their overexposure to mercury. In addition to its agitation for strong enforcement activities, union officials strove to help devise health standards with right-to-know provisions. Both Mazzocchi and colleague Steven Wodka frequently participated in standard-setting proceedings.[8]

When Mazzocchi testified in 1969 in support of federal responsibility for safeguarding workers' health and safety, the tone of his advocacy was a measured one. Along with some other unionists, such as those representing farm workers, he refused to look to any government-centered regulatory system as a panacea. The OCAW expected to rely primarily on the self-help mechanisms operating through direct action in the workplace. Negotiation and enforcement of strong contract language constituted the centerpiece of the strategy. Yet in embracing self-help, Mazzocchi and his comrades departed from the common tendency of unionists to go it alone in the familiar arena of collective bargaining, failing to reach out to possible allies. Just as he had enlisted Ralph Nader in 1967, Mazzocchi turned to Nader's crew of activists to help build a knowledge base for negotiating and other tactics. At a 1969 discussion in New Jersey, he advised members of OCAW District 8 of the value of this resource: "I'm going to solicit the help of some of our friends—guys like Ralph Nader—who's been consistently on our side. He has recruited a bunch of young kids out of the universities, who've done more work on this subject in the last year than any thousand guys like myself and other people that I know. They've come out. They're bright, they're forceful, they can't be bought off, at this point in life, anyhow, and they've been willing to go forward with the facts. And we in the labor movement have been missing out." Also indicative of this receptivity to outside support was the presence of experts from medicine and science at the New Jersey conference and at other similar events.⁹

Connections with environmental groups, another outside force to which the union appealed, led to support in one critical engagement. In the bargaining round with the major oil companies in late 1972, OCAW pushed for advances on a number of health and safety issues, including production and distribution of information. One objective was to emulate a gain it had made earlier that year at a Kawecki Berylco plant in Pennsylvania, where the union had won the right to conduct its own air-sampling program for beryllium hazards. In the oil industry negotiations, all but one firm settled on terms that extended workers' rights to obtain company-held information and to generate its own data through hazard monitoring. In January 1973, the union struck the holdout, Shell Oil, and launched a national boycott of its products. In an unprecedented move, eleven mainstream environmental groups rallied to the union's defense and actively promoted its consumer boycott. The formation of this alliance contributed to a resolution of this dispute that brought the establishment of a joint health and safety committee and gave OCAW access to Shell's morbidity and mortality records. The strike marked a breakthrough in relations between the labor and environmental movements. In the domain of contract administration, the union won a historic arbitration case in 1973 that guaranteed a right to know the actual chemical names of substances with which its members worked. This arbitrator's decision compelled pharmaceutical manufacturer Ciba-Geigy to hand over chemical names for the hundreds of substances present in its McIntosh, Alabama, plant.¹⁰

Besides the manifest consciousness-raising effects of its work in the political and economic realms, OCAW carried out a wide-ranging educational program. Together with Mazzocchi and others, the chemist Jeanne Stellman organized an ambitious ten-week training course for workers at Rutgers University. Stellman and the physician Susan Daum converted the material for the course into a book, *Work Is Dangerous to Your Health*, that provided workers with a comprehensive practical guide to the recognition, evaluation, and control of workplace hazards. Appearing in 1973 (under the imprint of Vintage Books, a respected New York publishing house), *Work Is Dangerous to Your Health* instantly sold tens of thousands of copies. Workers' empowerment through self-help stood out as the volume's main theme. The authors emphasized that "it is the workers' own interest to gain more control over their working conditions and to strive to change them. Uncontrolled and unpressured, industries and government will do little or nothing to eliminate pollution either within the workplace or in the general environment." This perspective, as well as the material presented in the book, drew heavily on the authors' experiences with OCAW. This was particularly the case regarding an awareness of the centrality of gaining knowledge and then utilizing the knowledge acquired. Stellman continued with this orientation after joining the OCAW staff. Both the union's own in-house publications and its other opportunities to communicate reinforced this message. In a 1975 interview with OSHA's monthly magazine, Mazzocchi expressed doubt that nonunion workers could obtain hazard information. He held that unionized workers needed to "extract the information through collective-bargaining agreements that give them the right to know what they work with and the right to act on that knowledge." Mazzocchi told the interviewer that union involvement in OSHA's standard-setting process "makes workers aware of the problems they face." This pioneering organization took a broad view of its educational role and the ways to fulfill it.[11]

Anger and, beyond that, righteous indignation provide potent fuel for social movements, both in mobilizing those directly aggrieved and in attracting conscientiously sympathetic supporters. In the early 1970s, the germinating right-to-know campaign benefited from a series of muckraking exposés of corporate abuse and government negligence. Unsurprisingly, the first salvo of the barrage came from the OCAW. In 1970, Ray Davidson, the editor of the union's newspaper, published *Peril on the Job: A Study of Hazards in the Chemical Industries*. The book brought to life the daily working realities of exposure to hazards while in possession of limited information, no information, or misinformation about those often-lethal risks. Davidson discovered that the Manufacturing Chemists' Association (MCA) had produced safety datasheets on fewer than one hundred substances, obviously a tiny fraction of the many thousands in commercial use. He also found it "very rare that a company makes any of the data sheets available to industrial workers. To do this would raise annoying questions and well might interfere with the flow of production." When Jack Stagner, the chair of the safety committee at the Atlantic Richfield oil refinery in Houston, Texas, inquired about why management had painted over information on barrels and replaced it with meaningless code, he was told that if workers knew what the barrels contained, they would not handle them. At its plant in Texas City, Texas, the American Oil Company stopped releasing a hazard compendium. That move led Harold Hardage, an employee at the facility, to conjecture that the company was simply afraid to keep putting out dangerous facts. The deficiencies in employer-run training programs came in for criticism, especially for covering topics such as off-the-job safety risks instead of on-the-job health risks. Davidson brought to light the unwillingness of company doctors to diagnose occupational disease and their readiness to blame disorders on workers' lifestyles. He also described the impossibility of obtaining reports filed by federal inspectors enforcing the Walsh-Healey Act. His suggested route to a satisfactory right to know was through the collective-bargaining process. Contracts could compel disclosure of identities of chemicals, results of all hazard monitoring, and findings of medical examinations.[12]

Whereas Davidson tried to win outsiders' sympathetic assistance by vividly describing the chemical workers' plight, his colleague from the United Auto Workers (UAW), Franklin Wallick, turned to guilt to motivate support from his readers. Wallick's 1972 book, *The American Worker: An Endangered Species*, castigated environmentalists whose sympathies too seldom extended to working-class human beings. "Only a few halting steps," he declared, "have been taken by environmentalists to discover and do something about the vast and hidden workplace environment where millions are trapped by pollution which frequently exceeds the pollution which befouls our cities." A refrain throughout the work was the unfortunate preoccupation with the problems of the ambient environment at the expense of addressing the working environment. For this imbalance, he blamed not only ecological activists but also oblivious journalists, who were interested only in publicizing dramatic catastrophes like mine explosions, not the more subtle ravages of chronic disease. Wallick applauded the UAW local branch whose latest contract secured the right to use its own equipment to measure noise levels. He looked forward to the day when locals had "air-quality or shop-environment stewards" to gather hazard data and use it to remedy problems. In all probability, his optimism about the potential for the sort of worker-student alliances being fostered by Nader came from his relations with Nader's Raider Gary Sellers, the first attorney Nader ever hired. Wallick reprinted Sellers's "Workers' Bill of Rights," which enumerated several information entitlements. Beyond the usual demands for access to hazard records and personal medical records, this manifesto sought "easy access to all epidemiological and environmental data collected by the company or its consultants." It also aimed to empower workers to photograph or measure all hazards.[13]

Predictably, the 1973 report *Bitter Wages: Ralph Nader's Study Group Report on Disease and Injury on the Job*, written by Joseph A. Page and Mary-Win O'Brien, condemned the failings of corporate management and government bureaucrats and conveyed the message that those parties were hopeless. Regarding organized labor, Page and O'Brien struck a critical but somewhat optimistic tone, based on the behavior of the OCAW. Page and O'Brien urged other unions to follow the OCAW precedent of delivering hazard warning material via their newspapers. Given that only four of forty labor organizations surveyed kept any records on the occurrence of occupational disease within their jurisdiction, the reporters worried that "unions may have insufficient information to bargain intelligently." They approved of the recent decision of the United Rubber Workers (URW) to sponsor its own research program, but they expressed disappointment in the general lack of institutional capacity to take on this responsibility. Few unions had a health and safety department; none of those surveyed had an industrial hygienist on its staff. Instead meager resources were inordinately allocated to maintaining a bureaucracy focused on injury, not disease, prevention. The authors contrasted invidiously that orientation with the OCAW's grassroots approach and prioritizing of occupational disease. The Nader's Raiders argued that "unions have an obligation to inform their members about the hidden dangers of the work environment." Drawing on solid empirical research, Page and O'Brien presented a sharp challenge to the leadership of labor organizations. Beyond the unionized setting, they maintained that all employees "have a right to know the risks they are facing on their jobs." Their analysis concluded that "the key to real progress lies in the cultivation of worker involvement." It urged outsiders who came to assist at-risk workers to aim for "the fundamental goal of worker education and worker control." From this radical point of view, the value of OSHA lay mainly in its establishment for workers and unions of novel rights to know and act, not in its policing functions. Giving the newborn federal system no grace period, the authors cautioned that "history teaches the folly of overreliance on bureaucracy." Suffused with the polemical skepticism of established national institutions that characterized the Nader perspective in general, *Bitter Wages* reinforced both the imperative for self-help and the importance, albeit subordinate, of sympathetic outside expertise.[14]

In her account of widespread victimization published in 1974 under the title *Muscle and Blood*, the investigative journalist Rachel Scott discovered numerous instances of public health agencies' obstruction of access to their unpleasant findings. In Montana, the administrator of the state occupational health program claimed that the results of a study of exposure to cadmium, lead, and other hazards at a lead smelter were secret. In Ohio, the Textile Workers Union got the state to investigate the ketone solvents that were causing neurological disorders among its members. But the Department of Health then refused to divulge the facts found. The union representing aluminum workers in upstate New York experienced the same impediment from state agents who examined the hazards that had precipitated a two-months-long strike. The alternative to the futility of dependence on government sources of information, as Scott learned from Mazzocchi, was to get the unions more involved with this issue and for unorganized workers to form unions.[15]

Expanding on work first appearing in the *New Yorker*, Paul Brodeur in 1974 brought out *Expendable Americans: The Incredible Story of How Tens of Thousands of American Men and Women Die Each Year of Preventable Industrial*

Disease. The facts presented by the author fully warranted his sensational title. Concentrating primarily on the disaster caused by asbestos, Brodeur, like Scott, illuminated the deficiencies in state and federal protection of the workforce (as well as the irresponsibility of corporate management), with a strong emphasis on the withholding of vital information. He elucidated in florid detail the attempts by OCAW to prod public health officials to explore the hazards rampant at the asbestos insulation plant operated by Pittsburgh Corning Corporation in Tyler, Texas. His analysis of that situation and several others captured not just the key roles played by the familiar figures Mazzocchi and Wodka but also by shopfloor leaders.[16]

A series of dramatic events involving Steven Wodka became the subject of articles in *Rolling Stone*. In the countercultural magazine's issue of March 27, 1975, Howard Kohn discussed the highly suspicious death of Karen Silkwood on November 13, 1974, when she was apparently run off the road on her way to a meeting with Wodka and the *New York Times* reporter David Burnham. A folder of documents that Silkwood planned to present at that meeting disappeared from her wrecked car. Those documents would have supplied evidence that her employer, Kerr-McGee Corporation, was falsifying inspection records regarding the carcinogenic plutonium hazard at its nuclear fuel production facility near Cimarron City, Oklahoma. No mere victim of corporate violence, Silkwood was a fearless activist in the OCAW local at her plant. After her story also appeared in *Ms.* in 1975, she came to be seen as a feminist martyr. The National Organization for Women (NOW) declared the first anniversary of her death Karen Silkwood Memorial Day. A second exposé by Kohn in January 1977 dealt with the obstacles, amounting to a systematic cover-up, that blocked investigations of the Silkwood case.[17]

Bischloromethyl ether (BCME), a toxic chemical used in the synthesis of resins, became the subject of an in-depth study by the freelance writers Willard Randall and Stephen Solomon. They were alerted to the mounting toll in lung cancer cases at the Rohm and Haas Company factory in Philadelphia by a public announcement in 1974 by Nader's Health Research Group. Their digging into the human dimension of the more than fifty cancer fatalities and the employer malfeasance that caused them yielded first a lengthy article in the *Philadelphia Inquirer* in 1975 and then a book the following year. By focusing tightly on one hazard at one worksite, Randall and Solomon could delve more deeply into multiple dimensions of the manufacture of ignorance. They demonstrated how the Rohm and Haas Company impeded scientific research on the carcinogenicity of BCME. They described how the company prevailed on city health administrators to conceal the findings for their employees who participated in a lung cancer screening program. Randall and Solomon found that the firm failed to comply with an OSHA standard that mandated the posting of signs warning of a cancer hazard. They captured how workers and their families, despite these obstructions, came to believe that the frequent cancer deaths could not all be attributed to smoking, as management claimed. Among the many other chilling details they brought to light, the authors noted that employees had taken to calling the building where they made BCME "the Death House." Published by Little, Brown under the title *Building 6: The Tragedy at Bridesburg*, Randall and Solomon's book, like almost all the other muckraking volumes, carried the presumption of credibility accorded works brought forth by highly reputable, well-established publishing houses.[18]

The disturbing, often shocking revelations of the 1970s muckrakers gave visibility to previously hidden tragedies of the workplace. They also posed the possibility that the tragedies thus far exposed were but the tip of an iceberg. The critiques all reinforced the themes of employer opacity and the consequent necessity of transparency. Perhaps most important, some of these works elucidated starkly the cost of secrecy in human suffering. Because these narratives were far more likely to reach relatively unendangered middle-class readers, not the members of the working class most at risk, in all probability they served primarily to encourage individuals in the health and legal professions to come forward to assist the embryonic workers' counter-institutions.

In no small part, the search for alternative institutions stemmed from the mistrust of established ones. Like the muckraking writers, radical institution builders took it for granted that they could place no trust at all in corporate management and little in bureaucratized union leadership. As the 1970s unfolded, a great deal of skepticism also surrounded OSHA. From its inception, the agency existed under the control of Republican presidents, which raised doubts. The deep structural flaw inscribed in the law that permitted states to retain regulatory authority if they met (or appeared to meet) certain performance and resource benchmarks engendered further doubts, if not outright dismissal of the entire system. In the context of widespread social movement ferment, dissatisfaction with top-down bureaucracies fostered the clear-cut alternative of bottom-up organizations. New Left activists were especially excited by the spectacle of the black-lung insurgency, in which tens of thousands of coal miners engaged in a rowdy and effective three-week wildcat strike in 1969 over occupational disease grievances. Radicals of various stripes proceeded to craft a constellation of participatory organizations, the COSH groups, devoted to a diverse reform agenda, of which expanding the right to know constituted a foundational component.[19]

A series of projects arising under the auspices of preexisting progressive entities lay the groundwork for establishing full-blown organizations. In Boston, Urban Planning Aid (UPA), a group of planners who operated as radical community organizers, initiated its Industrial (or sometimes Occupational) Health and Safety Project in March 1970. On the right-to-know front, these activists attacked the failure of Massachusetts inspectors to share hazard data they had collected. Rather than foster overdependence on unresponsive government agents, the project worked with more than twenty local unions to train workers to function as inspectors who would develop their own hazard-reporting system. These shopfloor experts were encouraged to share their knowledge with at-risk coworkers and to use wider awareness as a lever for control of working conditions. Besides promoting the collection of hazard data, UPA assisted a local union in conducting pulmonary function tests for its asbestos-exposed members.[20]

Moving to fill a vacuum, UPA produced publications full of practical guidance that propounded a straightforward message of the necessity of carefully collecting evidence to enable enlightened decision making. A 1971 pamphlet stressed that "it is important that each local and each International Union develop methods for gathering information about hazards." This work also publicized the labeling requirements established in the newly enacted federal law, as well as the duty of employers to advise employees of hazard exposure levels that exceeded legal limits. A manual entitled *How to Look at Your Plant* began with this liberating declaration: "You don't have to be an expert to inspect your workplace. The people who are best qualified to identify dangerous situations are the ones who have to deal with them every day." This publication delivered a menu of tactics that union activists could deploy to force remedial action based on their discoveries. It presented a case study in which women at a fluorescent lamp factory dealt with mercury poisoning through a work stoppage that brought both additional hazard controls and access to employer-administered biweekly urine tests. The project's monthly newsletter, *Survival Kit*, offered a stream of suggestions along these lines. In December 1972, the newsletter announced that the printing pressmen's union at the *Washington Post* had done its own hearing tests on members and utilized the findings to win noise control measures. The same issue noted similar advances at a Massachusetts manufacturing facility after UPA loaned its noise meter to union grievance handlers. This emphasis on direct action at the worksite implied a lack of confidence in government protection. An editorial in *Survival Kit* in April 1974 made that attitude explicit: "OSHA lacks the personnel and the will to clean up workplaces adequately.... Better working conditions will not come without action on the shop floor and at the bargaining table. From the rank and file to international officers, workers need to be aware of threats to their health and be ready to do whatever is necessary to get rid of them." The UPA factsheet on solvents urged that all containers bear meaningful labels and that this arrangement be contractually guaranteed. It said nothing about seeking help from either OSHA or the National Institute for Occupational Safety and Health (NIOSH) in gaining information. Frank Wallick cited this factsheet in praising the group's ability to make complex scientific and technical phenomena comprehensible to workers: "These kids up in Boston are living on food stamps and in cold-water flats. And they've taken all this high-powered stuff and they've reduced it down to the kind of information that anybody can understand." In the same vein, by the mid-1970s, the project had studied enough union behavior to put out a guide with model contract language. This pioneering group's consistent advocacy of militant collective self-help exerted a potent formative influence on the movement.[21]

The Labor Occupational Health Project (LOHP) was, from its founding in 1974, another prolific source of agitational materials that promoted the right to know. Based at the University of California, Berkeley, a well-known launching pad for social justice initiatives, LOHP shared the anti-elitist predisposition of progressives at that moment. The founding director Donald Whorton declared at the outset that the purpose of LOHP was to help workers and unions to "develop their own organizational skills and capabilities" in a supportive, not directive, capacity. One of the first products of the project was *A Guidebook for Local Union Health and Safety Committees* by the staff member Bob Fowler, a former International Association of Machinists activist. The guidebook reprinted Gary Sellers's workers' bill of rights manifesto, with its claims of entitlement to various forms of information. Subsequent publications by the attorney Morris Davis and the OCAW veteran Andrea Hricko offered tools for empowering individuals at various levels of the labor movement. At one conference in January 1976, which was attended by more than one hundred local unionists, Davis and Hricko led a session devoted to employee rights that covered entitlement to information. Hricko's overview of issues facing women workers addressed the importance of extracting hazard data and medical findings from management, as well as the methods for doing so. Her survey of issues facing women workers, *Working for Your Life*, published in 1976, worked through practical methods for obtaining such critical information. Both Hricko's illumination of a previously neglected array of problems and her advocacy of collective self-help reflected the feminist orientation of the burgeoning women's health movement. (Beyond Berkeley, the same feminist energy propelled Jeanne Stellman's 1977 overview, *Women's Work, Women's Health*.)[22]

In the early 1970s, the International Brotherhood of Teamsters was an unlikely launching pad for radical initiatives. Yet its Local 688, a sizable branch centered in Saint Louis and led by maverick Harold Gibbons, proved a most hospitable host for one adventurous project. In the summer of 1971, the local brought in Daniel Berman, a graduate student in political science at Washington

University, to try an experiment in self-help at a plant that made steel pipe. Berman and his collaborators in the local gathered a body of data that identified and prioritized the hazards in the plant. This exercise involved training and unleashing a team of rank-and-file workers to produce the facts regarding the risks present and then surveying the factory's employees to determine their foremost concerns. Because the hazard recognition procedure both oriented and activated the workforce, it then facilitated a participative method for pursuing control measures such as improved ventilation. Local 688 turned to the traditional device of collective bargaining to control hazards, avoiding a resort to the policing power of OSHA. The aims of negotiations encompassed both entitlement to information and freedom to take self-protective action: "The collective bargaining agreement should require that the union know the chemical composition of all the substances its members work with, the containers be labeled with chemical composition information, and that the members be given the right to refuse to work with hazardous materials or under hazardous conditions." Preliminary indications of the efficacy of this approach and of its promise of wider applicability led to a sweeping assessment about the forces for ameliorative change. In a report on their work released on August 24, 1971, Berman and his colleagues declared, "Industrial health and safety problems are not going to be solved by corporate benevolence, 'safety contests,' the incentives of Workmen's Compensation, inspections by government officials or by expensive 'experts' who make reports and leave. The system presented here is based on the supposition that working conditions can be improved only by the organization and self-education of the workers affected by those conditions, under the leadership of their unions." In a pragmatic appeal to union leaders, Berman touted this program as a way to upgrade conditions inexpensively.[23]

The experiment in St. Louis soon took Daniel Berman well beyond the jurisdiction of one Teamsters local. Berman secured a place on the program of the national convention of the Medical Committee for Human Rights (MCHR), an organization composed primarily of liberal physicians. Formed in 1964 to assist the African American freedom struggle in the South, the group was broadening its agenda by the early 1970s. That MCHR chose to hold its semiannual convention in October 1971 in Lexington, Kentucky, was quite fortuitous for activists interested in promoting involvement in occupational health. The meeting witnessed not only Berman's presentation on the St. Louis Teamsters program but also that of representatives of the militant Black Lung Association of disabled coal miners. Building on the predisposition of Old Left elements within the organization to pursue struggles of the industrial working class, these messengers from the workplace battlefield prompted MCHR to commit itself to serious engagement in this problem area. Before the year was out, the organization had initiated its Occupational Health Project, which at once launched a newsletter and published a guide for members on possible opportunities to lend assistance to workers in need. Besides the straightforward potential for physicians to diagnose and treat cases of work-related disease, this guidance pamphlet suggested the value of agitation to get legislation enforced and improved. It urged those venturing into the internal politics of organized labor to ally themselves with rank-and-file workers. Placing medical expertise in an ancillary role, MCHR set as its goal "to provide the support to allow workers to determine their own health destiny" by performing research, creating practical publications, convening meetings, and raising public awareness of the importance of work-induced disorders.[24]

Beyond encouragement to its individual members and local chapters, the project, operating out of the committee's national office in Chicago, set out on a course of action that would, more than any other factor, propel the mobilization process that culminated in a national right-to-know movement. The formative experience that gave direction to the incipient project was the organization of a conference in Chicago in January 1972, cosponsored with the University of Illinois and the UAW. Approximately two hundred workers, along with numerous health professionals and union officials, participated in the two-day event. Quentin Young, MCHR's national chair who had a number of progressive labor leaders in the Chicago area as his patients, facilitated union participation and supported this project in other ways. The opening session featured a tribute to Alice Hamilton, who had begun her immersion in the field while at Hull House, the settlement house located near the meeting site. Conference organizers allocated a sizable block of time for workers to describe the hazards they encountered daily. Frieda Jordan expressed outrage at the failure of hospital administrators to warn lower-status workers about the biological agents they faced when dealing with patients. "These people, and that means housekeepers, too," Jordan insisted, "have a right to know what kind of illnesses they are exposed to." Those revelations were supplemented by the presentations on hazards and their adverse health effects by medical specialists. The physician Donald Whorton, a member of the project leadership team, condemned employers who hid behind the assertion of trade secrets. The Teamsters Local 688 activist Art Button outlined the methods he and his comrades had devised to curtail threats to their well-being. The discussion of manifold hazards and creative abatement interventions generated a sense of urgency. The conferees set up a continuation committee that, in short order, launched the Chicago Area Committee on Occupational Safety and Health (CACOSH). This coalition of concerned health-care workers, union officials, and at-risk workers became the prototype for groups that formed thereafter, just as holding a sizable conference became the standard precipitating event for their formation.[25]

Not every seed germinated. A meeting sponsored by MCHR's chapter in New Haven, Connecticut, in February 1972, did not bring forth a durable working coalition. At that session, Lionel Williams of the International Brotherhood of Boilermakers, pointed out, "What we as workers would like to have is some nuts and bolts information. Your polemics are very interesting but we can't apply them to our situation." A conference in Ashland, Kentucky, the following month featured the firebrand black lung activist physician I. E. Buff, whose stock in trade was flamboyant tirades against company doctors and corporate domination of the political system. True to form, Buff used this occasion to claim, "I've never met an honest politician." Buff apparently had forgotten meeting Kenneth Hechler, a member of the US House of Representatives from his own state of West Virginia who had bravely defied the coal operators and contributed significantly to landmark black lung reforms. Despite cosponsorship by the area's Central Labor Council and the big USW local that hosted the event, this exploratory gathering failed to give birth to a COSH organization.[26]

These stumbles came despite warnings and other facilitative work by MCHR's occupational health task force. In an editorial in the March 1972 issue of *Health Rights News*, the task force member Whorton announced that his team was trying to educate MCHR members about this issue. Reflecting the often fraught political environment of the moment, both within the organization and in progressive circles more broadly, Whorton pleaded for ecumenicalism: "We insist that the occupational health effort not become the basis of factionalism." Those with diverse political tendencies were welcome, but they were asked to set sectarian squabbles aside. In the single decision that did the most to push their fledgling venture forward, the MCHR leaders hired Daniel Berman to run the project. Among the many information-generating chores to which Berman applied his considerable energies was the production of publications. He distributed copies of a description of the program that he and the Teamsters had invented in St. Louis. The first issue of the project's newsletter that appeared after his hiring highlighted the pathbreaking work of UPA, based on that group's assumption that "informed workers are their own best health and safety inspectors." The issue also announced that a new pamphlet series on hazards would have workers, not physicians, as its target audience. The newsletter's coverage of the MCHR convention in April 1972 quoted Tony Mazzocchi on the need for unions to place right-to-know clauses in their collective-bargaining agreements. Berman also operated a national clearinghouse on relevant resources, marshalling scarce literature and materials and distributing resource guides. Franklin Wallick's book publicized this "work environment information center" and its holdings on collective-bargaining issues. Within a year of hiring, Berman had filled about 250 requests for literature. Regular mailings went out to a list that soon reached roughly two thousand names.[27]

Berman repeatedly attempted to improve the chances that an educational conference would pave the way to the founding of a viable COSH organization. He gave local MCHR chapters detailed coaching on the planning of such events. Organizers needed to line up cosponsors—an MCHR chapter, "a friendly union," and a local academic medical institution. They had to bring together diverse groups, including environmentalists, but to be sure to "allow workers to speak for themselves." The suggested format called for a concluding strategy session that would, it was hoped, lead directly to the establishment of a COSH-type entity. At that session, Berman warned that "discussion should be led by the workers. Don't push your own politics." The first attempt to follow this blueprint succeeded, at least in the short run. The Pittsburgh MCHR unit enlisted the Allegheny County Labor Council, several of its affiliates, and the Graduate School of Public Health at the University of Pittsburgh to join it in hosting an event in December 1972. A reporter from a management-oriented safety magazine bemusedly took in the scene: "Bearded MCHR docs and long-haired students mixed and mingled with eighty local union safety committeemen, shop stewards, and business managers." Some conferees criticized OSHA as "slow, undermanned, underfunded, and politically incapable of strong action" and argued that progress was possible through collective bargaining. This attitude prompted a stern rebuttal from John Sheehan, the USW legislative director. Sheehan had worked hard to help secure passage of the federal law and feared that the already embattled agency would soon need strong backing in order to withstand impending attacks from the hostile business community. Notwithstanding this disagreement, the hierarchy of the powerful USW union did not stand in the way of the creation of the Pittsburgh Area Committee on Occupational Safety and Health (PACOSH) a month later.[28]

The disenchantment with OSHA and embrace of private solutions was obvious in the issue of Berman's *Occupational Health Project Report* whose appearance coincided with the Pittsburgh conference. An editorial condemned the "extremely lax" enforcement of the law and maintained that "government stalling and inaction on health and safety issues has thrown the burden of cleaning up the shop environment back on the collective bargaining process." The newsletter reprinted the recent demands formulated by a district branch of the Amalgamated Meat Cutters with MCHR assistance. These called for several rights to information of the union health and safety committee, including the chemical composition of all substances used or created in the workplace and copies of all existing data on working conditions. The Amalgamated Meat Cutters also sought to obtain rights for individual members to see all their company medical records. Some organizers feared that excessive criticism of OSHA and related leftist polemics would alienate mainstream unionists. In March 1973, Will Shortell of CACOSH explained how activists should proceed in forming relations with local unions. At the critical first meeting, he advised, "DO NOT go in depth into your own analysis of OSHA, or the exploitation of the working class, or socialism, etc." Instead, activists should stress the value of practical educational services that would enable workers to understand hazards and try to control them. Shortell gave this summary of the approach taken in Chicago: "We avoid becoming involved in internal union disputes, and work with all worker organizations as long as that is feasible."[29]

Whatever lack of confidence he shared with other activists about OSHA's regulatory efficacy, Berman appreciated that the landmark statute established important entitlements. In an article straightforwardly titled "The Worker's Right to Know" in MCHR's *Health Rights News* in April 1973, he characterized these as "the most innovative new rights" set forth in the law. After enumerating the legal rights to access to hazard and medical information, he did, however, attach the qualifier that at present these were "mostly paper rights." Retreating from a prior critique of experts, Berman observed that MCHR was now receiving help from the National Lawyers Guild. He concluded that "further progress on the worker's right to know about health hazards on the job can best be accomplished by coalitions of workers with legal and medical people, using the expertise of all three." The newfound availability of legal aid prompted an interest in promoting lawsuits against company doctors who concealed diagnoses. In part, the prior minimizing of conventional professional expertise had been an attempt to make a virtue of necessity, based on the premises that experts were unsympathetic to workers and unaffordable to unions. Berman's repeated issuance of guides to resources from other organizations reflected in part the relative paucity of resources emanating directly from his own project. With its parent organization collapsing but one of its local chapters offering free office space, the Occupational Health Project, its director working without a salary, relocated to San Francisco in mid-1973.[30]

The little project continued to have an outsized impact. This was evident in its contribution to framing the issue as one of democratization of knowledge to enable self-protection. The June 1974 issue of OSHA's in-house magazine carried a piece titled "The Worker's Right to Know," which quoted Berman on the imperative to arm working people with the information necessary to abate the risks they endured. At a time when rights claims still got traction with relative ease in American political culture, this sort of assertion resonated.

The article heralded the emergence of "a growing occupational health movement based on a loose alliance among young activists, old-line activists, and rank and file workers." It went on to call attention to Berman's operation functioning "on a shoestring budget," as well as to note the work of UPA and PACOSH's distribution of more than one hundred copies of Stellman and Daum's *Work Is Dangerous to Your Health*, among other movement activities that both spread knowledge and elevated the value of expanding such knowledge. Along the same lines, Donald Whorton's pamphlet on byssinosis, issued a few months later in the MCHR series, underscored the central message: "Workers who must expose themselves to the dangers of cotton dust must also know of its hazards. It is their right." All these endeavors shaped the emerging discourse by recasting needs as rights. From this perspective, workers were not abjectly needy victims but rather righteous actors.[31]

Institution building remained the primary objective of the MCHR project, despite the time and energy absorbed by serving as a clearinghouse. This proved to be a challenging chore. In both southwestern Pennsylvania and northern California, incipient COSH groups failed to thrive. In Pittsburgh, as of 1973 the home of the MCHR national office, PACOSH antagonized cautious union leaders, especially in the USW, despite gaining the active support of a number of labor organizations. Daniel Hannan, no stodgy business unionist, was disgusted with the reckless shenanigans of I. E. Buff, whom PACOSH brought in for a speech in January 1974. Creating a crossfire, leftists criticized this COSH's devotion to reformist service functions as insufficiently revolutionary. Similar difficulties doomed the first incarnation of the Bay Area Committee on Occupational Safety and Health (BACOSH). Too many local unions kept their distance from a committee pervaded with leftist sectarianism. As local observer Berman put it in his postmortem assessment, "The quickest way to destroy a COSH group is for it to denounce all union leadership in the name of a self-appointed 'rank-and-file.'"[32]

Organizers had far better luck in the tristate area surrounding Philadelphia, where the MCHR crew set up an occupational health task force in February 1975. At the outset, one participant in this task force had been carrying out a project that did much to lay the groundwork for the founding of a COSH. For more than a year, Rick Engler, a fresh college graduate employed by OCAW, had been leading a participative study of the conditions in five oil refineries in the Delaware Valley. The project was Mazzocchi's idea. Together with OCAW District 8, MCHR activists hosted a well-attended public meeting on May 29, 1975, in part to attract medical and legal talent to provide technical assistance and to help develop an educational program. The success of a six-week course offered that summer led to the birth of the Philadelphia Area Project on Occupational Safety and Health (PhilaPOSH).[33]

From its founding, PhilaPOSH understood the value of collecting and disseminating information. Engler's study of the oil refineries, released in 1975, plainly embodied this value. That document was suffused with his mentor Mazzocchi's right-to-know perspective as well his thoroughgoing militance. Engler bluntly asserted, "Workers have a right to know the identities of the substances they work with. Code names prevent this." He attacked the recent exonerative work of management consultants because "no information is provided to the operator of a particular refinery process about his or her likelihood of getting a disease." He wondered if the consultants' findings of elevated rates of respiratory system cancer accounted for the American Petroleum Institute's refusal to publicize their study. In his analysis, workers' enhanced knowledge made possible successful struggles to eradicate hazards, especially when local health and safety committees were contractually empowered. In early 1976, the first issue of the PhilaPOSH newsletter, *Safer Times*, put it simply: "To win a safe workplace, knowledge is a necessary first step to power." The organization signaled its receptivity to militant tactics by reporting on an Illinois UAW local's use of a strike threat to extract from International Harvester the chemical names of all hazardous substances present in the plant. The project's guide to acquiring hazard information endorsed forceful methods: "When possible, direct action (strikes, slowdowns, other job actions) is the best weapon to use to obtain needed information. It is faster and much more reliable than NIOSH, grievance procedures, or the NLRB [National Labor Relations Board]." Where circumstances permitted, PhilaPOSH did not hesitate to promote an aggressive brand of activism.[34]

The Philadelphia area organizers strove to convey a sense of crisis around the right to know. The announcement of an upcoming conference referred to "death at Rohm and Haas," invoking the recently uncovered local cover-up of the carcinogen BCME. More than two hundred people came to this event in March 1976, where PhilaPOSH gave the regional OSHA administrator a hard time. Demands included opening the agency's library to the public in the evening and on weekends and having OSHA run regular educational sessions. Obviously, denial of opportunities to gain knowledge gained additional visibility in this confrontation, one in which the federal official made no immediate concessions. The experience thus served to reaffirm the necessity of self-help through union channels. Gaining the support of numerous progressive unions in the metropolitan area made this strategy viable. In this approach, PhilaPOSH saw CACOSH as exemplary. From the outset, Philadelphia activists sought buy-in from local unions, especially in the manufacturing sector. A critical self-assessment during the formative phase captured the tension involved in operating inside the house of labor: "Even though we work with existing trade unions, we want to so far as possible take a rank and file approach."

However, promoting rank-and-file demands for enhanced access to health-related information might place union leaders under unwelcome added pressure to address complicated, thorny problems at a time when hazard-filled unionized industries were increasingly plagued by layoffs and runaway shops. PhilaPOSH and its counterparts in other northern industrial centers often faced a delicate balancing act in difficult circumstances.[35]

In winning the support of local unions in the Delaware Valley, nothing beat evidence of practical problem solving. *Safer Times* seized on successful initiatives that displayed an activated rank and file. An early issue detailed the work of the health and safety committee of the UAW local at an ITE-Imperial Corporation electrical manufacturing facility in Philadelphia. The committee investigated hazards, studied control methods, bought literature to start a library, and filed grievances. These actions forced the substitution of less hazardous chemicals for more hazardous ones and the installation of a new ventilation system. At the Kawecki Berylco plant in southeastern Pennsylvania, management refused to help a local union officer investigating a pattern of nosebleeds, rashes, and open sores. Rather than reveal the identities of the chemicals suspected of causing these ailments, the company blamed poor personal hygiene. However, the combination of assistance from PhilaPOSH and the employers' fear of a strike brought about a contract that made gains. The International Chemical Workers local obtained a list of all chemicals used, the labeling of all containers, and an employee training program.[36]

Despite a preference for confronting employers in the economic arena, PhilaPOSH did not abandon agitation in the political arena. Although quite critical of this weak bureaucratic weapon, the Philadelphia group never set aside the option of turning to OSHA for assistance. The most important political undertaking in which PhilaPOSH played a crucial leadership role was its advocacy of an OSHA standard creating a right to know. This COSH group joined the petition to OSHA filed by the Health Research Group and US Representative Andrew Maguire seeking a hazard communication rule. In no small part, this move stemmed from a failed attempt by Local 785 of the URW to require Lee Tire Company to release the chemical names of the substances to which it exposed its employees. Over the course of more than a year, beginning in early 1976, the URW branch used the grievance process and contract bargaining to try to force the company to supply this information, without success. After exhausting these avenues, Local 785 and PhilaPOSH pressured OSHA to extract this evidence, also without success. The lesson of this exercise in futility was the necessity for a specific regulatory mandate in OSHA's arsenal. But along with that realization came an awareness that a proposed regulation covering the identification of hazardous materials had long been stalled.[37]

In the spring of 1977, plans for overcoming the impasse began to take shape. The idea of mounting a major campaign to advance this cause originated with Dudley Burdge of the Service Employees International Union. In May 1977, Burdge proposed starting a mass petition drive to turn up the heat on the federal agents in Washington, DC. Burdge argued that an OSHA standard on hazard information represented "the foundation stone without which no effective pro-worker health and safety program can be built." He contended that such a standard was especially important for unorganized workers, who were "completely at the mercy of management" regarding access to the facts of their exposures. At that time, PhilaPOSH hired Jim Moran to coordinate the right-to-know drive. Moran had led his UAW local's efforts to pry loose information at ITE-Imperial and was later fired for his purported instigation of a wildcat strike. Moran was not alone in having a commitment forged by unfortunate personal experience. John Windfelder, a rank-and-file member of URW Local 785 who had come to PhilaPOSH with a list of meaninglessly codenamed chemicals and who had fought Lee Tire Company's adamant refusal to give out their real names, also became very active in the petition drive for a standard. PhilaPOSH legal advisers drafted a petition that called on OSHA to force employers to release chemical names, hazard-monitoring data, and employee medical records, and to post hazard warnings. To facilitate wider participation by workers, the petition also requested that OSHA hold regional hearings on the proposal, with the Delaware Valley as one site. The work of circulating petitions in workplaces was underway by July in the Philadelphia area.[38]

To intensify the pressure on Washington, PhilaPOSH sought to extend the scope of the campaign. It invited the other COSH groups—from Chicago, Massachusetts, Rhode Island, and North Carolina—to a meeting to discuss rights to hazard and medical information, along with other mutual interests. At a session on July 30, 1977, PhilaPOSH made its case for opening a national campaign for a standard. Dudley Burdge's pitch portrayed this as an important national issue that needed grassroots support. The right to know would give the COSHes a chance to work together for the first time. This was seen as a winnable issue given the generally hospitable attitude of the Jimmy Carter administration's OSHA, led by progressive toxicologist Eula Bingham. Although each group had to take the proposition back to its decision makers for authorization, the prevailing sentiment was that advocacy of informational rights represented a timely challenge worth at least exploring. All the organizations soon got on board. Bob Holt of the USW and CACOSH, reported, "It was the consensus of the board that this campaign is the ideal issue for our groups to work together on."[39]

A simple plan of action emerged from the meeting. Each group would print its own petition forms, with the PhilaPOSH form serving as a template.

Organizers distributed these in workplaces, union meetings, and elsewhere. By mid-November 1977, PhilaPOSH held more than one hundred petitions containing about 2,500 signatures. For the North Carolina Occupational Safety and Health Project (NCOSH), based in an area with little union presence, this meant soliciting signatures at street fairs and in chapters of the Carolina Brown Lung Association. The Massachusetts Coalition for Occupational Safety and Health (MassCOSH) produced a flyer to recruit supporters who would circulate petitions, casting this drive as furthering "the right of working people to informed participation in all decisions affecting their safety and health." Activists used their existing networks of union affiliations and relations to pursue formal organizational endorsements. In November, MassCOSH secured an expression of support from the Massachusetts American Federation of Labor and Congress of Industrial Organizations (AFL-CIO). NCOSH won endorsements of sympathetic environmental and community organizations. PhilaPOSH delegations met with congressional members from Pennsylvania and New Jersey and got legislators to ask OSHA for both expedited standard setting and regionalized hearings. When New Jersey congressional representative James Florio expressed his support in October 1977, he made note of the elevated cancer rates in industrial centers of his state. Florio's declaration plainly indicated that the movement's framing of this issue as a matter of entitlement had taken hold: "The workers have a right to know what they are handling so they can deal with the risks involved."[40]

An effective division of leadership responsibilities operated from the outset. PhilaPOSH coordinated activities on the ground among the five participating groups. Jim Moran dispensed guidance and kept the participants informed of one another's work. Peter Greene of the Health Research Group, based in Washington, DC, took care of making connections and monitoring developments there. He reported at length on the performance of a top OSHA official at the symposium on labeling and warning systems held by the American Conference of Governmental Industrial Hygienists (ACGIH) in November. Venturing outside the Washington, DC, area, Greene spoke at the September PhilaPOSH meeting, where he stressed the national significance of the rights campaign. In a visit to the nation's capital in November, the COSHes met with Assistant Secretary of Labor Eula Bingham, who promised that a proposed standard was imminent. At the annual meeting of the American Public Health Association, organizers collected signatures on petitions and convinced the association to endorse their initiative. By the end of the year, the COSHes and their allies had begun to build momentum for reform on a number of levels.[41]

This was the first occasion on which the COSH groups functioned as a unified force on the national stage, and it was the first time these activists managed to enlist the formal nationwide cooperation of organized labor. Creation of a national movement marked a critical turning point in the marathon fight for greater transparency regarding lethal risks in the American workplace. Although obdurate opposition by powerful interests and an increasingly conservative general political environment would foreclose any easy success, it was a major breakthrough to have established a matrix of movement organizations engaged in a concerted, sustained effort. The decades of scattered and often isolated voices calling for transparency were at an end, replaced by a determined and militant set of counter-institutions, capable of mobilizing a range of conscientious supporters. Just as Alice Hamilton, the grandmother of the movement, had initially needed the resources of Hull House (in a sense, another forerunner of the subsequent alt-labor organizations) and of the larger Progressive movement, the activists of the 1970s depended on the capacity of the COSH groups to attract and allocate various resources necessary to sustain their struggle.

EPILOGUE
Turning the Tide on Toxic Chemical Ignorance

> **The most effective means of finally achieving worker and community knowledge has been through the local efforts of multiple local coalitions of public health activists, local labor unions, citizens, and even certain business leaders who are turning the tide on toxic chemical ignorance.**
>
> —Eula Bingham, 1983

Turned out of office by the Ronald Reagan administration, Eula Bingham was back in Cincinnati, Ohio, in the early 1980s, teaching toxicology at the University of Cincinnati. There she had an excellent vantage point from which to assess recent gains in the struggle for the right to know. Along with the Ohio River Valley Committee on Occupational Safety and Health and diverse other insurgents, she helped pass a municipal ordinance in 1982 that granted a right of access to chemical hazard information. In a brief commentary in the *American Journal of Public Health*, she proudly identified the Cincinnati reform as part of a "legislative revolution" that had won not only local ordinances but also statutes in ten states. Although she astutely predicted that conservative US Occupational Safety and Health Administration (OSHA) leaders would at last finalize a weak federal standard on hazard communication, Bingham still found much to celebrate in the progress of the movement toward an expanded right to know about carcinogens and other health threats.[1]

The decade after the coalitions on occupational safety and health (COSH groups) undertook their national right-to-know campaign produced a harvest of progressive change. The events during this brief interval of progressive change, and subsequent developments as well, have received some scholarly attention and merit much more. The modest aim here is to illuminate salient aspects of the dynamics of change and of the milestones achieved (leaving lots of room for future research to fill in the picture more satisfactorily). To that end, we consider activists' coalition-building skills, organizational infrastructure, tactical repertoire, and strategic resourcefulness.[2]

Proponents of transparency operated in an inhospitable environment. The long economic boom that most Americans enjoyed for roughly thirty years after World War II finally ended. In the manufacturing sector, where fears of toxic materials were most acute, rampant deindustrialization and accelerated flight from union strongholds left workers in a weaker position. With increasing frequency, US capital fled to third world sites where dangerous working conditions were less likely to be challenged. A recessionary contraction of the economy in the early 1980s left workers in an especially precarious state. Unions withered, sometimes to utter impotence. At the same time, the political climate became markedly more conservative. The rise of the New Right and the persistence of potent elements of the Old Right, epitomized by the election and reelection of Ronald Reagan, dimmed prospects for government intervention to regulate the transfer of any business-related information. An ideological devotion to deregulation, buttressed by a resurgence of radical individualism that sometimes veered into outright social Darwinism, guided public policy. The fact that right-to-know proponents made substantial gains against these headwinds is extraordinary.[3]

In contrast to the unfavorable political and economic circumstances, the context regarding societal awareness of work-induced illness served to validate and thus help to promote receptivity to reforms. The steady accumulation of revelations regarding the magnitude of the plague of occupational disease and, in some instances, the nefarious methods by which that phenomenon had been concealed continued unabated. In 1977, the National Institute of Occupational Safety and Health (NIOSH) admitted that it had failed to notify tens of thousands of workers about its findings that they had been, and in many cases still were, exposed to carcinogens. The following year, Daniel Berman's *Death on the Job: Occupational Health and Safety Struggles in the United States* began with the story of asbestos worker Marcos Vela, whose diagnosis of asbestosis was kept from him by the physicians retained by his employer, the Johns Manville Corporation. The massive wave of product liability lawsuits by victims of asbestos-induced diseases or by their surviving families generated a good deal of media attention. These legal battles and the concealment of hazard evidence that inspired them received thorough treatment in Paul Brodeur's unsparingly titled book, *Outrageous Misconduct: The Asbestos Industry on Trial*. In a major Hollywood production that starred Meryl Streep, the film *Silkwood* in 1983 dramatized the lengths to which corporate cover-ups might go. No event during this period did more to illuminate the risks borne by communities near hazardous workplaces than the gas leak in December 1984 at a pesticide plant in Bhopal, India, run by a subsidiary of Union Carbide

Corporation. This worst-ever industrial catastrophe, which killed thousands in the plant and in surrounding areas, received prominent news coverage for a protracted period of time, in part because the firm operated a similar facility in West Virginia. Whether they took a restrained reportorial stance or a sharp accusatory one, the drumbeat of incidents, revelations, and indictments lent legitimacy to demands for hazard transparency.[4]

Widespread public recognition of carcinogens and other dangers and the possibility of their concealment particularly aided occupational health activists in their quest to build coalitions. Union and COSH activists were at pains to stress that theirs was not simply a labor problem. Proving that risks were not confined to the workplace drew support from environmentalists and residents of communities located close to industrial sources of ambient pollution. The results of systematic recruitment of allies were often impressive. The Philadelphia Area Project on Occupational Safety and Health (PhilaPOSH) and other parties set up the Delaware Valley Toxics Coalition (DVTC) in 1979. The DVTC soon grew to more than forty member organizations, including Friends of the Earth, local branches of the Audubon Society and the Sierra Club, the League of Conservation Voters, and other environmentalist groups. DVTC also brought in many community associations—the Philadelphia Council of Neighborhood Organizations and a number of its affiliates from hard-hit working-class areas. Immediately upon winning for Philadelphia the nation's first municipal ordinance granting information rights to both workers and the general public in January 1981, the Delaware Valley group was bombarded by far-flung requests for guidance. This leadership position created an opportunity to disseminate a model for reform in which the appeal of a community right to know led to the formation of class-bridging coalitions. The presence of DVTC agitators in southern New Jersey contributed substantially to the labor-environmental coalition that won the New Jersey Worker and Community Right-to-Know Act of 1983. Caron Chess of DVTC produced a handbook for activists that conveyed not only the lessons of the Philadelphia breakthrough but also the experiences of several other winning campaigns across the country. Those experiences invariably involved coalition building as a crucial aspect of organizing. In Cincinnati, reformers enlisted the local chapters of the National Association for the Advancement of Colored People (NAACP) and the Sierra Club, the League of Women Voters, and the social justice arm of the Catholic archdiocese.[5]

The much-strengthened infrastructure of the right-to-know movement gave agitators a sizable supply of human resources in numerous sites. The primary catalyst for growth in institutional capacity was the New Directions education and training program initiated by the Jimmy Carter administration. From the beginning of her tenure as the head of OSHA, Eula Bingham understood the value of promoting worker education. Shortly after her appointment as assistant secretary of labor for occupational safety and health, Bingham offered a fresh perspective to a congressional committee examining her agency's lackluster past performance: "We must reach employees, every employee, to inform them of possible workplace dangers which they face and their rights under OSHA. A workforce which is sensitized to the work environment is the frontline in any campaign to eradicate workplace hazards." Such a declaration could not have come from any of her Republican predecessors. The New Directions program aimed to help implement this policy principle of promoting worker self-help. By the end of the 1970s, almost half of the twenty COSH groups in existence had New Directions grants. Organized labor was arguably an even bigger beneficiary of this stream of federal funding. Numerous national unions and other components of the labor movement received grants. Newly acquired in-house expertise enabled unions to support their local health and safety committees, promote COSH participation, negotiate over access to information, and engage in other tasks related to winning entitlements to information.[6]

Tactical ingenuity also distinguished the right-to-know offensive of the 1980s. Creative, militant actions energized adherents to the movement, attracted media attention, and embarrassed political decision makers. In one widely publicized maneuver at a sensitive formative moment for the movement, Phila-POSH found a novel way to influence the Philadelphia City Council. On October 6, 1980, the United Auto Workers (UAW) activist Bill Kane arrived at hearings of the council's Health and Welfare Committee with a gas canister meaninglessly labeled X17. When Kane flipped a lever releasing the mysterious contents (compressed air), the legislators scattered and pleaded for information as to what they were inhaling, to the amusement of the more than two hundred right-to-know supporters in attendance. The committee voted to support the DVTC bill before it. Challengers elsewhere wore full-body protection while delivering large steel drums full of pro-reform letters and mounted raucous public demonstrations.[7]

The tactical repertoire advanced a pragmatic strategy. Advocates of a national right to know made a significant gain in 1980 when OSHA produced a standard that opened access to some employer-held records, although it did not mandate the creation of such records. Workers, retired workers, and their designated representatives obtained the right to see medical and hazard-monitoring documents. On the question of a broader entitlement to information, however, the paralysis continued. The first act of the Reagan administration's OSHA leadership was to withdraw their predecessors' last-minute proposal for a hazard communication standard. Faced with this impasse, activists adopted a strategy that amounted to federalism from the bottom up. Numerous legislative advances took place at the local, county, and state levels. As of August 1983, New York, California, and eight other states had enacted statutes, and several other states were discussing proposed measures. Although the laws and ordinances exhibited many similarities, each had its peculiarities. This plethora of differing requirements was a nightmare for chemical firms and other enterprises subject to these strictures while operating in a nationwide market. As a result, the deregulators set aside their antipathy for centralized bureaucratic government in order to put in place a rule to preempt as many of the existing lower-level requirements as possible. Despite its preemptive effect and other limitations, the hazard communication standard issued on November 25, 1983, did impose long-awaited obligations on employers to label containers of hazardous materials, make available material safety datasheets, administer educational and training programs, and take other steps to expand employees' knowledge of health risks. Subsequent litigation forced OSHA to revise its standard to eliminate some flaws. A decade after the COSH groups launched their campaign for transparency, American workers possessed a potentially formidable legal right to know what might kill them on the job. Daniel Berman celebrated this exception to the tendency for federalism to pit states against one another to ensure freedom from regulation. In his view, the American system of fragmented public authority had given "the new social movements and labor the space to regroup and continue their bureaucratic guerilla wars over control of the chemical industry." Continuing the guerilla warfare, organizers intensified efforts to build on this victory by attempting to establish a right to act on hard-won knowledge.[8]

Since the turn of the twentieth century, challengers have taken on the sponsors and beneficiaries of toxic ignorance. This book has sought to identify the wide range of men and women who helped to invent the right to know—government officials like Eula Bingham and Irma West, unionists like Daniel Hannan and Anthony Mazzocchi, COSH activists like Rick Engler and Dan Berman, and others who had multiple affiliations like Alice Hamilton and Herbert Abrams. It has tried to describe and explain the obstacles that those insurgents faced, and the creativity and determination with which they fought to overcome those obstacles. It has tried to demonstrate that many of the advocates of transparency saw their cause not only as a humanitarian endeavor but also as an integral part of the larger project of establishing human rights that expanded the scope of democracy, especially in the generally undemocratic realm of employment relations.

Despite the considerable progress made thus far, partisans of democratization of access to hazard information and to decision-making power still have unfinished business. In waging the battles that remain, contemporary activists might draw a bit of encouragement from the knowledge that they carry on a long tradition. This pattern of engagement originated with a small number of dissidents but eventually grew into a sizable, successful national movement, which should indeed be encouraging.

Notes

INTRODUCTION

Epigraph: OSHA, "Informal Public Hearing on Proposed Standard for Coke Oven Emissions," December 18, 1975, 3233 (Pughsley quotation), Docket H-017, document 153.18, OSHA Technical Data Center, Perkins Building, Washington.

1. Ibid., 3232, 3243, 3246, 3289; OSHA, "Informal Public Hearing on Proposed Standard for Coke Oven Emissions," December 16, 1975, 2978, 2980, Docket H-017, document 153.16; J. William Lloyd, "Long-Term Mortality Study of Steelworkers: V. Respiratory Cancer in Coke Plant Workers," *Journal of Occupational Medicine* 13, no. 2 (February 1971): 53–68.

2. Richard M. Nixon, *The President's Report on Occupational Safety and Health* [for 1971] (Washington, DC: United States Government Publishing Office [GPO], 1972), 111; US House of Representatives, Committee on Government Operations, Manpower and Housing Subcommittee, *Control of Toxic Substances in the Workplace: Hearings*, 94th Cong., 2d sess., 1976 (Washington, DC: GPO, 1976), 55–61.

3. UCLA Labor Center, *Fast Food Frontline: COVID-19 and Working Conditions in Los Angeles* (Los Angeles: The Center, 2022), 16 (quotation), 3, 7–9, 15–16; California Occupational Safety and Health Standards Board, "COVID-19 Prevention," *General Industrial Safety Orders*, November 20, 2020, 3, 5, 6, 10, https://www.dir.ca.gov/OSHSB/documents/COVID-19-Prevention-Emergency-apprvdtxt.pdf; Tamar Lapin, "Amazon Workers at Staten Island Warehouse to Stage Walkout over Coronavirus," *New York Post*, March 29, 2020, https://nypost.com/2020/03/29/amazon-workers-on-staten-island-walkout-over-coronavirus/; Ginia Bellafante, "Amazon Workers Are Feeling Vulnerable," *New York Times*, April 5, 2020, sec. MB, 3; Jodi Kantor and Karen Weise, "How Two Friends Birthed Union inside Amazon," *New York Times*, April 3, 2022, 1, 20. For the right-to-know provisions of the 2021 federal rule that, until invalidated by a judicial decision within a few months, compelled larger employers to notify at-risk employees of cases among coworkers with whom they might have been in contact, see OSHA, "COVID-19 Vaccination and Testing: Emergency Temporary Standard," *Federal Register* 86, no. 212 (November 5, 2021): 61475, 61536, 61542–44, 61547–48, 61554–55.

4. Robert N. Proctor, "Agnotology: A Missing Term to Describe the Cultural Production of Ignorance (and Its Study)," in *Agnotology: The Making and Unmaking of Ignorance*, ed. Proctor and Londa Schiebinger (Stanford, CA: Stanford University Press, 2008), 2 (quotation), 8–20; idem, *Cancer Wars: How Politics Shapes What We Know and Don't Know about Cancer* (New York: Basic Books, 1995), esp. 36–48, 110–32; David Michaels, *Doubt Is Their Product: How Industry's Assault on Science Threatens Your Health* (New York: Oxford University Press, 2008); idem, *The Triumph of Doubt: Dark Money and the Science of Deception* (New York: Oxford University Press, 2020), 77–101, 117–40, 240–47; David E. Lilienfeld, "The Silence: The Asbestos Industry and Early Occupational Cancer Research—A Case Study," *American Journal of Public Health* (*AJPH*) 81, no. 6 (June 1991): 791–800; Paul Brodeur, *Outrageous Misconduct: The Asbestos Industry on Trial* (New York: Pantheon, 1985); Gerald Markowitz and David Rosner, *Deceit and Denial: The Deadly Politics of Industrial Pollution* (Berkeley: University of California Press, 2002); David Egilman and Samantha Howe, "Against Anti-Health

Epidemiology: Corporate Obstruction of Public Health via Manipulation of Epidemiology," *International Journal of Occupational and Environmental Health* 13, no. 1 (January–March 2007): 118–24; Egilman, Tess Bird, and Caroline Lee, "Dust Diseases and the Legacy of Corporate Manipulation of Science and Law," *International Journal of Occupational and Environmental Health* 20, no. 2 (April 2014): 115–25; Marianne Sullivan, "Contested Science and Exposed Workers: ASARCO and the Occupational Standard for Inorganic Lead," *Public Health Reports* 122, no. 4 (July–August 2007): 541–47.

5. David Rosner and Gerald Markowitz, "A 'Gift of God'? The Public Health Controversy over Leaded Gasoline during the 1920s," *AJPH* 75, no. 4 (April 1985): 344–52; idem, "Workers, Industry, and the Control of Information: Silicosis and the Industrial Hygiene Foundation," *Journal of Public Health Policy* 16, no. 1 (Spring 1995): 29–58; Paul Blanc, *Fake Silk: The Lethal History of Viscose Rayon* (New Haven, CT: Yale University Press, 2016), 78–109, esp. 82, 85, 98. For insights into the nature of the capitalist state, see, among others, Bob Jessop, *State Theory: Putting the Capitalist State in Its Place* (University Park, PA: Penn State University Press, 1990); idem, *State Power: A Strategic-Relational Approach* (Malden, MA: Polity, 2007); Michael B. Lax, "Falling Short: The State's Role in Workplace Safety and Health," *New Solutions: A Journal of Environmental and Occupational Health Policy* 18, no. 3 (2020): 27–41.

6. Lani Watson, *Epistemic Rights and Why We Need Them* (New York: Routledge, 2021), viii (quotation).

1. A VERY GENERAL IGNORANCE

Epigraph: Illinois Legislature, "Joint Resolution of the Legislature and the Subsequent Acts," March 12 and 20, 1907, in Illinois Commission on Occupational Diseases, *Report* (Chicago: Warner, 1911), 5.

1. James Quesada, Laurie Kain Hart, and Phillippe Bourgois, "Structural Vulnerability and Health: Latino Migrant Laborers in the United States," *Medical Anthropology* 30, no. 4 (July 2011): 339–62. For my previous treatment of developments in this period, one that leaves the issues of ignorance and transparency in the shadows, see Alan Derickson, "Naphtha Drunks, Lead Colic, and the Smelter Shakes: The Inordinate Exposure of Immigrant Workers to Occupational Health Hazards at the Turn of the Twentieth Century," *Journal of American Ethnic History* 37, no. 2 (Winter 2018): 37–61.

2. Massachusetts, *Acts and Resolves . . ., 1907* (Boston: Wright and Potter, 1907), 518–20; Massachusetts State Board of Health, *Fortieth Annual Report* [for the fiscal year ended November 30, 1908] (Boston: Wright and Potter, 1909), 674, 681 (Washburn quotation); idem, *Forty-Second Annual Report* [for the fiscal year ended November 30, 1910] (Boston: Wright and Potter, 1911), 529 (Hanson quotations), 512 (Hanson quotation), 512–13, 521–31.

3. Barbara Sicherman, *Alice Hamilton: A Life in Letters* (Cambridge, MA: Harvard University Press, 1984), 156–58, 180–81; Matthew C. Ringenberg, William C. Ringenberg, and Joseph D. Brain, *The Education of Alice Hamilton: From Fort Wayne to Harvard* (Bloomington: Indiana University Press, 2019), 34–83, esp. 50, 81; Earl R. Beckner, *A History of Labor Legislation in Illinois* (Chicago: University of Chicago Press, 1929), 272–76; Alice Hamilton, *Exploring the Dangerous Trades: The Autobiography of Alice Hamilton, M.D.* (1943; Boston: Northeastern University Press, 1985), 125 (quotation), 120–26, 138–39, 157–59; idem, "Lead-Poisoning in Illinois," *JAMA* 56, no. 17 (April 29, 1911): 1240–41 (quotation), 1240–44; idem, "Lead Poisoning in Illinois," *American Economic Review* 1, no. 2 (April 1911): 264 (quotation), 257–64; idem, "Lead Poisoning in Illinois," *American Labor Legislation Review* (*ALLR*), January 1911, 25 (quotation—identical to that in *American Economic Review*), 17 (quotation), 17–26; Illinois Commission on Occupational Diseases, *Report*, 35 (Hamilton quotation), 42 (Hamilton

quotation), 22–46, 48. On the saliency of the lead threat at this time, see Christian Warren, *Brush with Death: A Social History of Lead Poisoning* (Baltimore, MD: Johns Hopkins University Press, 2000), 64–115.

4. Illinois Commission on Occupational Diseases, *Report*, 98 (quotation), 52–98.

5. Charles R. Henderson, "Illinois Commission on Occupational Diseases," in American Association for Labor Legislation, *First National Conference on Industrial Diseases* (New York: The Association, 1910), 25–26 (quotation), 21–22; Illinois Commission on Occupational Diseases, *Report*, 16 (quotation), 20 (quotations), 15–17.

6. Illinois Commission on Occupational Diseases, *Report*, 160 (quotation), 165–71; Illinois, *Laws . . ., 1909* (Springfield: Illinois State Journal, 1909), 211–12; idem, *Laws . . ., 1911* (Springfield: Illinois State Journal, 1911), 334.

7. Richard A. Greenwald, *The Triangle Fire, the Protocols of Peace, and Industrial Democracy in New York* (Philadelphia: Temple University Press, 2005); David Von Drehle, *Triangle: The Fire That Changed America* (New York: Atlantic Monthly Press, 2003); David R. Colburn, "Al Smith and the New York Factory Investigating Commission, 1911–1915," in *Reform and Reformers in the Progressive Era*, ed. David R. Colburn and George E. Pozzetta (Westport, CT: Greenwood, 1983), 25–45, esp. 32–35.

8. New York Factory Investigating Commission, *Preliminary Report of the Factory Investigating Commission*, 3 vols. (Albany, NY: Argus, 1912), 1: 549 (Pratt quotation), 544, 365–556, 3: 677, 683–84; idem, *Second Report of the Factory Investigating Commission*, 4 vols. (Albany, NY: J. B. Lyon, 1913), 2: 1137 (Graham-Rogers and Vogt quotation), 1116 (Graham-Rogers and Vogt quotation), 1116–17, 1137–39, 3: 688f (Bliss quotation), 679–88f. On a subsequent nondisclosure issue in Niagara Falls, see Jim Morris, *The Cancer Factory: Industrial Chemicals, Corporate Deception, and the Hidden Deaths of American Workers* (Boston: Beacon, 2024), 83, 106, 128.

9. Idem, *Second Report*, 1: 245 (quotation), 248, 251, 2: 467 (Price quotation), 476 (Price quotations), 477 (Price quotation), 466–77, 1160–61, 3: 630–41; idem, *Preliminary Report*, 2: 467 (Vogt quotation), 460–62; idem, *Second Report*, 2: after 462 (quotation), 3: 465–66; idem, *Preliminary Report*, 3: 1938–44.

10. Idem, *Preliminary Report*, 1: 401 (Pratt quotation), 396–401, 553 (Pratt quotation), 549–55; idem, *Second Report*, 2: 486, 1137, 1139, 1: 254, 298–320, 388–89.

11. New York, *Laws . . ., 1913*, 4 vols. (Albany, NY: J. B. Lyon, 1913), 1: 243–62.

12. New York Department of Labor (NYDoL), *Thirteenth Annual Report of the Commissioner of Labor for the Twelve Months Ended September 30, 1913* (Albany, NY: The Department, 1914), 15 (Lynch quotation), 15–16, 20; "Industrial Diseases," *New York Labor Bulletin*, March 1913, 64–65.

13. E. R. Hayhurst, *A Survey of Industrial Health-Hazards and Occupational Diseases in Ohio* (Columbus, OH: F. J. Heer, 1915), 109 (quotation), xv–xviii, 51–113, esp. 112.

14. Hayhurst, *A Survey of Industrial Health-Hazards*, 129, 134, 136 (quotation), 148, 154, 183 (quotations), 112 (quotation), 117–356 passim on workers' ignorance and personal habits.

15. Ibid., 164, 208, 228–29, 107 (quotation), 208, 228, 229, 294, 349.

16. Ibid., v, 406 (quotation), 402–7, esp. 403; Ohio, *Legislative Acts Passed and Joint Resolutions Adopted . . ., 1913* (Springfield, OH: Springfield Publishing, 1913), 822; Terence L. Chorba et al., "Mandatory Reporting of Infectious Diseases by Clinicians," *JAMA* 262, no. 21 (December 1, 1989): 3018.

17. Paul S. Peirce, "Industrial Diseases," *North American Review*, October 1911, 540 (quotation), 529–40; "The Prevention of Industrial Disease, (editorial), *JAMA* 57, no. 23 (December 2, 1911): 1842; John B. Andrews to Ernst Freund, October 21, 1910, American Association for Labor Legislation Records, reel 4, Kheel Center for Labor-Management Documentation, Catherwood Library, Cornell University, Ithaca, NY; Andrews to Paul

Watrous, October 28, 1910, ibid.; Andrews to Erich C. Stern, January 10, 1911, ibid.; Great Britain, *Public General Statutes ...*, *1895* (London: William Clowes, 1895), 83–84; idem, *Public General Statutes ...*, *1901* (London: William Clowes, 1901), 93; "Discussion of Immediate Problems," *ALLR*, January 1911, 74, 82–83. For one characteristic expression of outsized enthusiasm for education, see Edmund J. James, "The Economic Significance of a Comprehensive System of National Education: Annual Address of the President," *American Economic Review* 1, no. 2 (April 1911): 1–25.

18. Connecticut, *Public Acts ...*, *1911* (Hartford: Connecticut Press, 1911), 1425; New York, *Laws ...*, *1911*, 3 vols. (Albany, NY: J. B. Lyon, 1911), 1: 646; California, *The Statutes of the State of California and Amendments to the Codes ...*, *1911* (San Francisco: Bancroft-Whitney, 1911), 953; Michigan, *Public Acts ...*, *1911* (Lansing, MI: Wynkoop Hallenbeck Crawford, 1911), 179; Illinois, *Laws, 1911*, 331; Wisconsin, *Session Laws, Acts, Resolutions and Memorials ...*, *1911* (Madison, WI: Democrat Printing, 1911), 256; John B. Andrews, "The Beginning of Occupational Disease Reports," *ALLR*, December 1911, 108 (quotation), 107–11; idem, "Industrial Diseases and Physicians," *JAMA* 56, no. 15 (April 15, 1911): 1133 (quotation), 1132–34; New Jersey, *Acts ...*, *1912* (Trenton, NJ: MacCrellish and Quigley, 1912), 603–4; New Jersey Board of Health, *Thirty-Sixth Annual Report, 1912* (Union Hill, NJ: Dispatch, 1913), 39; Maryland, *Laws ...*, *1912* (Baltimore, MD: King Brothers, 1912), 330–31. Andrews's call to physicians echoed one made little more than a year earlier in the same forum. See David L. Edsall, "Some of the Relations of Occupations to Medicine," *JAMA* 53, no. 23 (December 4, 1909): 1873–81, esp. 1879, 1881.

19. W. Gilman Thompson, "Occupational Poisoning in Chemical Trades," *Journal of Industrial and Engineering Chemistry* 4, no. 6 (June 1912): 454–57; [John B. Andrews] to Leonard W. Hatch, October 2, 1912 (quotation), AALL Records, reel 8; Andrews to Gertrude Felker, October 18, 1912, ibid.

20. C.-E. A. Winslow, "Occupational Disease and Economic Waste," *Atlantic Monthly*, May 1909, 684 (quotation); Joint Board of Sanitary Control in the Cloak, Suit and Skirt Industry, *Second Annual Report* (New York: The Board, 1912), 12–13; John B. Andrews to Gertrude Felker, October 18, 1912, AALL Records, reel 8. On the garment workers' union and the Joint Board of Sanitary Control, see Greenwald, *The Triangle Fire*, 25–79; George M. Price, "A General Survey of the Sanitary Conditions of the Shops in the Cloak Industry," in Joint Board of Sanitary Control in the Cloak, Suit and Skirt Industry, *First Annual Report* (New York: The Board, 1911), 35–72; Daniel E. Bender, *Sweated Work, Weak Bodies: Anti-Sweatshop Campaigns and Languages of Labor* (New Brunswick, NJ: Rutgers University Press, 2004), 75–154.

21. Diana Chapman Walsh, *Corporate Physicians: Between Medicine and Management* (New Haven, CT: Yale University Press, 1987), 33–49; Angela Nugent, "Fit for Work: The Introduction of Physical Examinations in Industry," *Bulletin of the History of Medicine* 57, no. 4 (Winter 1983): 578–95; Harry E. Mock, "Industrial Medicine and Surgery—A Resume of Its Development and Scope," *Journal of Industrial Hygiene* 1, no. 1 (May 1919): 1–8. On welfare capitalism, see, among many others, Stuart Brandes, *American Welfare Capitalism, 1880–1940* (Chicago: University of Chicago Press, 1976), esp. 52–65; Andrea Tone, *The Business of Benevolence: Industrial Paternalism in Progressive America* (Ithaca, NY: Cornell University Press, 1997).

22. Harry E. Mock, *Industrial Medicine and Surgery* (Philadelphia: W. B. Saunders, 1919), 141 (quotation), 142–43 (quotation); Hamilton, *Exploring the Dangerous Trades*, 4 (quotation).

23. Hamilton, *Exploring the Dangerous Trades*, 153 (quotation—lead), 152–53, 197 (quotation—TNT); idem, "In Retrospect," in American Labor Health Association, *Papers and Proceedings of the National Conference on Labor Health Services* (Washington, DC: The Association, 1958), 162 (quotation), 161–62; Josephine W. Bates, *Mercury Poisoning*

in the Industries of New York City and Vicinity (New York: National Civic Federation, New York and New Jersey Section, n.d. [ca. 1912]), 31.

24. W. Irving Clark, "Medical Supervision of Factory Employees," *JAMA* 60, no. 7 (February 15, 1913): 508-9; C. H. Watson, "Physical Examinations: A Resume," in National Industrial Conference Board, *The Physician in Industry: A Symposium* (New York: The Board, 1922), 25; Eugene L. Fisk, *The Periodic Physical Examination of Employees* (New York: Life Extension Institute, [1915]), 5 (quotation), 14; National Industrial Conference Board, *Health Service in Industry* (New York: The Board, 1921), 6, 39-41; W. Irving Clark, *Health Service in Industry* (New York: Macmillan, 1922), 82, 98.

25. J. W. Schereschewsky, "Physical Examination of Workers," *Public Health Reports* 29, no. 47 (November 20, 1914): 3109 (quotation), 3109-12; C. D. Selby, "Physicians in Industry," in National Safety Council, *Proceedings of the Seventh National Safety Congress, 1918* (n.p., n.d.), 329-30 (quotation), 329-31; idem, *Studies of the Medical and Surgical Care of Industrial Workers* (Washington, DC: US Government Printing Office [GPO], 1919), 5 (quotation), 5-9, 61-63; NYDoL, Bureau of Statistics and Information, *European Regulations for Prevention of Occupational Diseases* (Albany, NY: J. B. Lyon, 1916), 21.

26. George M. Price, *The Modern Factory: Safety, Sanitation and Welfare* (New York: John Wiley, 1914), 483-85; Thomas Darlington, "Practical Health Work for the Industries, Large and Small," in National Safety Council, *Proceedings of the Seventh National Safety Congress, 1918* (n.p., n.d.), 249 (quotation), 249-57; idem, "Model Yard Conditions at the Bethlehem Steel Company's Works," *Monthly Bulletin of the American Iron and Steel Institute*, January 1913, 4-5; idem, "Why Have Bathing Facilities in Industrial Plants?," ibid., July 1913, 199-207; idem, "The Importance of Mouth Hygiene," ibid., September 1914, 240-42; Magnus W. Alexander, "The Physician in Industry," *Safety Engineering*, May 1916, 299-304, esp. 303.

27. C. E. Ford, "Health Instruction," in National Safety Council, *Proceedings of the Sixth National Safety Congress, 1917* (n.p., n.d.), 246-49; Michael M. Davis and Linda James, "Industrial Medicine and the Immigrants," *Journal of Industrial Hygiene* 2, no. 11 (March 1921): 399-401; Michael M. Davis, *Immigrant Health and the Community* (New York: Harper, 1921), 350 (quotation), 348-53, 361.

28. Alice Hamilton, *Lead Poisoning in the Smelting and Refining of Lead*, BLS Bulletin 141 (Washington, DC: GPO, 1914), 50 (quotation), 50-51 (quotation), 10, 50-53, 72; idem, *Exploring the Dangerous Trades*, 5 (quotation), 5-6, 153-54; Alan M. Kraut, *Silent Travelers: Germs, Genes, and the "Immigrant Menace"* (New York: Basic Books, 1994); Amy L. Fairchild, *Science at the Borders: Immigrant Medical Inspection and the Shaping of the Modern Industrial Labor Force* (Baltimore, MD: Johns Hopkins University Press, 2003); Howard Markel, *When Germs Travel: Six Major Epidemics That Have Invaded America since 1900 and the Fears They Have Unleashed* (New York: Pantheon, 2004), 13-140; Mark Aldrich, *Safety First: Technology, Labor, and Business in the Building of American Work Safety, 1870-1939* (Baltimore, MD: Johns Hopkins University Press, 1997), 116 (quotation), 115-16.

29. Brandes, *American Welfare Capitalism*, 52-65; Tone, *Business of Benevolence*, 158-61; Susan F. Martin, *A Nation of Immigrants* (New York: Cambridge University Press, 2010), 123-30; Aneta Pavlenko, "'We Have Room for but One Language Here': Language and National Identity in the U.S. at the Turn of the 20th Century," *Multilingua* 21, nos. 1-2 (April 2002): 163-96. On Americanization more broadly, see James R. Barrett and David Roediger, "Inbetween Peoples: Race, Nationality and the 'New Immigrant' Working Class," *Journal of American Ethnic History* 16, no. 3 (Spring 1997): 3-44; Edward G. Hartmann, *The Movement to Americanize the Immigrant* (New York: Columbia University Press, 1948); Gerd Korman, "Americanization at the Factory Gate,"

Industrial and Labor Relations Review 18, no. 3 (April 1965): 396–419; idem, *Industrialization, Immigrants, and Americanizers: The View from Milwaukee, 1866–1921* (Madison: State Historical Society of Wisconsin, 1967).

30. US Immigration Commission, *Reports*, 42 vols. (Washington, DC: GPO, 1911), 1: 474–79; Homer Hoyt, "The Relation of the Literacy Test to a Constructive Immigration Problem," *Journal of Political Economy* 24, no. 5 (May 1916): 452; Pennsylvania Department of Labor and Industry, *First Annual Report of the Commissioner of Labor and Industry, 1913, Part I* (Harrisburg, PA: William Stanley Ray, 1915), 255–56; Marion K. Clark, "Americanization and Safety," *Bulletin of the Chamber of Commerce of the State of New York*, June 1918, 46 (quotation), 45–49.

31. Korman, *Industrialization, Immigrants, and Americanizers*, 102–5, 147; "Combining Americanization with Safety First in the Plant of the American Car and Foundry Company at Berwick," *Monthly Bulletin of the Pennsylvania Department of Labor and Industry*, January 1917, 13 (quotation), 13–17; Charles H. Paull, "Development of Americanization Project: Experiment and Experience at Solvay Process," *Industrial Management*, March 1919, 213–17, esp. 214; George F. Quimby and Charles H. Paull, *English of Leather Making: Lessons for Adult English Classes* (Boston: Associated Industries of Massachusetts, 1919), n.p., Lesson 3 (quotation), and passim.

32. Robert Shaw, "Discussion," in National Safety Council, *Proceedings of the Sixth National Safety Congress, 1917* (n.p., n.d.), 236–37; Stephen Meyer III, *The Five Dollar Day: Labor Management and Social Control at the Ford Motor Company, 1908–1921* (Albany: State University of New York Press, 1981), 156–61; Peter Roberts, "The Roberts Method of Teaching English to Foreigners," *Illinois Miners' and Mechanics' Institutes Bulletin*, November 16, 1914, 37–52; idem, "The YMCA Teaching Foreign-Speaking Men," *Immigrants in America Review*, June 1915, 18–22; Peter Roberts, *The New Immigration: A Study of the Industrial and Social Life of Southeastern Europeans in America* (New York: Macmillan, 1912), 81 (quotation), 91; Korman, *Industrialization, Immigrants, and Americanizers*, 143–46; Howard C. Hill, "The Americanization Movement," *American Journal of Sociology* 24, no. 6 (May 1919): 638 (Ford management quotation); Esther E. Lape, "The 'English First' Movement in Detroit," *Immigrants in America Review*, September 1915, 46–50; National Americanization Committee, *Americanizing a City: The Campaign for the Detroit Night Schools Conducted in August–September, 1915* (New York: National Americanization Committee and Committee for Immigrants in America, 1915), 10, 12, 19; "Educate Alien Workmen, Prevent Accidents and Increase Your Plant's Efficiency," *Spokesman-Review* (Spokane, WA), August 27, 1916, 2; Frank V. Thompson, *Schooling of the Immigrant* (New York: Harper, 1920), 56 (quotation), 55–56, 104. On Roberts's wider agenda, see Paul McBride, "Peter Roberts and the YMCA Americanization Program, 1907–World War I," *Pennsylvania History* 44, no. 2 (April 1977): 145–62, esp. 150–52.

33. L. P. Worthington, "The Non-English Speaking Workman in Shop Safety Organization," in New York Industrial Commission, *Proceedings of the Third Industrial Safety Congress . . ., 1918* (Albany, NY: Bureau of Statistics and Information, n.d.), 184–86; J. L. Gerson, "General Discussion," in New York Industrial Commission, *Proceedings of the Third Industrial Safety Congress . . ., 1918* (Albany, NY: Bureau of Statistics and Information, n.d.), 195; "Americanization Questionnaire Gives Interesting Facts," *Personnel*, October 1919, 3; Chester S. Carney, "National Conference on Americanization in Industries," *Journal of Applied Psychology* 3, no. 3 (September 1919): 269–70.

34. Pennsylvania, *Laws . . ., 1913* (Harrisburg, PA: C. E. Aughinbaugh, 1913), 1366; Pennsylvania Industrial Board, "Minutes," July 5, 1917, "Industrial Board Minutes, 1914–1918, 285–86, RG-16: Records of the Department of Labor and Industry, Minutes

of the Industrial Board, 1914–1932, box 1, Pennsylvania State Archives, Harrisburg; Pennsylvania Industrial Board, "Employment of Non-English Speaking Persons," *Monthly Bulletin of the Pennsylvania Department of Labor and Industry*, July 1917, 52; J. B. Douglas, "Address by Chairman," in National Safety Council, *Proceedings of the Sixth National Safety Congress, 1917*, 485; "Benzol Poisoning," *Monthly Bulletin of the Pennsylvania Department of Labor and Industry*, February 1916, 14; Pennsylvania Industrial Board, "Safety Standards: Plants Manufacturing or Using Explosives," in National Safety Council, *Proceedings of the Sixth National Safety Congress, 1917* (n.p., n.d.), May 1917, 52–53; "Suggested Practices for the Manufacture of Nitro and Amido Compounds as Evolved by the Industrial Board with the Aid of the Division of Industrial Hygiene and Engineering and a Committee of Representatives of Plants Manufacturing Explosives," in National Safety Council, *Proceedings of the Sixth National Safety Congress, 1917* (n.p., n.d.), September 1917, 48–50; Pennsylvania Council of National Defense, Americanization Bureau, *Americanization in Pennsylvania: Methods of Teaching English to the Non-English-Speaking Foreign-Born* (Philadelphia: The Bureau, n.d. [ca. 1918]), Lesson IV; Lizabeth Cohen, *Making a New Deal: Industrial Workers in Chicago, 1919–1939*, 2nd ed. (New York: Cambridge University Press, 2008), 163; C. W. Hammond, "Getting Close to the Men: Intensive Instruction by Foremen," in National Safety Council, *Proceedings of the Seventh National Safety Congress, 1918*, 897–98; Francis D. Patterson, "The Functions of the State in Enforcing Industrial Hygiene Legislation," *Public Health Reports* 37, no. 42 (October 10, 1922): 2630 (quotation), 2625–31.

35. "Occupational Hygiene," *ALLR*, December 1914, 544; New Jersey, *Acts of the One Hundred and Thirty-Eighth Legislature* [1914] (Union Hill, NJ: Dispatch, 1914), 301 (quotations); Massachusetts State Board of Labor and Industries, *Rules and Regulations Suggested for Safety in the Manufacture of Benzene Derivatives and Explosives* (Boston: Wright and Potter, 1916), 10 (quotation); M. G. Overlock, "Education for the Prevention of Industrial Diseases," *ALLR*, June 1912, 333 (quotation), 332–33. The federal government publicized the Massachusetts regulation that called for multilingual notices. See Alice Hamilton, *Industrial Poisoning in Making Coal-Tar Dyes and Dye Intermediates*, BLS Bulletin 280 (Washington, DC: GPO, 1921), 77.

36. Meyer, *The Five Dollar Day*, 56; J. A. Smith, "How the Employer Feels about It," in New York Industrial Commission, *Proceedings of the Second Industrial Safety Congress . . ., 1917* (n.p., n.d.), 61; "Discussion," in National Safety Council, *Transactions of the National Safety Council Sixteenth Annual Safety Congress, 1927*, 3 vols. ([Chicago]: The Council, 1928) 1: 518–19; Charles H. Paull, *Americanization: A Discussion of Present Conditions with Recommendations for the Teaching of Non-Americans* (Syracuse, NY: Solvay Process, 1918), 28–29; "General Round Table," in National Safety Council, *Proceedings of the Fifth National Safety Congress, 1916* (n.p., n.d.), 125; John Train, "Motion Pictures—The Universal Language," in New York Industrial Commission, *Proceedings of the Fourth Industrial Safety Congress . . ., 1919* (Albany, NY: Bureau of Statistics and Information, n.d.), 235–40; Vincent Colelli, "How to Reach the Non-English Speaking Workman," *Monthly Bulletin of the Pennsylvania Department of Labor and Industry*, March 1917, 26–27; Alice Hamilton, "The Fight against Industrial Diseases: The Opportunities and Duties of the Industrial Physician," *Pennsylvania Medical Journal* 21, no. 6 (March 1918): 380 (quotation).

37. William Conibear, "System of Safety Inspection of the Cleveland-Cliffs Iron Company," in Association of Iron and Steel Electrical Engineers, *Proceedings of the First Cooperative Safety Congress, 1912* (n.p., n.d.), 85, 87; Frank McKee, "Accident Prevention in Foundry and Machine Shop," in Association of Iron and Steel Electrical Engineers, *Proceedings of the First Cooperative Safety Congress, 1912* (n.p., n.d.), 228; New

York Division of Industrial Hygiene, *Health Hazards of the Chemical Industry*, Special Bulletin 96 (Albany, NY: J. B. Lyon, 1920), 33; Carl M. Hansen, *Universal Safety Standards: A Reference Book of Rules, Drawings, Tables, Formulae, Data and Suggestions for Use of Architects, Engineers, Superintendents, Foremen, Inspectors, Mechanics and Students*, 2nd ed. (New York: Workmen's Compensation Service Bureau, 1914), 36 (quotation), 36–38; "General Round Table," in National Safety Council, *Proceedings of the Fifth National Safety Congress, 1916*, 125; "Discussion," in National Safety Council, *Proceedings of the Sixth National Safety Congress, 1917*, 235 (Schereschewsky quotation), 234–36.

38. John Roach, "Hygienic and Sanitary Equipment," *Industrial Management*, October 1917, 20–29; Aldrich, *Safety First*, 116–20; Lucian W. Chaney, "The Engineering Factor in Safety Work," in New York Industrial Commission, *Proceedings of Safety Congress, 1917*, 47–53; Royal Meeker, "General Discussion," in New York Industrial Commission, *Proceedings of Safety Congress, 1917*, 63 (quotation); Bernard J. Newman, "Industrial Health," in US Department of the Interior, Bureau of Education, *Proceedings, Americanization Conference . . ., 1919* (Washington, DC: GPO, 1919), 182–89.

39. Hamilton, *Exploring the Dangerous Trades*, 131–32, 141–43, 155–60; Illinois Commission on Occupational Diseases, *Report*, 24, 26–27, 32–34, 47–48; Alice Hamilton, *Poisons Used in the Rubber Industry*, BLS Bulletin 179 (Washington, DC: GPO, 1915), 48; idem, *Lead Poisoning in the Smelting and Refining of Lead*, 6 (quotation), 5–9, 21, 28, 31–42, 46–49; idem, *Lead Poisoning in Potteries, Tile Works, and Porcelain Enameled Sanitary Ware Factories*, Bureau of Labor Bulletin 104 (Washington, DC: GPO, 1912), 15, 26, 30, 33–36.

40. Crystal Eastman, *Work-Accidents and the Law* (New York: Charities Publication Committee, 1910), 90–104; Lucian W. Chaney and Hugh S. Hanna, *The Safety Movement in the Iron and Steel Industry, 1907 to 1917*, BLS Bulletin 234 (Washington, DC: GPO, 1918), 165 (quotation), 176–77; Chaney, "The Engineering Factor in Safety Work," 47 (quotation); Arthur H. Young, "Practical Aspects of the Safety Movement," *Industrial Management*, October 1917, 32 (quotations), 30–35; L. A. DeBlois, "Some Hazards of the Chemical Industry and Their Prevention," *Monthly Bulletin of the Pennsylvania Department of Labor and Industry*, March 1917, 112 (quotation), 108, 112–13; Daniel M. Berman, *Death on the Job: Occupational Health and Safety Struggles in the United States* (New York: Monthly Review Press, 1978), 21–23.

41. Charles L. Close, "Safety in the Steel Industry," *Annals of the American Academy of Political and Social Science* 123 (January 1926): 86–92; "Plant Safety Committees," *Bulletin* (US Steel Committee/Bureau of Safety, Sanitation and Welfare), July 1, 1911, n.p.; Young, "Practical Aspects of the Safety Movement," 30; Aldrich, *Safety First*, 91–93; Thompson, "Occupational Poisoning in the Chemical Trades," 457; R. W. Campbell, "Safety in the Iron and Steel Industry," in Association of Iron and Steel Electrical Engineers, *Proceedings of Safety Congress, 1912*, 279–91; R. J. Young, "Our Foreigner: What We Are Doing to Help Him Help Himself," in Association of Iron and Steel Electrical Engineers, *Proceedings of Safety Congress, 1912*, 302–6; C. W. Price, "Safety as Insured by State Bureaus," in National Council for Industrial Safety, *Proceedings of the Second Safety Congress . . ., 1913* (n.p., n.d.), 110.

42. Illinois Commission on Occupational Diseases, *Report*, 92–93; Young, "Our Foreigner," 302–6; "The National Tube Company: Description of Educational Work—Lorain, Ohio," *Bulletin* (US Steel), December 1914, 93; "National Tube Company—Riverside Works: Teaching English to Foreigners," *Bulletin* (US Steel), December 1914, 92; "Lessons for Teaching Foreigners English by the Roberts Method," *Bulletin* (US Steel), December 1914, November 1913, 8–9; Campbell, "Safety in the Iron and Steel Industry," 289; Robert

J. Young, "How to Reach the Man and Reduce Accidents," *Monthly Bulletin of the American Iron and Steel Institute*, April 1914, 91.

43. "The Universal Danger Sign," *Bulletin* (US Steel), August 1912, front cover (quotation); "Bureau of Safety, Sanitation and Welfare," *Bulletin* (US Steel), August 1912, 4; "The Universal Danger Sign," *Monthly Bulletin of the American Iron and Steel Institute*, February 1913, 51; "United States Steel Corporation, Gary Plant," *Monthly Bulletin of the American Iron and Steel Institute*, March 1913, back cover; "Signs and Their Value in the Prevention of Accidents," *American Industries* (National Association of Manufacturers), May 1914, supplement, 4; William H. Tolman and Leonard B. Kendall, *Safety: Methods for Preventing Occupational and Other Accidents and Disease* (New York: Harper, 1913), 48.

44. W. L. Chandler, "Report of the Subcommittee on Universal Danger Emblem," in National Safety Council, *Proceedings of the Fifth Annual Safety Congress . . ., 1916* (n.p., n.d.), 146 (quotation), 152 (quotation), 146–57; "Discussion," National Safety Council, *Proceedings. . ., 1916*, 168–81; "The Committee of Safety," *Bulletin* (US Steel), October 1, 1910, n.p.; "Electric Danger Sign All May Read," *Popular Mechanics*, May 1913, 724; Charles P. Neill, *Report on Conditions of Employment in the Iron and Steel Industry in the United States*, 4 vols., vol. 4: *Accidents and Accident Prevention* (Washington, DC: GPO, 1913), following 234; Stewart J. Owen, Jr., "Warning Signs—Their Use and Maintenance," *National Safety News*, January 1928, 25–31.

45. New York Division of Industrial Hygiene, *Health Hazards of the Chemical Industry*, 9 (quotation), 3.

46. Alan Derickson, "The United Mine Workers of America and the Recognition of Occupational Respiratory Diseases, 1902–1968," *American Journal of Public Health* (*AJPH*) 81, no. 6 (June 1991): 782–85; idem, *Workers' Health, Workers' Democracy: The Western Miners' Struggle, 1891–1925* (Ithaca, NY: Cornell University Press, 1988), 136, 162–69, 180–82; Illinois Commission on Occupational Diseases, *Report*, 38; Christopher A. Eldridge, "Poisoned Painters: Organized Painters' Responses to Lead Poisoning in Early 20th-Century America," *Bulletin of Science, Technology and Society* 18, no. 4 (August 1998): 266–80; Angela Nugent, "Organizing Trade Unions to Combat Disease: The Workers' Health Bureau, 1921–1928," *Labor History* 26, no. 3 (Summer 1985): 426–37.

47. Hamilton, *Lead Poisoning in the Smelting and Refining of Lead*, 75; Tolman and Kendall, *Safety*, 277 (quotation); Selby, *Studies of the Medical and Surgical Care*, 10; Roberts, *The New Immigration*, 87.

48. Massachusetts State Board of Health, *Thirty-Eighth Annual Report* [for the fiscal year ended November 30, 1906] (Boston: Wright and Potter, 1907), 555; Hamilton, *Lead Poisoning in the Smelting and Refining of Lead*, 72–73, 76; idem, "Dangers Other Than Accidents in the Manufacture of Explosives," *Journal of Industrial and Engineering Chemistry* 8, no. 11 (November 1916): 1066 (quotation), 1065–67; idem, *Industrial Poisons Used or Produced in the Manufacture of Explosives*, BLS Bulletin 219 (Washington, DC: GPO, 1917), 10–22, 96 (quotation); Hayhurst, *A Survey of Industrial Health-Hazards*, 228 (quotation), 227–28, 287, 293 (quotation), 121, 136, 183, 201, 206, 217, 219, 317, 319, 334–36, 341, 347, 349.

49. DeBlois, "Some Hazards of the Chemical Industry," 108 (quotation); Hamilton, *Exploring the Dangerous Trades*, 131 (quotation), 139, 141; Hayhurst, *A Survey of Industrial Health-Hazards*, 206, 228.

50. Gordon Thayer (pseudonym of Lillian Erskine), "The Lead Menace," *Everybody's Magazine*, March 1913, 331; Hamilton, "Lead Poisoning in Illinois," *ALLR*, 19.

51. Alice Hamilton, "Occupational Diseases," in National Conference of Charities and Correction, *Proceedings of the Thirty-Eighth Annual Session, 1911* (Fort Wayne, IN: Fort Wayne Printing, 1911), 199 (quotation), 197–207.

2. WIDER USE OF EXISTING KNOWLEDGE

Epigraph: Alice Hamilton, "Lead Poisoning in the United States," *American Journal of Public Health (AJPH)* 4, no. 6 (June 1914): 477-78.

1. Christopher Sellers, "The Public Health Service's Office of Industrial Hygiene and Sanitation and the Transformation of Industrial Medicine," *Bulletin of the History of Medicine* 65, no. 1 (Spring 1991): 42-73; William T. Moye, "BLS and Alice Hamilton: Pioneers in Industrial Health," *Monthly Labor Review*, June 1986, 24-27; Barbara Sicherman, *Alice Hamilton: A Life in Letters* (Cambridge, MA: Harvard University Press, 1984), 357-58, 375.

2. David Rosner and Gerald Markowitz, "Research or Advocacy: Federal Safety and Health Policies during the New Deal," *Journal of Social History* 18, no. 3 (Spring 1985): 365-81; Gerald Markowitz and David Rosner, "More Than Economism: The Politics of Workers' Safety and Health, 1932-1947," *Milbank Quarterly* 64, no. 3 (1986): 331-54.

3. Ralph C. Williams, *The United States Public Health Service, 1798-1950* (Washington, DC: Commissioned Officers Association of the United States Public Health Service, 1951), 279-86; S. C. Hotchkiss, "Occupational Diseases in the Mining Industry," *American Labor Legislation Review (ALLR)*, February 1912, 133 (quotation), 132 (quotation), 131-39

4. J. W. Schereschewsky, "The Educational Function of Industrial Physicians," in American Association of Industrial Physicians and Surgeons," *First Annual Meeting, 1916* (n.p., n.d.), 34 (quotations); George Price, "Discussion [of Schereschewsky]," ibid., 35 (quotation); J. A. Watkins, *Health Conservation at Steel Mills*, Bureau of Mines Technical Paper 102 (Washington, DC: US Government Printing Office [GPO], 1916), 34 (quotation), passim throughout, esp. 31-34; Bernard J. Newman et al., *Lead Poisoning in the Pottery Trades*, Public Health Bulletin 116 (Washington, DC: GPO, 1921), 70-71, 76-77, 129-33, 171-72; A. J. Lanza, "Physiological Effects of Siliceous Dust on the Miners of the Joplin District," in Edwin Higgins et al., *Siliceous Dust in Relation to Pulmonary Disease among Miners of the Joplin District, Missouri*, Bureau of Mines Bulletin 132 (Washington, DC: GPO, 1917), 63 (quotation). For the focus on disease-preventive personal behavior, see (besides the work of Thomas Darlington and others cited in chapter 1), Hibbert W. Hill, *The New Public Health* (New York: Macmillan, 1916). On the preliminary groundwork for the individualistic orientation, see Nancy Tomes, "The Private Side of Public Health: Sanitary Science, Domestic Hygiene, and the Germ Theory, 1870-1900," *Bulletin of the History of Medicine* 64, no. 4 (Winter 1990): 509-39.

5. A. J. Lanza and J. H. White, *How a Miner Can Avoid Some Dangerous Diseases*, Bureau of Mines Miners' Circular 20 (Washington, DC: GPO, 1916), 25 (quotation), passim throughout, esp. 24-25; US Surgeon General, *Annual Report... for the Fiscal Year 1918* (Washington, DC: GPO, 1918), 43; Joseph S. Lawrence, "The Place of Venereal-Disease Control in Industry," *Public Health Reports* 37, no. 42 (October 20, 1922): 2609-13.

6. John B. Andrews, "Phosphorus Poisoning in the Match Industry in the United States," *Bulletin of the Bureau of Labor* 20 (January 1910): 31-146; David A. Moss, "Kindling a Flame under Federalism: Progressive Reformers, Corporate Elites, and the Phosphorus Match Campaign of 1909-1912," *Business History Review* 68, no. 2 (Summer 1994): 255-56n20; Christopher Sellers, *Hazards of the Job: From Industrial Disease to Environmental Health Science* (Chapel Hill: University of North Carolina Press, 1997), 121-35; Byron R. Newton to Chairman, Senate Committee on Education and Labor, February 3, 1914, RG 174: General Records of the Department of Labor, General Records, 1907-42, box 15, file 8/27, National Archives, Archives II, College Park, MD; Byron R. Newton to Secretary of Labor, February 7, 1914, ibid.; US House of Representatives, Committee on Labor, *Bureau of Labor Safety*, 63rd Congress, 2nd session, 1914, House of Representatives Report 167 (Washington, DC: GPO, 1914), 12 (Bremner

quotation), 1–5, 11–14. On the deepening commitment of the PHS to scientific research at this time, see (besides the foregoing citation of Sellers) Allan M. Brandt and Martha Gardner, "Antagonism and Accommodation: Interpreting the Relationship between Public Health and Medicine during the 20th Century," *AJPH* 90, no. 5 (May 2000): 710; Fitzhugh Mullan, *Plagues and Politics: The Story of the United States Public Health Service* (New York: Basic Books, 1989), 61–75.

7. J. W. Kerr, "Relation of the Public Health Service to Problems of Industrial Hygiene," *AJPH* 7, no. 9 (September 1917): 782; Sellers, *Hazards of the Job*, 136; Alan Derickson, *Black Lung: Anatomy of a Public Health Disaster* (Ithaca, NY: Cornell University Press, 1998), 73–76; J. J. Bloomfield et al., *Anthraco-Silicosis among Hard Coal Miners*, Public Health Bulletin 221 (Washington, DC: GPO, 1935), 1; Newman et al., *Lead Poisoning in the Pottery Trades*, 14–15; C. D. Selby, "Physicians in Industry," in National Safety Council, *Proceedings of the Seventh National Safety Congress . . ., 1918* (n.p., n.d.), 329–30. On the extremely stable labor relations that facilitated the pottery workers' investigation, see Marc J. Stern, "Industrial Structure and Occupational Health: The American Pottery Industry, 1897–1929," *Business History Review* 77, no. 3 (Autumn 2003): 417–45. For managerial willingness to tell examinees of their diagnoses, see Charles F. Willis, "Physical Examination Previous to Employment," *Coal Age*, August 21, 1919, 315; Harry E. Mock, *Industrial Medicine and Surgery* (Philadelphia: W. B. Saunders, 1919), 380–81; National Industrial Conference Board, *Health Service in Industry* (New York: The Board, 1921), 39, 41; W. Irving Clark, *Health Service in Industry* (New York: Macmillan, 1922), 82, 98–99; Frank L. Rector, "Physical Examinations in Industry," *Monthly Labor Review*, April 1926, 768; Hart E. Fisher, "Periodic Medical Examinations," *Industrial Medicine* 1, no. 1 (October 1932): 2, 4, 5.

8. Angela Nugent Young, "Interpreting the Dangerous Trades: Workers' Health in America and the Career of Alice Hamilton, 1910–1935" (PhD diss., Brown University, 1982), 84–85; Grant Hamilton, "Uncle Sam's Industrial Doc: Working Conditions Service of the Department of Labor Prescribes for Ills in Industrial Plants," *New York Times*, May 18, 1919, 48; F. C. MacDonald to Hywel Davies, January 23, 1925, RG 174, General Records, 1907–42, box 46, file 16/336; US House of Representatives, Committee on Labor, *Division of Safety: Hearings . . . on HR 11886 and HR 12263*, 69th Cong., 1st sess., 1926 (Washington, DC: GPO, 1926), 69–70.

9. US Bureau of Labor Statistics, "Minimum Requirements for the Health, Safety and Comfort of Workers in Manufacturing Industries," February 19, 1934, 8 (quotation), RG 174, Office of the Secretary, General Subject File, 1933–1941, box 50, folder: Conference on Standards for Safety and Health of Workers; Committee on Safety and Health Standards for NRA Codes, "Minutes," February 19, 1934, ibid.

10. James L. Gernon, "Necessity for Educating Employers and Employees in Factories and Mercantile Establishments," in New York Industrial Commission, *Proceedings of the First Industrial Safety Congress of New York State, 1916* (Albany, NY: J. B. Lyon, 1917), 41 (quotation), 42 (quotation), 43, 46; "Industrial Diseases," *New York Labor Bulletin*, March 1913, 64–65; New York Department of Labor, *Annual Report for the Twelve Months Ended June 30, 1924* (Albany, NY: J. B. Lyon, 1925), 124–26; Leland L. Cofer, "The Underlying Object of the *Industrial Hygiene Bulletin*," *Industrial Hygiene Bulletin* (New York Division of Industrial Hygiene), July 1924, 1–3; "New Bulletin on Silicosis," ibid., September 1925, 12; Lester Roos, "General Discussion," in New York Industrial Commission, *Proceedings of the Second Industrial Safety Congress of New York State, 1917* (n.p., n.d.), 33 (quotation), 33–34; "Industrial Hygiene Division," *Industrial Bulletin* (New York Industrial Commission), November 1923, 58; "Foods for Energy and Warmth," *Industrial Hygiene Bulletin*, April 1926, 37, 39.

11. Marian K. Clark, "The English for Safety Campaign by the State Industrial Commission," *Safety: Bulletin of the American Museum of Safety*, February–March 1918, 34–38; New York Division of Industrial Hygiene, *Dangers in Manufacture of Paris Green and Scheele's Green*, Special Bulletin 83 (Albany, NY: New York Department of Labor [NYDoL], 1917), 16–17; idem, *Health Hazards of the Chemical Industry*, Special Bulletin 96 (Albany, NY: J. B. Lyon, 1920), 33–34; William J. Burke, "Accidents and Health Hazards in the Chemical Industries," in International Association of Industrial Accident Boards and Commissions, *Proceedings of the Sixteenth Annual Meeting . . ., 1929* (Washington, DC: GPO, 1930), 151 (quotation), 151–52; John Train, "Motion Pictures—the Universal Language," in New York Industrial Commission, *Proceedings of the Forth Industrial Safety Congress of New York State, 1919* (Albany, NY: NYDoL, n.d.), 235–40; Louis I. Dublin, "Conditions of Industry Which Unfavorably Affect the Health of Workers," in idem, *Proceedings of the Eighth Industrial Safety Congress of New York State, 1924* (Albany, NY: J. B. Lyon, 1925), 206 (quotation), 206–7; Louis I. Dublin and Philip Leiboff, *Occupation Hazards and Diagnostic Signs: A Guide to Impairments to Be Looked for in Hazardous Occupations*, BLS Bulletin 306 (Washington, DC: GPO, 1922), 20 (quotation); May R. Mayers, "Preventive Medicine and Industrial Hygiene," *Industrial Hygiene Bulletin*, December 1927, 23 (quotation).

12. "Discussion of Immediate Problems," *ALLR*, January 1911, 74–76, 82–83; Josephine W. Bates, *Mercury Poisoning in the Industries of New York City and Vicinity* (New York: National Civic Federation, [1912]), 1 (quotation), 4, 9, 34, 90–129; Leonard W. Hatch, "Compulsory Reporting by Physicians," *ALLR*, June 1912, 264, 279; F. L. Hoffman, "List of Recommendations Made by the Committee on Industrial Diseases," December 28, 1912, American Association for Labor Legislation Records, reel 8, Kheel Center for Labor-Management Documentation, Catherwood Library, Cornell University, Ithaca, NY; Alice Hamilton to Charles Verrill, Alice Hamilton Papers, box 2, folder 29, Schlesinger Library, Radcliffe Institute for Advanced Study, Harvard University, Cambridge, MA; American Association for Labor Legislation (AALL), *Uniform Reporting of Occupational Diseases* (New York: The Association, [1913]), Section 3 [unpaginated]; Connecticut, *Public Acts . . ., 1913* (Hartford: Connecticut Press, 1913), 1634; Ohio, *Legislative Acts . . ., 1913* (Springfield, OH: Springfield Publishing, 1913), 185; New Hampshire, *Laws . . ., 1913* (Concord: Ira C. Evans, 1913), 607; New Jersey, *Acts of the One Hundred Forty-Eighth Legislature* [1924] (Trenton, NJ: MacCrellish and Quigley, 1924), 403. For the reporting laws passed in 1911–1912, see note 18 in chapter 1.

13. New York, *Laws . . ., 1913*, 4 vols. (Albany, NY: J. B. Lyon, 1913), 1: 257; New York Department of Labor, *Fourteenth Annual Report for the Year Ended September 30, 1914* (Albany, NY: J. B. Lyon, 1915), 107–8; C. T. Graham-Rogers, "Occupational Diseases and the Physician," *Industrial Hygiene Bulletin*, January 1926, 1; Commissioners on Uniform State Laws, *Proceedings of the Twenty-Fourth Annual Conference, 1914* (n.p., n.d.), 89, 276–77; May R. Mayers, "Industrial Diseases and Compensation," in International Association of Industrial Accident Boards and Commissions, *Proceedings of the Sixteenth Annual Meeting, 1929*, BLS Bulletin 511 (Washington, DC: GPO, 1930), 47–56, esp. 53.

14. NYDoL, Bureau of Statistics and Information, *A Plan for Shop Safety, Sanitation, and Health*, Special Bulletin 91 (Albany, NY: The Department, 1919), 6 (quotation), passim throughout, esp. 6–12, 18–24, 28, 32.

15. New York Division of Industrial Hygiene, *Health Hazards of the Chemical Industry*, 67 (quotation), 3, 9, 22; New York Industrial Commission, *New York State Industrial Code, 1920* (n.p., n.d.).

16. "Symposium on Occupational Diseases in Chemical Trades," *Journal of Industrial and Engineering Chemistry* 8, no. 10 (October 1916): 946; New Jersey Department of Labor, *Report, 1916* (Trenton, NJ: MacCrellish and Quigley, 1917), 42–43; Andrew F.

McBride, "Progress the State of New Jersey Has Made in Coping with Occupational Diseases," in Association of Governmental Officials in Industry of the United States and Canada, *Fifteenth Annual Convention, 1928*, BLS Bulletin 480 (Washington, DC: GPO, 1929), 145–46 (quotation), 146 (quotation), 145–47; New Jersey Department of Labor, *Report, July 1, 1924 to June 30, 1925* (n.p., n.d.), 9 (McBride quotation). On the tetraethyl lead disaster, see David Rosner and Gerald Markowitz, "A 'Gift of God'? The Public Health Controversy over Leaded Gasoline during the 1920s," *AJPH* 75, no. 4 (April 1985): 345–46.

17. Donald W. Rogers, *Making Capitalism Safe: Work Safety and Health Regulation in America, 1880–1940* (Urbana: University of Illinois Press, 2009), 153–57; Industrial Commission of Wisconsin, *General Orders on Sanitation, Including Ventilation, Toilet Rooms, and General Sanitation, Revision Effective 1921* (n.p., [1921]), 22–23 (quotation), 23 (quotation), 22–33.

18. Massachusetts State Board of Labor and Industries, *First Annual Report, January 1915* (Boston: Wright and Potter, 1914), 10–11; idem, *Rules and Regulations Suggested for the Prevention of Anthrax*, Industrial Bulletin 6 (Boston: Wright and Potter, 1916), 5 (quotation), 9–10; idem, *Rules and Regulations Suggested for Safety in the Manufacture of Benzene Derivatives and Explosives*, Industrial Bulletin 11 (Boston: Wright and Potter, 1916); idem, *Fifth Annual Report, January 1918* (Boston: Wright and Potter, 1918), 55. Like New York, Massachusetts made physicians' reports of occupational disease cases available for use in its workers' compensation proceedings. See Massachusetts, *Acts and Resolves . . ., 1913* (Boston: Wright and Potter, 1913), 901. However, in 1935, state law denied any public access to the reports. See idem, *Acts and Resolves . . ., 1935* (Boston: Jordan and More, 1935), 373.

19. Theodore L. Hazlett and William W. Hummel, *Industrial Medicine in Western Pennsylvania, 1850–1950* (Pittsburgh, PA: University of Pittsburgh Press, 1957), 199; "Posters for Workrooms Where Lead Products Are Handled," *Monthly Bulletin of the Pennsylvania Department of Labor and Industry*, October 1914, 39–40; "Benzol Poisoning," ibid., February 1916, 14; Pennsylvania, Department of Labor and Industry, "Safety Standards . . ., Plants Manufacturing or Using Explosives," ibid., May 1917, 52–54; Francis D. Patterson, "The Functions of the State in Enforcing Industrial Hygiene Legislation," *Public Health Reports* 37, no. 42 (October 20, 1922): 2630; William B. Fulton et al., *Asbestosis: Part II. The Nature and Amount of Dust Encountered in Asbestos Fabricating Plants, Part III: The Effects of Exposure to Dust Encountered in Asbestos Fabricating Plants on the Health of a Group of Workers*, Special Bulletin 42 (Harrisburg: Pennsylvania Department of Labor and Industry, 1935), esp. 3; Alice Hamilton, "The Fight against Industrial Diseases: The Opportunities and Duties of the Industrial Physician," *Pennsylvania Medical Journal* 21, no. 6 (March 1918): 380 (quotation), 378.

20. William Graebner, "Federalism in the Progressive Era: A Structural Interpretation of Reform," *Journal of American History* 64, no. 2 (September 1977): 333; Alba M. Edwards, "The Labor Legislation of Connecticut," *Publications of the American Economic Association* (3d ser.) 8, no. 3 (1907): 708–11; Duane Lockard, *New England State Politics* (Princeton, NJ: Princeton University Press, 1959), 247, 286; Robert Asher, "Connecticut's First Workmen's Compensation Law," *Connecticut History* 32 (November 1991): 25–44, esp. 25, 43; Connecticut, *Public Acts, 1913*, 1735–51, 1634 (quotation); idem, *Public Acts, 1917* (Hartford, CT: The State, 1917), 2557–59.

21. John T. Black and E. K. Root, "Recommendations," *Connecticut Health Bulletin*, January 1919, 7 (quotation), 7–8; Connecticut, *Public Acts, 1923* (Hartford, CT: The State, 1923), 1923; idem, *Public Acts, 1927* (Hartford, CT: The State, 1927), 4460–61; Connecticut State Department of Health, *Forty-Third Report . . . for the Year Ending June 30, 1928* (Hartford, CT: n.p., 1928), 10, 35, 207–8; idem, *Forty-Fourth Report . . . for the*

Year Ending June 30, 1928 (Hartford, CT: n.p., 1929), 409–35; idem, *Forty-Fifth Report . . . for the Year Ending June 30, 1930* (Hartford, CT: n.p., 1930), 243–74; Connecticut, *Public Acts, 1931* (Hartford, CT: The State, 1931), 174. On the PHS and Hooverian corporatism, see Alan Derickson, "'On the Dump Heap': Employee Medical Screening in the Tri-State Zinc-Lead Industry," *Business History Review* 62, no. 4 (Winter 1988): 655–77; Rosner and Markowitz, "A 'Gift of God'?," 344–52.

22. Connecticut, *Public Acts, 1929* (Hartford, CT: The State, 1929), 4487; Industrial Hygiene Committee, Conference of State and Provincial Health Authorities of North America, *Industrial Hygiene Committee Reports* (n.p.: [1937?], 59, 60, 62 (Thompson quotation), 62–63; Connecticut, State Department of Health, *Forty-Eighth Report . . . for the Year Ending June 30, 1933* (Hartford, CT: n.p., 1933), 13, 105–6.

23. David Rosner and Gerald Markowitz, *Deadly Dust: Silicosis and the On-Going Struggle to Protect Workers' Health*, 2nd ed. (Ann Arbor: University of Michigan Press, 2006), 75–124; Martin Cherniack, *The Hawk's Nest Incident: America's Worst Industrial Disaster* (New Haven, CT: Yale University Press, 1986), 55–74; Derickson, *Black Lung*, 87–108.

24. Wesley M. Graff, "The Responsibility of the Health Department for Occupational Disease Control," in Conference of State and Provincial Health Authorities of North America, *Proceedings of the Forty-Ninth Annual Meeting, 1934* (n.p., n.d.), 100 (quotation), 104 (quotations), 99–105; Industrial Hygiene Committee, "Tentative Report, 1934," in ibid., 127 (quotation), 127–32; "Discussion," in ibid., 132–36; Connecticut State Department of Health, *Forty-Ninth Report . . . for the Year Ending June 30, 1934* (Hartford, CT: n.p., 1934), 498 (Gray quotation), 497–98. For a PHS attempt to underscore to the public health community the value of the Connecticut program and its confidential reporting practices, see J. J. Bloomfield and W. Scott Johnson, "Potential Problems of Industrial Hygiene in a Typical Industrial Area," *AJPH* 25, no. 4 (April 1935): 415–24, esp. 423–24. For a dramatic appeal to public health professionals to rescue industrial hygiene from the "mess" that labor bureaucrats had made of state programs, see Emery R. Hayhurst, "The Industrial Hygiene Section, 1914–34," *AJPH* 24, no. 10 (October 1934): 1042 (quotation), 1041–42.

25. Judson E. MacLaury, "The Division of Labor Standards: Laying the Groundwork for OSHA," *Applied Industrial Hygiene* 3, no. 12 (December 1988): F8–F11; Markowitz and Rosner, "More Than Economism," 336–38. On Frances Perkins in Albany and her early work in Washington, see Kirstin Downey, *The Woman behind the New Deal: The Life and Legacy of Frances Perkins—Social Security, Unemployment Insurance, and the Minimum Wage* (New York: Anchor, 2009), 75–217.

26. Irving Bernstein, *A Caring Society: The New Deal, the Worker, and the Great Depression* (Boston: Houghton Mifflin, 1985), 59; US, *United States Statutes at Large*, vol. 49 (Washington, DC: GPO, 1936), 634–35; US House of Representatives, Committee on Ways and Means, *Economic Security Act: Hearings . . . H.R. 4120*, 74th Cong., 1st sess., 1935 (Washington, DC: GPO, 1935), 353; A. J. Chesley to William M. Graff, June 4, 1935 (quotation), Conference of State and Provincial Health Authorities of North America Archives (Modern Manuscripts Collection, History of Medicine Division, National Library of Medicine, Bethesda, MD), box 1, folder 11. On the Social Security system as a component of evolving federalism, see James T. Patterson, *The New Deal and the States: Federalism in Transition* (Princeton, NJ: Princeton University Press, 1969), 85–101.

27. R. R. Sayers and J. J. Bloomfield, "Industrial Hygiene Activities in the United States," *AJPH* 26, no. 11 (November 1936): 1087–95, esp. 1094–95; H. F. Easom and M. F. Trice, "Development of an Industrial Hygiene Program in a State Health Department," *AJPH* 28, no. 5 (May 1938): 610–15; Connecticut State Department of Health, *Fifty-First Report . . . for the Year Ended June 30, 1936* (Hartford, CT: n.p., 1936), 221; US Surgeon General,

Annual Report . . . Fiscal Year 1937 (Washington, DC: GPO, 1937), 45–46; William B. Fulton, *Control of Occupational Diseases in Pennsylvania* (Harrisburg: Pennsylvania Department of Health, 1937), 9; Rosner and Markowitz, "Research or Advocacy," 370.

28. Sayers and Bloomfield, "Industrial Hygiene Activities," 1091; PHS, Division of Industrial Hygiene, *But Flu Is Tougher* (Washington, DC: GPO, 1941); idem, *Leonard's Appendix and How It Burst* (Washington, DC: GPO, 1941); idem, *What You Don't Know Can Hurt You* (Washington, DC: GPO, 1943).

29. Rhode Island Department of Public Health, Division of Industrial Hygiene, *Annual Report, 1937* (n.p., n.d.), 3 (quotation), 11 (quotation), 4, 11–12; Colorado State Board of Health, *Evaluation of the Industrial Hygiene Problem of Colorado* (Denver, CO: The Board, 1939), 11–13, 31; J. J. Bloomfield et al., *A Preliminary Survey of the Industrial Hygiene Problem in the United States*, Public Health Bulletin 259 (Washington, DC: GPO, 1940), 94 (quotation), 87–120.

30. PHS, Division of Industrial Hygiene and Utah State Board of Health, *The Working Environment and Health of Workers in Bituminous Coal Mines, Nonferrous Metal Mines, and Nonferrous Metal Smelters in Utah* (n.p., 1940), 3, 16–19, 21; J. J. Bloomfield and W. M. Gafafer, "The Public Health Administrator's Responsibility in the Field of Occupational Disease Legislation," *Public Health Reports* 56, no. 42 (October 17, 1941): 2036 (quotation), 2033–41; Tennessee, *Public Acts . . ., 1945* (Nashville: Rich, n.d.), 398–404, esp. 402.

31. Rogers, *Making Capitalism Safe*, 166; Harry A. Nelson, "The Administration of an Occupational Disease Law," in International Association of Industrial Accident Boards and Commissions, *Discussion of Industrial Accidents and Diseases: 1937 Convention of the International Association of Industrial Accident Boards and Commissions*, Division of Labor Standards Bulletin 17 (Washington, DC: GPO, 1938), 55 (quotation), 54–56.

32. Frances Perkins to John B. Andrews, March 4, 1936 (quotation), AALL Records, reel 54; New York, *Laws . . ., 1936*, 2 vols. (Albany, NY: J. B. Lyon, 1936), 2: 1995; Rosner and Markowitz, *Deadly Dust*, 91–96; NYDoL, *Annual Report of the Industrial Commissioner, 1936* (Albany, NY: J. B. Lyon, 1937), 24, 67; Leonard Greenburg, "Some Aspects of the Problem of Occupational Disease Diagnosis," in International Association of Industrial Accident Boards and Commissions, *Discussion of Industrial Accidents and Diseases: 1937*, 100–4; Clara M. Beyer, "Memorandum on Training Courses for Factory Inspectors," April 16, 1936, Clara M. Beyer Papers, box 13, folder 193, Schlesinger Library, Radcliffe Institute for Advanced Study, Harvard University, Cambridge, MA; Frieda S. Miller, *Workers' Health Hazards—Today and Tomorrow: Detection and Control of Silicosis and Other Occupational Diseases* (Albany, NY: NYDoL, 1940), 9, 12, Appendix; NYDoL, *Annual Report of the Industrial Commissioner, 1937* (Albany, NY: J. B. Lyon, 1938), 36–38, 108; NYDoL, *Annual Report of the Industrial Commissioner, 1938* (Albany, NY: J. B. Lyon, 1939), 42–44, 47, 191; May R. Mayers and Minnie M. McMahon, *Lead Poisoning in Industry and Its Prevention*, Special Bulletin 195 (Albany, NY: NYDoL, 1938), 55 (quotation).

33. Rosner and Markowitz, "Research or Advocacy," 365–81, esp. 368; Jean A. Flexner, *The Work of an Industrial Hygiene Division in a State Department of Labor*, DLS Bulletin 31 (Washington, DC: GPO, 1939), 13–21.

34. Division of Labor Standards (DLS), *Arsenic Poisoning: Its Cause and Prevention* (Washington, DC: GPO, 1935); DLS, *Chromium Poisoning: Its Cause and Prevention* (Washington, DC: GPO, 1935); DLS, *Mercury Poisoning: Its Cause and Prevention* (Washington, DC: GPO, 1935); DLS, *Wood Alcohol Poisoning (Methyl Alcohol and Methanol): Its Cause and Prevention* (Washington, DC: GPO, 1937), 3; DLS, *Carbon Tetrachloride Poisoning: Its Cause and Prevention* (Washington, DC: GPO, 1937), 3–4; DLS, *The Causes and Prevention of Nitrous Fumes Poisoning* (Washington, DC: GPO,

1939), 4; National Silicosis Conference, *Report on Medical Control: Final Report of the Committee on the Prevention of Silicosis through Medical Control*, DLS Bulletin 21, Part 1 (Washington, DC: GPO, 1938), 70–71; idem, *Report on Engineering Control: Final Report of the Committee on the Prevention of Silicosis through Engineering Control*, DLS Bulletin 21, Part 2 (Washington, DC: GPO, 1938), 57–58.

35. "Safety and Health [Discussion]," in National Conference on Labor Legislation, *Proceedings of the Fourth Conference . . ., 1937*, DLS Bulletin 18 (Washington, DC: GPO, 1938), 54–57; US Interdepartmental Committee to Coordinate Health and Welfare Activities, *The Nation's Health: Discussion at the National Health Conference* (Washington, DC: GPO, 1939), 24–26.

36. James E. Murray, "The National Health Bill," *ALLR*, March 1940, 9–16; US Senate, Committee on Education and Labor, Subcommittee on S. 1620, *To Establish a National Health Program: Hearings . . . on S. 1620*, 76th Cong., 1st sess., 1939 (Washington, DC: GPO, 1939), 229–30, 256 (Greenburg quotation), 250–60, 315 (McCord quotation), 311–18, 445, 666, 868 (Zimmer quotation), 862–68. For the Michigan legislation sequestering records of investigations, see Michigan, *Public and Local Acts . . ., 1937* (Lansing, MI: Franklin DeKleine, 1937), 335.

37. V. A. Zimmer to James E. Murray, February 8, 1940, James E. Murray Papers, box 352, folder 4, Archives and Special Collections, Mansfield Library, University of Montana, MT; Clara M. Beyer to Mr. [Marshall E.] Dimock, September 28, 1939, Beyer Papers, box 4, folder 52; Frances Perkins to Bureau of the Budget, April 25, 1940 (quotations), RG 90: Records of the Public Health Service, General Correspondence, 1936–44, box 88, file 0875-96, National Archives II, College Park, MD; W. F. Draper to Surgeon General, April 30, 1940, ibid., box 568, file [0875-]96.

38. Rosner and Markowitz, "Research or Advocacy," 370–77; US Senate, Committee on Education and Labor, Subcommittee on S. 3461, *Prevention of Industrial Conditions Hazardous to the Health of Employees: Hearings . . . on S. 3461*, 76th Cong., 3rd sess., 1940 (Washington, DC: GPO, 1940), 59–61, 70, 100, 111, 117, 3, 14 (Gray quotation), 14–21. For the bitter-end phase of the turf war, see US House of Representatives, Committee on Labor, Subcommittee on H.R. 2800, *To Establish Safe and Healthful Working Conditions in Industry: Hearings . . . on H.R. 2800*, 78th Cong., 1st sess., 1943 (Washington, DC: GPO, 1943); International Association of Governmental Labor Officials, *Labor Laws and Their Administration: Proceedings of the Thirty-Fourth Convention . . ., 1951*, Bureau of Labor Standards Bulletin 155 (Washington, DC: GPO, 1952), 125–26.

39. Robert T. Legge, "Objectives of the Institutes of Wartime Industrial Health," *California and Western Medicine* 57, no. 4 (October 1942): 233; James G. Townsend, "Industrial Health at the State's Level," *Pennsylvania's Health*, April 1942, 23–28; Ohio Department of Health, Adult Hygiene Division, *Industrial Survey of the State of Ohio: Evaluation of Industrial Hygiene Problems* (Columbus, OH: The Department, 1940), 25; Carey P. McCord, "Industry's Manpower: Its Conservation," *California and Western Medicine* 57, no. 4 (October 1942): 237 (quotation), 237–38; J. J. Bloomfield, "Teamwork for Industrial Health," *AJPH* 36, no. 3 (March 1946): 261–68; Elna I. Perkins, "Worker Health Education: Present Outlook among Industrial Workers," *Industrial Medicine* 13, no. 7 (July 1944): 577 (quotation), 575–77; [Editorial], "A Modern Concept of Industrial Hygiene," *Industrial Hygiene Newsletter*, December 1946, 2 (quotations), 2–3; Leonard J. Goldwater, "The Future of Industrial Medicine," *AJPH* 37, no. 10 (October 1947): 1247–55. For evidence that the industrial health communication strategy formed an integral part of the larger human relations movement in midcentury labor-management relations, see "Health Education in Industry," *Industrial Hygiene Newsletter* (PHS), November 1948, 6–7; Caesar Branchini, "Health Education for Industrial Employees at the Hanford Atomic Products Operation," *Public Health Reports* 69, no. 9 (September 1954):

883–88; Raymond J. Murray, "Effective Educational Techniques in Industrial Health Counseling," in Industrial Hygiene Foundation of America, *Twenty-First Annual Meeting . . ., 1956*, Transactions Bulletin 30 (Pittsburgh, PA: The Foundation, n.d.), 95–102. On the human relations movement, see Robert Wood Johnson, "Human Relations in Modern Business," *Harvard Business Review* 27, no. 5 (September 1949): 521–41; Douglas McGregor, *The Human Side of Enterprise* (New York: McGraw-Hill, 1960).

40. Markowitz and Rosner, "More Than Economism," 347–50; Rosner and Markowitz, "Research or Advocacy," 368, 375–76. On union growth, see Leo Troy, *Trade Union Membership, 1897-1962* (New York: National Bureau of Economic Research, 1965), 1.

41. Alice Hamilton, "Some New and Unfamiliar Industrial Poisons," *New England Journal of Medicine* 215, no. 10 (September 3, 1936): 426 (quotation), 425–27; Alice Hamilton, *Exploring the Dangerous Trades: The Autobiography of Alice Hamilton, M.D.* (1943; Boston: Northeastern University Press, 1985), 387–94; Pennsylvania Department of Labor and Industry, Occupational Disease Prevention Division, *Survey of Carbon Disulphide and Hydrogen Sulphide Hazards in the Viscose Rayon Industry* (Harrisburg, PA: The Department, 1938); Alice Hamilton, *Occupational Poisoning in the Viscose Rayon Industry*, DLS Bulletin 34 (Washington, DC: GPO, 1940), esp. vii; DLS, *Carbon Bisulphide Poisoning (Carbon Disulphide): Its Cause and Prevention* (Washington, DC: GPO, 1937), 3 (quotations); "Workers' Education as a Legislative and Administrative Aid [Discussion]," in National Conference on Labor Legislation, *Proceedings, 1937*, 116 (Beyer quotation). For an uncharacteristic endorsement of worker education that may well have reflected the influence of the rival DLS, see PHS Division of Industrial Hygiene, "Carbon Disulfide: Its Toxicity and Potential Dangers," *Public Health Reports* 56, no. 12 (March 21, 1941): 579. For the engineering controls implemented as a result of this government-union initiative, see "Develop Methods to Check Poison," *Textile Labor* (Textile Workers Union of America), December 1939, 5. For the comprehensive history of this hazard, see Paul D. Blanc, *Fake Silk: The Lethal History of Viscose Rayon* (New Haven, CT: Yale University Press, 2016).

3. THE PATH OF SELF-CORRECTION

Epigraphs: W. L. Chandler, "Report of the Subcommittee on Universal Danger Sign," in National Safety Council, *Proceedings of the National Safety Council Fifth Annual Safety Congress, 1916* (n.p., n.d.), 147–48; Labels and Precautionary Information Committee (LaPIC), Manufacturing Chemists' Association (MCA), "Minutes of Meeting," May 17, 1944, L-5 (Granch quotation), Toxic Docs, https://www.toxicdocs.org/d/6nbVrpmr279RbNxJ1p5wrqqm, Center for the History and Ethics of Public Health, Columbia University and the Graduate Center, City University of New York.

1. David Egilman and Susanna Rankin Bohme, "A Brief History of Warnings," in *Handbook of Warnings*, ed. Michael S. Wogalter (Mahwah, NJ: Erlbaum Associates, 2006), 11 (quotation); Edwin A. Jaggard, *Hand-Book of the Law of Torts*, 2 vols. (St. Paul, MN: West Publishing, 1895), 2: 1007 (quotation), 990–91, 1002–7; William B. Hale, *Handbook of the Law of Torts* (St. Paul, MN: West Publishing, 1896), 504, 509–10; William L. Prosser, *Handbook of the Law of Torts* (St. Paul, MN: West Publishing, 1941), 509; "General Discussion," *American Labor Legislation Review* (*ALLR*), March 1913, 78; C. G. Farnum, "The Ideal Industry from the Standpoint of Health and Safety," in National Safety Council, *Proceedings of the National Safety Council Sixth Annual Safety Congress, 1917* (n.p., n.d.), 223–31; Charles Baskerville, "Report of the Committee on Occupational Diseases in the Chemical Trades," *Journal of Industrial and Engineering Chemistry* 12, no. 5 (May 1920): 440; National Industrial Conference Board, *Health Service in Industry* (New York: The Board, 1921), 39–41; Louis I. Dublin, "The Effect of Physical Examinations on the Health and Welfare of Employees," in National Safety

Council, *Proceedings of the National Safety Council Twelfth Annual Safety Congress, 1923* (n.p.: The Council, 1924), 366–67. On the assumption-of-risk rule, see John F. Witt, *The Accidental Republic: Crippled Workmen, Destitute Widows, and the Remaking of American Law* (Cambridge, MA: Harvard University Press, 2004), 50–51.

2. US, *United States Statutes at Large*, vol. 36 (Washington, DC: US Government Printing Office [GPO], 1910), 333; Minnesota, *General Laws . . ., 1905* (Minneapolis, MN: Harrison and Smith, 1905), 56; Massachusetts, *Acts and Resolves . . ., 1905* (Boston: Wright and Potter, 1905), 149; New Hampshire, *Laws . . ., 1911* (Concord, NH: John B. Clarke, 1911), 17; Connecticut, *Public Acts . . ., 1917* (Hartford, CT: The State, 1917), 2338; W. Gilman Thompson, "Occupational Poisoning in Chemical Trades," *Journal of Industrial and Engineering Chemistry* 4, no. 6 (June 1912): 457 (quotation), 454–57; New York Factory Investigating Commission, *Second Report*, 4 vols. (Albany, NY: J. B. Lyon, 1913), 1: 254, 297, 393–94, 4: 1589; New York Division of Industrial Hygiene, *Dangers in the Manufacture and Industrial Uses of Wood Alcohol*, Special Bulletin 86 (Albany, NY: J. B. Lyon, 1917), 3 (quotation), passim, esp. 17. By 1895, thirty-one states mandated labeling pharmaceutical products deemed poisonous. See George B. Griffenhagen and Mary O. Bogard, *History of Drug Containers and Their Labels* (Madison, WI: American Institute of the History of Pharmacy, 1999), 93.

3. US, *United States Statutes at Large*, vol. 44 (Washington, DC: GPO, 1927), 1406–10; Grace M. Burnham, "Proposed Safeguards for the Protection of Workers in Shop Trades," in Workers' Health Bureau of America, *First National Labor Health Conference, 1927* (New York: The Bureau, [1927]), 33–34; Executive Committee, Workers' Health Bureau of America, "The Failure of Existing Legislative Machinery to Control Industrial Accidents and Diseases and Trade Union Demands for Safeguarding the Health of Workers," in Workers' Health Bureau of America, *First National Labor Health Conference, 1927* (New York: The Bureau, [1927]), 124; US Senate, Committee on Agriculture and Forestry, *Volatile Poisons: Hearing . . . on S. 3853*, 72nd Cong., 1st sess., 1932 (Washington, DC: GPO, 1932), 18, 31, 35, 43; Massachusetts, *Acts and Resolves . . ., 1933* (Boston: Jordan and More, 1933), 480 (quotation), 479–81.

4. "Safety Program for Manufacturing Chemists' Association," *Chemical and Engineering News*, November 20, 1934, 416; C. Joseph Stetler and Bernard E. Conley, "The Labeling of Dangerous Household Chemicals," *Food, Drug, Cosmetic Law Journal* 12, no. 12 (December 1957): 753; Thomas Parran to H. H. Schrenk, July 12, 1941, RG 90: Records of the Public Health Service, General Classified Records, 1936–1944, box 658, folder [0875-]096 Industrial Hygiene 1940–1944, Archives II, National Archives and Records Administration, College Park, MD; Warren W. Watson to J. G. Townsend, February 24, 1944 (quotation), Toxic Docs, https://www.toxicdocs.org/d/dYnKKz8menwdvzK7b60pOgXGq.

5. W. N. Watson to E. W. Webb, March 23, 1939 (quotation), Toxic Docs, https://www.toxicdocs.org/d/108N9bLQjrrkp3r8N4kqQE92a; MCA, *Guide to Precautionary Labeling of Hazardous Chemicals: Manual L-1*, 6th ed. (Washington, DC: The Association, 1961), 6 (quotation); James D. Kittelton, "Industry's Views on the Federal Hazardous Substances Labeling Act," *Food, Drug, Cosmetic Law Journal* 15, no. 2 (December 1960): 788; Executive Committee, MCA, minutes, May 9, 1944, unpaginated, Toxic Docs, https://www.toxicdocs.org/d/Xjva5OOr0n4ronvV3xvDgnZR.

6. MCA, *Product Caution Labels* (Washington, DC: The Association, 1945); MCA, "A Guide for the Preparation of Warning Labels for Hazardous Chemicals," *Chemical and Engineering News*, June 10, 1945, 992 (quotation), 992–94. On employer acceptance of responsibility for providing hazard information, see David Rosner and Gerald Markowitz, "'Educate the Individual . . . to a Sane Appreciation of the Risk': A History of Industry's Responsibility to Warn of Job Dangers before the Occupational Safety and Health Administration," *American Journal of Public Health (AJPH)* 106, no. 1 (January 2016): 28–35.

7. MCA, "Guide to Precautionary Labeling," 992 (quotations), 994 (quotation); Alice Hamilton, *Industrial Poisons in the United States* (New York: Macmillan, 1925), 1 (quotation); Alice Hamilton, *Industrial Toxicology* (New York: Harper, 1934); Christopher C. Sellers, *Hazards of the Job: From Industrial Disease to Environmental Health Science* (Chapel Hill: University of North Carolina Press, 1997), 155–86. Undercutting its narrow definition of poison, the initial compilation of model labels designated as dangerous poisons many substances that entered the body via the skin or respiratory system. See MCA, *Product Caution Labels*, 2 (acrylonitrile), 4 (aniline), 5 (benzene, calcium cyanide), 6 (carbon disulfide), 12 (liquid hydrocyanic acid, inorganic cyanides).

8. MCA, *Product Caution Labels*, 8 (quotations); Ludwig Teleky, "Occupational Cancer of the Lung," *Journal of Industrial Hygiene and Toxicology* 19, no. 2 (February 1937): 75–76; J. A. Campbell, "Cancer of the Human Lung and Animal Experiment," *Journal of Industrial Hygiene and Toxicology* 19, no. 8 (October 1937): 455; W. C. Hueper, *Occupational Tumors and Allied Diseases* (Springfield, IL: Charles C. Thomas, 1942), 410 (quotation), 415 (quotation), 410–15; W. C. Hueper, "Industrial Management and Occupational Cancer," *JAMA* 131, no. 9 (June 29, 1946): 740 (quotation), 738–41; James T. Patterson, *The Dread Disease: Cancer and Modern American Culture* (Cambridge, MA: Harvard University Press, 1987), 97–98, 111–13.

9. Dohrman H. Byers, "Solvent Sleuths at Work," *Occupational Health*, March 1953, 43; *Industrial Hygiene Newsletter*, September 1948, 16; California Division of Industrial Safety, *Danger Wears This Label: Labeling Orders for Hazardous Substances* (San Francisco: The Division, 1948), n.p.

10. MCA, *Warning Labels*, 2nd ed. (Washington, DC: The Association, 1946), 2, 5; MCA, *Warning Labels: A Guide for the Preparation of Warning Labels for Hazardous Chemicals*, 3rd ed. (Washington, DC: The Association, 1949), 5 (quotation), 14–15.

11. MCA, *Guide to Precautionary Labeling of Hazardous Chemicals*, 7th ed. (Washington, DC: The Association, 1970), 52–61; Willard Machle and Frederick Gregorius, "Cancer of the Respiratory System in the United States Chromate-Producing Industry," *Public Health Reports* 63, no. 35 (August 27, 1948): 1114–27; T. F. Mancuso and W. C. Hueper, "Occupational Cancer and Other Health Hazards in a Chromate Plant: A Medical Appraisal, I. Lung Cancers in Chromate Workers," *Industrial Medicine and Surgery* 20, no. 8 (August 1951): 358–63; Willard S. Randall and Stephen D. Solomon, *Building 6: The Tragedy at Bridesburg* (Boston: Little, Brown, 1977). On the wealth of evidence that forced the recognition of the carcinogenicity of benzidine and beta naphthylamine, see David Michaels, "Waiting for the Body Count: Corporate Decision Making and Bladder Cancer in the U.S. Dye Industry," *Medical Anthropology Quarterly* 2, no. 3 (September 1988): 215–32. For promotion of the MCA system as authoritative without acknowledgment of any need to warn about carcinogenicity, see Thomas W. Nale, "Label Statements for Hazardous Chemicals," *Archives of Environmental Health* 6, no. 2 (February 1963): 235–38.

12. "New Safety Manuals Prepared," *Industrial Hygiene Newsletter*, February 1947, 10; LaPIC, MCA, "Minutes of Meeting," April 21–22, 1947, L-156, Toxic Docs, https://www.toxicdocs.org/d/x5JGJ5rqo4rzypXLagv7N31rE; idem, "Minutes of Meeting," February 8–9, 1949, L-224, Toxic Docs, https://www.toxicdocs.org/d/zJOXND2wkaoNZL04NDvX7Yzn; idem, "Minutes of Meeting," May 7–8, 1952, L-22-23, Toxic Docs, https://www.toxicdocs.org/d/aBY9jynGwkK9xV7y7JxYkw1pY; idem, "Minutes of Meeting," March 12–13, 1953, L-38, Toxic Docs, https://www.toxicdocs.org/d/4QB23j43OLm9BYBVdN-gR31KDR; "Chemical Labeling Committee Reactivated," *Public Health Reports* 68, no. 1 (January 1953): 66–67.

13. LaPIC, MCA, "Minutes of Meeting," February 8–9, 1949, L-221 (emphasis in original), Toxic Docs, https://www.toxicdocs.org/d/zJOXND2wkaoNZL04NDvX7Yzn; idem, "Minutes of Meeting," March 28–29, 1946, L-139, Toxic Docs, https://www.toxicdocs

.org/d/4ajynXLbn82qxNRrbMN6aMB8R; Legal Advisory Committee, MCA, "Minutes of Meeting," January 6, 1950, 2-3, Toxic Docs, https://www.toxicdocs.org/d/8R9xwnGB0eQmBw2wjQw0dbMJd; Manfred Bowditch, "State and Territorial Warning Label Laws," January 1952, Toxic Docs, https://www.toxicdocs.org/d/JNwnaMYjVxj5y87pLOkKO45z6; LaPIC, MCA, "Minutes of Meeting," May 7-8, 1952, L-15, Toxic Docs, https://www.toxicdocs.org/d/aBY9jynGwkK9xV7y7JxYkw1pY.

14. LaPIC, MCA, "Minutes of Meeting," April 21-22, 1947, L-160, Toxic Docs, https://www.toxicdocs.org/d/x5JGJ5rqo4rzypXLagv7N31rE; idem, "Minutes of Meeting," November 15-16, 1948, L-216 (quotation), Toxic Docs, https://www.toxicdocs.org/d/LJ4wJ3gDZrd5Jq8RRearxrNg3; "State and Local News: Massachusetts," *Industrial Hygiene Newsletter*, April 1950, 8; California Division of Industrial Safety, *Danger Wears This Label*; LaPIC, MCA, "Minutes of Meeting," October 13 and 14, 1953, L-60, Toxic Docs, https://www.toxicdocs.org/d/xzNmY3zoNd1dqdkZ4pay0V0n6; idem, "Minutes of Meeting," September 27-28, 1950, 1, 4 (quotation), Toxic Docs, https://www.toxicdocs.org/d/NEBaoqXn261MjdEbYvQdj63Ew; idem, "Minutes of Meeting," May 7-8, 1952, L-15, Toxic Docs, https://www.toxicdocs.org/d/aBY9jynGwkK9xV7y7JxYkw1pY.

15. "Panel on Industrial Health and Safety," in International Association of Governmental Labor Officials, *Labor Laws and Their Administration: Proceedings of the Thirty-Sixth Convention of the International Association of Governmental Labor Officials . . ., 1953*, Bureau of Labor Standards Bulletin 169 (Washington, DC: GPO, 1954), 33 (Hill quotations), 33-34; Sanford Hill, "Report of the Subcommittee on Labeling Dangerous Substances," in International Association of Governmental Labor Officials, *Labor Laws and Their Administration: Proceedings of the Thirty-Eighth Convention of the International Association of Governmental Labor Officials . . ., 1955*, Bureau of Labor Standards Bulletin 184 (Washington, DC: GPO, [1956]), 121-24; Massachusetts, *Acts and Resolves . . ., 1955* (Boston: Wright and Potter, 1955), 386-88.

16. American Conference of Governmental Industrial Hygienists (ACGIH), *Transactions of the Fourteenth Annual Meeting, 1952* (n.p., n.d.), 102-4; ACGIH, *Transactions of the Seventeenth Annual Meeting, 1955* (n.p., n.d.), 70-71; Sanford J. Hill, "The Manufacturing Chemists' Association Labeling Program," *AMA Archives of Industrial Health* 12, no. 4 (October 1955): 382 (quotation), 378-82; LaPIC, MCA, "Minutes of Meeting," October 10-11, 1957, L-196, Toxic Docs, https://www.toxicdocs.org/d/82dopkq2JydjEVMRb6BNqKOjo; Hervey B. Elkins, "Labeling Requirements for Toxic Substances—The Governmental Industrial Hygienists' Viewpoint," in ACGIH, *Transactions of the Twentieth Annual Meeting, 1958* (n.p., n.d.), 72 (quotation), 72-78; Thomas W. Nale, "The Chemical Industry and Precautionary Labeling," in ibid., 79-87; Committee on Standard Labeling Procedures, "Report," in ACGIH, *Transactions of the Twenty-First Annual Meeting, 1959* (Cincinnati, OH: The Conference, 1959), 110 (quotation), 107-15; idem, "Report," in ACGIH, *Transactions of the Twenty-Second Annual Meeting, 1960* (n.p., n.d.), 57; idem, "Report," in ACGIH, *Transactions of the Twenty-Eighth Annual Meeting, 1966* (n.p., n.d.), 160.

17. US, *United States Statutes at Large*, vol. 36 (Washington, DC: GPO, 1911), 333; ibid., vol. 61 (Washington, DC: GPO, 1948), 165 (quotation),163-73; Christopher J. Bosso, *Pesticides and Politics: The Life Cycle of a Public Issue* (Pittsburgh: University of Pittsburgh Press, 1987), 10-11, 58-59; Marion Moses, "Farmworkers and Pesticides," in *Confronting Environmental Racism: Voices from the Grassroots*, ed. Robert D. Bullard (Boston: South End, 1993), 169 (quotation).

18. A. Gordon Ball and Earl O. Heady, "Trends in Farm and Enterprise Size and Scale," in *Size, Structure, and Future of Farms*, ed. Ball and Heady (Ames: Iowa State University Press, 1972), 40-58; Charles V. Moore and Gerald W. Dean, "Industrialized Farming," in ibid., 214-31; Michelle Mart, *Pesticides, a Love Story: America's Enduring*

Embrace of Dangerous Chemicals (Lawrence: University Press of Kansas, 2015), 11–56; David D. Vail, *Chemical Lands: Pesticides, Aerial Spraying, and Health in North America's Grasslands since 1945* (Tuscaloosa: University of Alabama Press, 2018), 1–109.

19. LaPIC, MCA, "Minutes of Meeting," October 4–5, 1945, L-63, Toxic Docs, https://www.toxicdocs.org/d/5L3aYG3w1GMJp8DnkyrN5pz3e; US Department of Agriculture, Production and Marketing Administration, "Regulations for the Enforcement of the Federal Insecticide, Fungicide, and Rodenticide Act," *Federal Register* 12, no. 193 (October 2, 1947): 6495–97; idem, "Regulations for the Enforcement of the Federal Insecticide, Fungicide, and Rodenticide Act: Interpretation with Respect to Warning, Caution and Antidote Statements Required to Appear on Labels of Economic Poisons," *Federal Register* 14, no. 223 (November 18, 1949): 6985–91; idem, "Regulations for the Enforcement of the Federal Insecticide, Fungicide, and Rodenticide Act: Exemption of Certain Economic Poisons," *Federal Register* 13, no. 15 (January 22, 1948): 309; Chester L. French, "Report of the Labels and Precautionary Information Committee," March 14, 1961, 2, Toxic Docs, https://www.toxicdocs.org/d/RGXV6NG5L25OxJp6JVxOvkza; LaPIC, MCA, "Minutes of Meeting," September 27–28, 1950, 3, Toxic Docs, https://www.toxicdocs.org/d/NEBaoqXn261MjdEbYvQdj63Ew; idem, "Minutes of Meeting," September 18–19, 1951, L-6, Toxic Docs, https://www.toxicdocs.org/d/ZBrBJe6zodDMY20JXea664DrL; Pete Daniel, *Toxic Drift: Pesticides and Health in the Post-World War II South* (Baton Rouge: Louisiana State University Press, 2005), 5 (quotation), 7, 130–34, 145.

20. [Albert B. Heagy], "Report of the Secretary," in Association of Economic Poison Control Officials, *Report . . ., 1948* (n.p., 1948), 1 (quotation), 28 (quotation), 1–2, 9–29.

21. Albert B. Heagy to All Economic Poison Control Officials, September 20, 1949, in Association of Economic Poison Control Officials, *Report . . ., 1949* (n.p., 1949), 1; Executive Committee, Association of Economic Poison Control Officials, "Report," in ibid., 36; "Persons in Attendance," in ibid., 81–84; John D. Conner, "Statement," in Association of Economic Poison Control Officials, *Report . . ., 1951* (n.p., 1951), 48 (quotation), 48–49; John D. Conner and George A. Burroughs, *Manual of Chemical Products Liability: An Analysis of the Law Concerning Liability Arising from the Manufacture and Sale of Chemical Products* (Washington, DC: MCA and National Agricultural Chemical Association, 1952), 37–47.

22. Walter J. Murphy, "Labels—An Ounce of Prevention," *Journal of Agricultural and Food Chemistry* 1, no. 5 (May 27, 1953), 353 (quotation); Floyd Roberts, "Preface," in Association of American Pesticide Control Officials, *Pesticide Official Publication and Condensed Data on Pesticide Chemicals, 1955* (College Park, MD: The Association, 1955), n. p.; idem, "Address of the President," in ibid., 35 (quotation), 31, 33.

23. Council on Pharmacy and Chemistry, American Medical Association, "Report of the Council: Committee on Pesticides," *JAMA* 142, no. 13 (April 1, 1950): 989–90; Bernard E. Conley, "The Relationship of Health and Regulatory Agencies in the Control of Economic Poisons," in Association of Economic Poison Control Officials, *Report . . ., 1950* (n.p., 1950), 56–59; Bernard E. Conley, "Incidence of Injury with Pesticides," *JAMA* 163, no. 15 (April 13, 1957): 1338–40; Bernard E. Conley, "Principles for Precautionary Labeling of Hazardous Chemicals," *JAMA* 166, no. 17 (April 26, 1958): 2154 (quotations), 2154–57; Bernard E. Conley, "Labels, Legislation and Our Expanding Chemical Environment," *The Sanitarian* 21, no. 4 (January–February 1959): 197 (quotations), 195–99. On the flight of government professionals to better-paying jobs in industry, see J. G. Townsend, "Industrial Hygiene for All Workers: Evaluation of Present Facilities," *Industrial Medicine* 16, no. 6 (June 1947): 282; PHS, *State Occupational Health Programs*, PHS Publication 605 (Washington, DC: GPO, 1958), 2.

24. Frederick R. Davis, *Banned: A History of Pesticides and the Science of Toxicology* (New Haven, CT: Yale University Press, 2014), 120; [Ira P. McNair], "The Editor

Comments," *Agricultural Chemicals*, October 1948, 19 (quotation); LaPIC, MCA, "Minutes of Meeting," April 20–22, 1955, L-119-20, Toxic Docs, https://www.toxicdocs.org/d/bOx9ZeBzk2xv6Rje954wjMNz6; Wayland J. Hayes, Jr., "Agricultural Chemicals and Public Health," *Public Health Reports* 69, no. 10 (October 1954): 895 (quotations); Vail, *Chemical Lands*, 100; L. S. Hitchner, "Remarks," in Association of American Pesticide Control Officials, in *Pesticide Official Publication and Condensed Data on Pesticide Chemicals, 1958* (College Park, MD: The Association, 1958), 14–15.

25. L. C. McGee in "Health Problems Involved in the Manufacture, Sale, and Use of Toxic Materials: A Panel Discussion," in Industrial Hygiene Foundation of America, *Twenty-First Annual Meeting, 1956*, Transactions Bulletin 30 (Pittsburgh, PA: The Foundation, n.d.), 268; Paul H. Leach, "Organic Phosphorus Poisoning in General Practice," *California Medicine* 78, no. 6 (June 1953): 491–95; Bernard E. Conley, "Morbidity and Mortality from Economic Poisons in the United States," *AMA Archives of Industrial Health* 18, no. 2 (August 1958): 126–33; US House of Representatives, Select Committee to Investigate the Use of Chemicals in Food Products, *Chemicals in Food Products: Hearings . . . Pursuant to H. Res. 323*, 81st Cong., 2nd sess., 1950 (Washington, DC: GPO, 1951).

26. LaPIC, MCA, "Minutes of Meeting," April 29–May 1, 1958, L-232-34, Toxic Docs, https://www.toxicdocs.org/d/gbbEKgBeJZ1Xkab4Eman261k3; William C. Wilentz to Philip Muccilli, September 2, 1958, Toxic Docs, https://www.toxicdocs.org/d/85EM82z2NVzNVaM1mYenXZvKm; "AMA Bill Hit," *Chemical and Engineering News*, August 4, 1958, 23 (quotation); Board of Directors, MCA, "Minutes," January 13, 1959, Toxic Docs, https://www.toxicdocs.org/d/k6VVJmavjZkr8Q97JdzOBV5dE.

27. LaPIC, MCA, "Minutes of Meeting," January 27–28, 1959, L-270-71, Toxic Docs, https://www.toxicdocs.org/d/G6dmQVGqrRn93bBNKK1o8E8oq; J. T. Fuess, "The American Medical Association Proposed Act for Labeling Hazardous Substances: An Industry Look at the Proposed Act," *AMA Archives of Industrial Health* 19, no. 3 (March 1959): 275 (quotations), 274–77.

28. US Senate, Committee on Interstate and Foreign Commerce, *Hazardous Substances for Household Use: Hearing . . . on S. 1283*, 86th Cong., 1st sess., 1959 (Washington, DC: GPO, 1960), 28 (Walker quotation), 8–30, 50–53.

29. US House of Representatives, Committee on Interstate and Foreign Commerce, Subcommittee on Health and Safety, *Federal Hazardous Substances Labeling Act: Hearing . . . on H.R. 5260*, 86th Cong., 2nd sess., 1960 (Washington, DC: GPO, 1960), 62 (Hunter quotation), 70 (Brown quotation), 43, 56–57, 62–64, 69–70.

30. US, *United States Statutes at Large, 1960*, vol. 74 (Washington, DC: GPO, 1961), 372–81; James D. Kittelton, "Industry's Views on the Federal Hazardous Substances Labeling Act," *Food, Drug, Cosmetic Law Journal* 15, no. 12 (December 1960): 790, 792.

31. Raymond J. Murray, "Effective Educational Techniques in Industrial Health Counseling," in Industrial Hygiene Foundation of America, *Twenty-First Annual Meeting, 1956*, 101 (quotations); Richard J. Sexton, "Health Information for Employees: Utilization of One of the Methods of Health Education and Its Application to Employees of a Chemical Plant," *AMA Archives of Industrial Health* 20, no. 4 (October 1959): 309 (quotation), 313 (quotation), 303–22; Margaret Hart, "Health Education in Industry," *Occupational Health* 13, no. 4 (April 1953): 57–58. It is unclear the extent to which managerial transparency reflected a sense of moral obligation and the extent to which it reflected, as David Rosner and Gerald Markowitz have maintained, a calculated attempt to preempt government intervention. See Rosner and Markowitz, "Educate the Individual," 28–35.

32. Committee on Industrial Hygiene Education, "Interim Report," in ACGIH, *Proceedings of the Eighth Annual Meeting, 1946* (n.p., n.d.), 49 (quotations), 49–50; Committee on Worker Health Information, "Report," in ACGIH, *Transactions, 1955*, 56

(quotation—emphasis in original); Committee on Worker Health Information, "Report," in ACGIH, *Transactions, 1959*, 153.

33. ACGIH, "Proposed Uniform Industrial Hygiene Code," *Industrial Hygiene Newsletter*, October 1948, 16 (quotation); Resolutions Committee, "Report," in International Association of Governmental Labor Officials, *Labor Laws and Their Administration: Proceedings of the Thirty-Second Convention of the International Association of Governmental Labor Officials . . ., 1949*, Bureau of Labor Standards Bulletin 120 (Washington, DC: GPO, 1950), 126–27; Victoria M. Trasko, *Occupational Health and Safety Legislation: A Compilation of State Laws and Regulations*, PHS Publication 357 (Washington, DC: GPO, 1954).

34. Donald E. H. Frear to Lea S. Hitchner, April 10, 1947 (quotation), Donald Frear Papers, box 1, folder: Aa-American Cyanamide, Special Collections Library, Pennsylvania State University, University Park; L. Gordon Utter to Frear, June 25, 1947, ibid.; Donald E. H. Frear to Charles L. Smith, May 28, 1948 (quotation), ibid.; Charles L. Smith to Donald E. H. Frear, June 1, 1948, ibid.; Donald E. H. Frear, *Pesticide Handbook: Entoma* (State College, PA: College Science Publishers, 1949); Donald E. H. Frear, *Pesticide Handbook: Entoma*, 20th ed. (State College, PA: College Science Publishers, 1968).

35. Joint Committee on Pesticides, American Medical Association (AMA), "Exploratory Meeting," October 26, 1949, Frear Papers, box 1, folder: Af-Az; Donald E. H. Frear to Bernard E. Conley, March 18, 1950 (quotation), ibid.; Donald E. H. Frear, *Newer Pesticides: Formulations, Hazards, Precautions and Compatibility* (State College: Pennsylvania State College, Agricultural Experiment Station, 1950).

36. Paul Scharrenberg and Wilton L. Halverson, "Plan of Integration and Definition of Responsibilities of the Departments of Industrial Relations and of Public Health with Respect to the Health and Safety of Industrial Workers in California," November 24, 1947, in International Association of Governmental Labor Officials, *Labor Laws and Their Administration: Proceedings of the Thirty-Third Convention of the International Association of Governmental Labor Officials . . ., 1950*, Bureau of Labor Standards Bulletin 145 (Washington, DC: GPO, 1951), 203–5; "California's Industrial Health Activities," *Industrial Hygiene Newsletter*, April 1948, 4–5. For a more complete account of Abrams's activities, see Alan Derickson, "Inventing the Right to Know: Herbert Abrams's Efforts to Democratize Access to Workplace Health Hazard Information in the 1950s," *AJPH* 106, no. 2 (February 2016): 237–45.

37. Herbert K. Abrams, "Adult Health—An Opportunity in Public Health," *California's Health* 5, no. 24 (June 30, 1948): 381 (Rosenau quotation), 381–86. On the rise of rights-based politics and policy, see Alan Brinkley, *The End of Reform: New Deal Liberalism in Recession and War* (New York: Alfred A. Knopf, 1995); Elizabeth Borgwardt, *A New Deal for the World: America's Vision for Human Rights* (Cambridge. MA: Belknap Press of Harvard University Press, 2005); Alan Derickson, "'Health for Three-Thirds of the Nation': Public Health Advocacy of Universal Access to Medical Care in the United States," *AJPH* 92, no. 2 (February 2002): 180–90.

38. Herbert K. Abrams, "Health Hazards Associated with Agricultural Chemicals," in ACGIH, *Transactions of the Eleventh Annual Meeting, 1949* (n.p., n.d.), 12 (quotations); Herbert K. Abrams, "Occupational Illness Due to Agricultural Chemicals, 1949," *California's Health*, September 15, 1950, 36 (quotation), 35–36; Conley, "Morbidity and Mortality from Economic Poisons," 126.

39. Herbert K. Abrams, "Labor, Management, and the Official Agency—Relationships Illustrated by a Plant Study," *AJPH* 42, no. 1 (January 1952): 40 (quotations), 41 (quotation), 38–43; Victoria M. Trasko, "The Work of State and Local Industrial Hygiene Agencies," *Public Health Reports* 64, no. 15 (April 15, 1949): 471–84; Trasko, *Occupational Health and Safety Legislation*, 17, 34, 36, 56, 87, 92, 125, 131, 132, 143, 153, 169, 214, 217, 224, 246, 249, 256, 264.

40. Robert T. Legge and Esther Rosencrantz, "Observations and Studies on Silicosis by Diatomaceous Silica," *AJPH* 22, no. 10 (October 1932): 1055–60; Herbert K. Abrams, "Some Hidden History of Occupational Medicine," *Environmental Research* 59, no. 1 (October 1992): 28–30; Lewis J. Cralley, "Occupational Health Study in the Diatomite Producing Industry: Environmental Aspects," in ACGIH, *Transactions of the Seventeenth Annual Meeting, 1955* (Cincinnati, OH: The Conference, 1955), 18; Herbert K. Abrams, "Diatomaceous Earth Silicosis," *American Journal of Industrial Medicine* 18, no. 5 (1990): 592; Herbert K. Abrams, "Practicing Social Medicine: Memoirs from the Neighborhoods," ca. 2003, Abrams family papers (copy in author's possession), 9, 161, 533. For the accumulating evidence on the risks of exposure to this silicious dust, see, among others, Enrico C. Vigliani and Giacomo Mottura, "Diatomaceous Earth Silicosis," *British Journal of Industrial Medicine* 5, no. 3 (July 1948): 148–60; Arthur J. Vorwald et al., "Diatomaceous Earth Pneumoconiosis," *The Proceedings of the Ninth International Congress on Industrial Medicine, 1948* (Bristol, UK: John Wright, 1949), 725–41.

41. Abrams, "Some Hidden History of Occupational Medicine," 30–32; [Robert Goe], "Death by Dust," *Search Magazine*, January 1952, 111 (quotation), 109–11; Nate Hale, "The Story of a Strange and Dangerous Dust," *San Francisco Chronicle*, January 13, 1952, 1, 15.

42. "Johns-Manville Employees Strike for Their Lives," *East Bay Labor Journal* (Oakland, CA), July 4, 1952, 8; Herbert K. Abrams, "Chemical Workers Face 'Death by Dust': Medic Report Proves Case for Local 146," *East Bay Labor Journal* (Oakland, CA), July 4, 1952, 8; John McReynolds, "Strike Looms after Twenty-Six Years of Labor Peace," *Lompoc Record*, March 4, 2007, http://lompocrecord.com/news/local/strike-looms-after-years-of-labor-peace/article/38f0df50-8792-5429-9236-1d2748b76136.html; "Strike at Johns-Manville Continues," *International Chemical Worker*, July 1952, 1, 8; H. A. Bradley, "An Urgent Appeal," *International Chemical Worker*, August 1952, 1; "Local 146 Wins Objectives in Strike Settlement," *International Chemical Worker*, December 1952, 5; International Chemical Workers Union (ICWU), *Proceedings of the Ninth Annual Convention, 1952* (n.p., n.d.), 46 (Rodrigues quotation), 45–50.

43. ICWU, *Proceedings of the Ninth Annual Convention, 1952*, 56–66, 89–91; Abrams, "Practicing Social Medicine," 535; Herbert K. Abrams, "Motivating Employees for Health," *International Chemical Worker*, July 1953, 3 (quotation); Johns Manville Products Corporation, Lompoc Plant, and Local 146, ICWU, "Agreement, 1953–54," International Chemical Workers Union Records, box F-55, microfilm roll E-10, Archival Services, University Libraries, University of Akron, Akron, OH. On the paucity of occupational health expertise for the unions, see "The New Activism on Job Health," *Business Week*, September 18, 1978, 146–50; Health Research Group, *Survey of Occupational Health Efforts of Fifteen Major Labor Unions* (Washington, DC: Health Research Group, 1976).

44. Herbert K. Abrams, "Motivating Employees for Industrial Health," *AMA Archives of Industrial Hygiene and Occupational Medicine* 8, no. 3 (September 1953): 246 (quotation), 247 (quotation), 246–49.

45. ICWU, *Proceedings of the Tenth Annual Convention, 1953* (n.p., n.d.), 62; Arch F. Blakey, *The Florida Phosphate Industry: A History of the Development and Use of a Vital Mineral* (Cambridge, MA: Harvard University Press, 1973), 51–52; Harvey Baker to Herbert K. Abrams, October 30, 1954 (quotation), ICWU Records, box I-6, folder: ICB-2baa Educational Programs—Local Unions—1954; ICWU, *Proceedings of the Thirteenth Annual Convention, 1956* (n.p., n.d.), 65.

46. Herbert K. Abrams, "ICWU Tackles Health Problems," *International Chemical Worker*, September 1954, 3; ICWU, *Proceedings of Convention, 1956*, 65; Harold J. Magnuson to Edward Moffett (with copy to Herbert K. Abrams), August 22, 1956, RG 90, Records of the Bureau of State Services, 1948–1963, Records of the Division of Special

Health Services, Occupational Health Subject Files, 1955–1957, box 43, folder: In; Harold J. Magnuson to Edward Moffett, November 7, 1956, ibid.; Henry Doyle to Abrams, March 4 and 14, 1957, ibid.; PHS and Florida State Board of Health, *Industrial Hygiene Survey of the Phosphate Industry in Polk County, Florida* (Washington, DC: PHS, 1958); Walter Mitchell to Henry Doyle, August 19, 1958 (quotations), reprinted in ICWU, *Proceedings, Fifteenth Annual Convention, 1958* (n.p., n.d.), 335; Herbert K. Abrams, "Labor Due Lion's Share Credit for Health Progress," *International Chemical Worker*, November 1962, 8; Wilhelm C. Hueper, "Adventures of a Physician in Occupational Cancer: A Medical Cassandra's Tale," 1976, 235 (quotation), W. C. Hueper Papers, box 1, folder 20, Archives and Modern Manuscripts Program, History of Medicine Division, National Library of Medicine, Bethesda, MD.

47. "Plan Phosphate Health Drive," *International Chemical Worker*, January 1959, 8; "Phosphate Planning Conference Charted," *International Chemical Worker*, February 1959, 6; "Phosphate Locals Plan Tactics, Point Up Health Hazards," *International Chemical Worker*, March 1959, 6; "Excessive Fluoride, Silica," *International Chemical Worker*, March 1959, 6; "Teamsters Pull Raid," *International Chemical Worker*, September 1960, 12; ICWU, *Proceedings, Sixteenth Annual Convention, 1959* (n.p., n.d.), 62, 183; ICWU, *Proceedings of the Seventeenth Annual Convention, 1960* (n.p., n.d.), 60, 265–67; H. O. Grant, "Pollution Control in a Phosphoric Acid Plant," *Chemical Engineering Progress*, January 1964, 53–55. On regulation of environmental pollution, see Scott H. Dewey, "The Fickle Finger of Phosphate: Central Florida Air Pollution and the Failure of Environmental Policy, 1957–1970," in *Other Souths: Diversity and Difference in the U.S. South, Reconstruction to the Present*, ed. Pippa Holloway (Athens: University of Georgia Press, 2008), 344–80.

48. "Doctor Abrams to Write Series of Articles on Health and Safety," *International Chemical Worker*, March 1953, 3; Herbert K. Abrams, "You and the Oath of Hippocrates," *International Chemical Worker*, October 1953, 4 (quotation); Herbert K. Abrams, "Diatomaceous Earth Pneumoconiosis: Some Sociomedical Observations," *AJPH* 44, no. 5 (May 1954): 597. On the distended prerogatives of capital in post–World War II employment relations, see Howell J. Harris, *The Right to Manage: Industrial Relations Policies of American Business in the 1940s* (Madison: University of Wisconsin Press, 1982). On subsequent objectionable behavior by Monsanto Corporation, see David Rosner and Gerald Markowitz, "'Ashamed to Put My Name on It': Monsanto, Industrial Bio-Test Laboratories, and the Use of Fraudulent Science, 1969–1985," *AJPH* 113, no. 6 (June 2023): 661–66.

49. Herbert K. Abrams, "Needed: Better Labelling of Poisonous Chemicals," *International Chemical Worker*, December 1958, 9 (quotation); Herbert K. Abrams, "Cancer at Work," *International Chemical Worker*, August 1954, 4 (quotation), 3–4; Herbert K. Abrams, "The 'Toxic Department' and Aniline," *International Chemical Worker*, May 1954, 5; Herbert K. Abrams, "Occupational Cancer of the Bladder," *International Chemical Worker*, November 1954, 3; Herbert K. Abrams, "Health Hazards in the Munitions Industry," *International Chemical Worker*, December 1954, 3.

50. "Safety Pamphlet Out, Praised by Local Officials," *International Chemical Worker*, April 1958, 8; Herbert K. Abrams to W. C. Hueper, July 9 and July 15, 1954, ICWU Records, box I-11, folder: IVD6 Chicago—1954; Herbert K. Abrams to Mr. Moffett et al., February 24, 1955, ICWU Records, box F-56, roll M-3; ICWU, *Proceedings of the Twelfth Annual Convention, 1955* (n.p., n.d.), 31 (Abrams quotations), 32–33 (Abrams quotation), 31–33, 155, 291–93. The booklet distributed at the 1954 convention was Wilhelm Hueper, *Environmental Cancer* (Bethesda, MD: National Cancer Institute, n.d. [1953?]).

51. ICWU, *Proceedings, 1959*, 187; Herbert K. Abrams, "Twin Problems: Health in the Plant, in Community," *International Chemical Worker*, December 1959, 9; Herbert

K. Abrams, "A New Four-Point Program for Growth and Strength," *International Chemical Worker*, May 1960, 3; Herbert K. Abrams, "Medical Ignorance, Faulty Laws, Scanty Research Hit," *International Chemical Worker*, June 1960, 7; ICWU, *Proceedings of the Seventeenth Annual Convention, 1960* (n.p., n.d.), 59–61; Herbert K. Abrams, "Lung Cancer and Chemical Workers," *International Chemical Worker*, February 1961, 9; Herbert K. Abrams, "How to Solve an Occupational Health Problem," *International Chemical Worker*, August 1962, 10 (quotation).

52. Abrams, "Practicing Social Medicine," 9–10; Herbert K. Abrams, "Comprehensive Plan Is Union Health Goal," *Local 25 Voice* (Chicago), June 11, 1953, 4; Herbert K. Abrams, "X-Rays, Solvents among Blood Hazards," *Local 25 Voice*, July 14, 1953, 4; Herbert K. Abrams, "Health Hazards on Janitor's Job," *Local 25 Voice*, September 22, 1953, 4; Herbert K. Abrams, "Labeling Will Help Prevent Chemical Poisonings," *Local 25 Voice*, December 1958, 4 (and on p. 2 in Polish as "Nalepki Pomoga Chronic Od Zatruc Chemicznych"); Herbert K. Abrams, "Health Resolutions for 1962," *Local 25 Voice*, January 1962, 4.

4. A MATTER OF INCREASINGLY PUBLIC RECORD

Epigraph: "Workers' Right to Know Is Law," *1557 Labor Journal* (Clairton, PA), August 1971, 4.

1. Frank Burke, "What Organized Labor Wants from Industrial Hygiene," in American Conference of Governmental Industrial Hygienists (ACGIH), *Transactions of the Twelfth Annual Meeting, 1950* (n.p., n.d.), 12 (quotations), 13 (quotations), 12–15.

2. Round Table Discussion, "Plant Conditions: To What Extent Should Official Findings Regarding Them Be Made Available to Workers?," in National Conference of Governmental Industrial Hygienists, *Transactions of the Seventh Annual Meeting, 1944* (n.p., n.d.), 25 (Bloomfield quotation), 23 (West quotation), 22–25; Herbert T. Walworth, "Worker Health Education: From the Viewpoint of the Engineer," National Conference of Governmental Industrial Hygienists, *Transactions of the Seventh Annual Meeting, 1944*, 11 (quotation), 9–11. On the influence of private parties over the ACGIH, see Jacqueline K. Corn, *Protecting the Health of Workers: The American Conference of Governmental Industrial Hygienists, 1938–1988* (Cincinnati, OH: ACGIH, 1989), 181. On the role of the Public Health Service (PHS) in the founding and early development of the ACGIH, see Ad Hoc Committee on Occupational Health Programs, "Report," in ACGIH, *Transactions of the Twenty-Ninth Annual Meeting, 1967* (n.p., n.d.), 87.

3. Leonard Woodcock, "Where Are We Going in Public Health? A Labor Leader's Appraisal," *American Journal of Public Health (AJPH)* 46, no. 3 (March 1956): 278; Victoria M. Trasko, *Occupational Health and Safety Legislation: A Compilation of State Laws and Regulations*, PHS Publication 357 (Washington, DC: US Government Printing Office [GPO], 1954), 17, 34, 36, 56, 87, 92, 125, 131, 132, 143, 153, 169, 214, 217, 224, 246, 249, 256, 264; PHS, *Occupational Health and Safety Legislation*, rev. ed., PHS Publication 357 (Washington, DC: GPO, 1971), 12, 22, 38, 48, 50, 58, 127, 147, 153, 154, 176, 194, 238, 246, 248, 272, 283, 299, 305; Tennessee, *Public Acts, 1945* (Nashville: Rich Printing, n.d.), 402; Texas, *General and Special Laws, 1967* ([Austin]: The State, n.d.), 443; Charles D. Yaffe, "Role of the Local Health Department in Occupational Health," in PHS, *The Local Health Officer in Occupational Health* (Washington, DC: GPO, 1959), 75 (quotation), 76 (quotation), 73–78.

4. Michael Schudson, *The Rise of the Right to Know: Politics and the Culture of Transparency, 1945–1975* (Cambridge, MA: Belknap Press of Harvard University Press, 2015), 6 (quotation), 1–102; David M. O'Brien, *The Public's Right to Know: The Supreme Court and the First Amendment* (New York: Praeger, 1981), passim, esp. 179–82; Pennsylvania, *Laws . . ., 1957* (Harrisburg: Pennsylvania General Assembly, 1957), 391.

5. Barry Commoner, *Science and Survival* (New York: Viking, 1966); Michael Egan, *Barry Commoner and the Science of Survival: The Remaking of American Environmentalism* (Cambridge, MA: MIT Press, 2007), 56–57, 75–78, 86–90; Rachel Carson, *Silent Spring* (Boston: Houghton Mifflin, 1962), 13 (Rostand quotation); Jean Rostand, "Popularization of Science," *Science* 131, no. 3412 (May 20, 1960): 1491 (quotation).

6. Carson, *Silent Spring*, 12 (quotation), 12–13, 18, 22, 26, 27, 36, 197–98, 229–30; US President's Scientific Advisory Committee, *Use of Pesticides: A Report of the President's Scientific Advisory Committee* (Washington, DC: GPO, 1963), 20 (quotation), 9–10, 23; US Senate, Committee on Government Operations, Subcommittee on Reorganization and International Organizations, *Interagency Coordination on Environmental Hazards (Pesticides): Hearings . . ., Coordination of Activities Relating to the Use of Pesticides*, 88th Cong., 1st sess., 1963–64 (Washington, DC: GPO, 1964), 1028 (Smith quotation), 1036 (Smith quotation), 560, 687, 699, 2401. On the influence of Carson's book and the reaction to it, see Mark H. Lytle, *The Gentle Subversive: Rachel Carson, Silent Spring, and the Rise of the Environmental Movement* (New York: Oxford University Press, 2007); Christopher J. Bosso, *Pesticides and Politics: The Life Cycle of a Public Issue* (Pittsburgh, PA: University of Pittsburgh Press, 1987), 115–33.

7. Alan Derickson, *Black Lung: Anatomy of a Public Health Disaster* (Ithaca, NY: Cornell University Press, 1998), 128–36; unidentified Pennsylvania Bureau of Industrial Hygiene employee, "Field Activity Report," August 14, 1957 (quotation), RG-43: Records of the Department of Environmental Resources, Bureau of Occupational Health, Investigative Reports (after Plant Closures) of Health Hazards in Industrial Plants, ca. 1941–1973, microfilm roll 7745, Pennsylvania State Archives, Harrisburg; Joseph L. Cohen and Thomas D. McBride to C. L. Wilbar, Jr., December 5, 1958, ibid.; Alan Derickson, "Leslie Falk: Oral History Interview on Coal Miners' Respiratory Diseases," July 12, 1991, Alan Derickson Research Interviews Concerning Black Lung Disease, box 2, folder 3, Historical Collections and Labor Archives, University Libraries, Pennsylvania State University, University Park. Lorin Kerr, the United Mine Workers of America (UMW) fund's authority on black lung issues, reportedly opposed informing the family doctors of those men found to have pneumoconiosis about their plight. Kerr worried that mining-town physicians would reveal this sensitive information to mine managers, and the worker-patient would lose his job. See Jan Lieben to C. L. Wilbar, Jr., August 5, 1959, RG-11: Records of the Department of Health, Office of the Secretary, General Correspondence and Related Records, 1930–1976, 1995–2001, carton 9, folder: Occupational Health, Pennsylvania State Archives, Harrisburg.

8. Jan Lieben to D. E. Hartman, May 12, 1959, RG-43, Bureau of Occupational Health, Investigative Reports (after Plant Closures) of Health Hazards in Industrial Plants, ca. 1941–1973, roll 7751; Roger J. Howell, "Dust Study Program by Pennsylvania Department of Mines and Mineral Industries," in Mine Inspectors' Institute of America, *Proceedings of the Fifty-First Convention, 1961* (n.p., n.d.), 89 (quotation), 93; Gordon E. Smith, "Coordination of Dust Conditions in Anthracite Mines," in Pennsylvania Governor's Conference on Pneumoconiosis (Anthraco-Silicosis), *Proceedings, 1964* (Harrisburg, PA: Department of Health, Department of Labor and Industry, and Department of Mines and Mineral Industries, 1964), 132 (quotation), 131–32.

9. Derickson, *Black Lung*, 133–39; US PHS, Division of Occupational Health, "Summary Report: Chest Diseases in Bituminous Coal Miners," n.d. [ca. November 1962], 22 (quotation), 10, 21–22, Russellton Miners' Clinic Records, box 1, folder 5, Historical Collections and Labor Archives, University Libraries, Pennsylvania State University, University Park; Alan Derickson, "Lorin Kerr: Oral History Interview on Coal Miners' Respiratory Diseases," June 26, 1989, Derickson Interviews Concerning Black Lung, box 2, folder 10.

10. Jan Lieben to C. Earl Albrecht, March 23, 1962, RG-11, Office of the Secretary, General Correspondence and Related Records, 1930–1976, 1995–2001, carton 9, folder: Occupational Health; C. Earl Albrecht to Jan Lieben, April 6, 1962 (quotation), ibid.; Marlin L. Brennan to Jan Lieben, March 11, 1965 (quotation), ibid.; Jan Lieben to C. L. Wilbar, Jr., March 22, 1965, ibid.; Rachel Scott, *Muscle and Blood* (New York: E. P. Dutton, 1974), 33–34. The published work in question may well have included Jan Lieben and Franz Metzner, "Epidemiological Findings Associated with Beryllium Extraction," *American Industrial Hygiene Association Journal* 20, no. 6 (December 1959): 494–99; Franz Metzner and Jan Lieben, "Respiratory Disease Associated with Beryllium Refining and Alloy Fabrication: A Case Study," *Journal of Occupational Medicine* 3, no. 7 (July 1961): 341–45. On the public relations campaign of the beryllium firms and their efforts to cultivate Jan Lieben and others, see David S. Egilman et al., "The Beryllium 'Double Standard' Standard," *International Journal of Health Services* 33, no. 4 (2003): 791–92. For a similar pattern of unhelpful behavior by state administrators in Massachusetts in the 1940s, see Craig Zwerling, "Salem Sarcoid: The Origins of Beryllium Disease," in *Dying for Work: Workers' Safety and Health in Twentieth-Century America*, ed. David Rosner and Gerald Markowitz (Bloomington: Indiana University Press, 1987), 103–18, esp. 110–13, 115.

11. Frank Burke to Haven Williams, May 5, 1966, RG-43, Bureau of Occupational Health, Investigative Reports (after Plant Closures) of Health Hazards in Industrial Plants, ca. 1941–1973, roll 7693; Haven Williams to Frank Burke, May 13, 1966, ibid.; Frank Burke to Haven Williams, May 16, 1966 (quotation), ibid.; Haven Williams to Frank Burke, May 26, 1966, ibid.; E. J. Baier to Frank Burke, August 9, 1967, ibid.; Jan Lieben to Frank Burke, June 8, 1966, ibid.; Ralph Dwork to Frank Burke, July 25, 1966, ibid.

12. Alan Derickson, "'Gateway to Hell': African American Coking Workers, Racial Discrimination, and the Struggle against Occupational Cancer," *Journal of African American History* 101, nos. 1–2 (Winter–Spring 2016): 126–49; Dennis C. Dickerson, *Out of the Crucible: Black Steelworkers in Western Pennsylvania, 1875–1980* (Albany, NY: SUNY Press, 1986), 17, 37, 121, 154, 188; E. W. Kenworthy "U.S. Steel Forced into Vast Antipollution Program," *New York Times*, August 27, 1972, F3.

13. W. C. Mawhinney, "Field Activity Report," October 18, 1967, RG-43, Bureau of Occupational Health, Investigative Reports (after Plant Closures) of Health Hazards in Industrial Plants, ca. 1941–1973, roll 7745; W. C. Mawhinney, "Investigation: U.S. Steel Corporation, Clairton Works," November 1, 1967, 2 (quotation), 1–3, ibid.; D. A. Tyler to R. R. Campbell, November 21, 1967, ibid. and in United Steelworkers of America, Local 1557 Records, box 1, folder 1, Historical Collections and Labor Archives, University Libraries, Pennsylvania State University, University Park.

14. A. W. Thomas, N. L. Fannick, and N. R. Brown, "Field Activity Report," n.d. [ca. May 7, 1969], RG-43, Bureau of Occupational Health, Investigative Reports (after Plant Closures) of Health Hazards in Industrial Plants, ca. 1941–1973, roll 7745; E. J. Baier to James L. Plasterer, June 13, 1969 (quotations), with Pennsylvania, Division of Occupational Health, "Coal Tar Pitch Volatile Concentrations," ibid.; E. J. Baier, "Relationships between Occupational Health Programs and Other State Agencies," in ACGIH, *Transactions of the Thirty-First Annual Meeting, 1969* (n.p., n.d.), 72 (quotation), 76. On the inadequacy of the ACGIH threshold limit value (TLV), see Alan Derickson, "Surviving a 'Carcinogen Rich Environment': Steelworkers' Democratic Intrusion into the Regulation of Coke-Oven Emissions," *Journal of Policy History* 27, no. 4 (2015): 561–91.

15. US Steel Corporation, Clairton Works, Joint Safety Committee, "Memorandum Minutes of Meeting," June 19, 1969 (quotation), USW Local 1557 Records, box 1, folder 28; Frank Rudman, "Safety Committee Report," *1557 Labor Journal*, May 1969, 3; J. L. Plasterer to Fellow Employee, June 20, 1969 (quotation), USW Local 1557 Records, box 1, folder 2.

16. Daniel Hannan to Edward Zemprelli, July 3, 1969 (quotation), USW Local 1557 Records, box 1, folder 2.

17. Daniel Hannan to Edward Zemprelli, July 3, 1969, USW Local 1557 Records, box 1, folder 2 (quotations); Edward Zemprelli to Daniel Hannan, July 24, 1969, ibid.; Daniel Hannan, "My Labor Diary," *1557 Labor Journal*, July 1969, 1 (quotation), 2; "Results of Survey on Batteries," ibid., 1–2; Legislative Committee of Pennsylvania, USW, "Facing the Seventies: Legislative Report," January 1970, 1, USW Legislative Department Records, box 111, folder 26, Historical Collections and Labor Archives, University Libraries, Pennsylvania State University, University Park.

18. W. C. Hueper, *A Quest into the Environmental Causes of Cancer of the Lung*, Public Health Monograph 36 (Washington, DC: GPO, 1955), 20, 32–33; Emerson Venable, "Inspection Trip—Clairton Works Coke By-Product Plant," August 10, 1960 (quotation), Emerson Venable Papers, box 14, folder 8, Detre Library and Archives Division, Heinz History Center, Pittsburgh, PA; Daniel Hannan, "My Labor Diary," *1557 Labor Journal*, November 1967, 1, 4; Daniel Hannan, "My Labor Diary," ibid., July 1969, 2; Daniel Hannan, "Testimony before the Allegheny County Commissioners," ibid., October 1969, 1, 3; US House of Representatives, Committee on Education and Labor, Subcommittee on Labor, *Occupational Safety and Health Act of 1969: Hearings . . . on HR 843, HR 3809, HR 4294, HR13373*, 91st Cong., 1st sess., 1969 (Washington, DC: GPO, 1970), 1004 (Hannan quotation), 1004–6; Howard Holmes, "On the Batteries," *1557 Labor Journal*, December 1969, 4 (quotation); Charles L. Stokes, "Ovens Zone 4," *1557 Labor Journal*, July 1968, 5.

19. J. William Lloyd and Antonio Ciocco, "Long-Term Mortality Study of Steelworkers: I. Methodology," *Journal of Occupational Medicine* 11, no. 6 (June 1969): 299–310; J. William Lloyd et al., "Long-Term Mortality Study of Steelworkers: IV. Mortality by Work Area," *Journal of Occupational Medicine* 12, no. 5 (May 1970): 151–57; J. William Lloyd, "Long-Term Mortality Study of Steelworkers: V. Respiratory Cancer in Coke Plant Workers," *Journal of Occupational Medicine* 13, no. 2 (February 1971): 53–68, esp. 62; Carol K. Redmond et al., "Long-Term Mortality Study of Steelworkers: VI. Mortality from Malignant Neoplasms among Coke Oven Workers," *Journal of Occupational Medicine* 14, no. 8 (August 1972): 621–29; Daniel Hannan, untitled autobiographical notes, n.d., Daniel W. Hannan Papers and Photographs, box 2, folder: United Steelworkers of America, Detre Library and Archives Division, Heinz History Center, Pittsburgh, PA.

20. Michael J. Zahorsky, USW Local 1211 meeting minutes, December 17, 1969, Minute Book 11, 61–62, USW Local 1211 Records, box 16, Historical Collections and Labor Archives, University Libraries, Pennsylvania State University, University Park; "Bills Introduced and Referred," *Legislative Journal* (Commonwealth of Pennsylvania), September 24, 1969, 612; Pennsylvania, *Laws . . ., 1957*, 391 (quotation); Legislative Committee of Pennsylvania, United Steelworkers (USW), "Facing the Seventies," January 1970, 1–3, USW Legislative Department Records, box 111, folder 26; Julius Uehlein to All Members of the Senate of Pennsylvania, December 4, 1969 (quotations), USW Local 1557 Records, box 1, folder 2.

21. Legislative Committee of Pennsylvania, USW, "Minutes of the Twelfth Annual Conference," January 30, 1970, 5, USW Legislative Department Records, box 111, folder 27; Pennsylvania, General Assembly, "Bill Information—History: House Bill 2408, Regular Session 1969–1970," https://www.legis.state.pa.us/cfdocs/billinfo/bill_history.cfm?syear=1969&sind=0&body=H&type=B&bn=2408; "Bills Introduced and Referred," *Legislative Journal* (Commonwealth of Pennsylvania), January 26, 1971, 53; "Steelworkers Pressed Successful Fight for State Safety Inspections," *Steel Labor*, August 1971, 17 (Shapp quotation); Pennsylvania, *Laws . . ., 1971* (Harrisburg, PA: By Authority [of the

General Assembly], 1971), 160 (quotation), 160–61; "Workers' Right to Know Is Law," *1557 Labor Journal*, August 1971, 4 (quotation).

22. "Landmark Compensation Award to Steelworker for Coke Oven Lung Disease," *Steel Labor*, October 1971, 4; Joseph Odorcich et al., "Memorandum of Agreement—Clairton Works, November 6, 1974, USW Safety and Health Department Records, box 23, folder: Daniel Hannan, 1977, Historical Collections and Labor Archives, University Libraries, Pennsylvania State University, University Park; US Steel Corporation, Clairton Works, Coking Department, "Door Repairs," January 13, 1975, ibid., box 13, folder 11; "Make a Coke Oven Work without Killing People," *Steel Labor*, February 1975, 7; Lawrence S. Bacow, *Bargaining for Job Safety and Health* (Cambridge, MA: MIT Press, 1980), 68–74.

23. John Gregory Dunne, *Delano*, rev. ed. (New York: Farrar, Straus and Giroux, 1971); Miriam Pawel, *The Union of Their Dreams: Power, Hope, and Struggle in Cesar Chavez's Farm Worker Movement* (New York: Bloomsbury, 2009), 5–65; Marshall Ganz, *Why David Sometimes Wins: Leadership, Organization, and Strategy in the California Farm Worker Movement* (New York: Oxford University Press, 2010), 119–228.

24. Robert T. Legge, "Occupational Hazards in the Agricultural Industries," *AJPH* 25, no. 4 (April 1935): 462 (quotation), 461–62; Bernard E. Conley, "Morbidity and Mortality from Economic Poisons in the United States," *AMA Archives of Industrial Health* 18, no. 2 (August 1958): 126; H. K. Abrams, "Increased Use of Agricultural Chemicals Serious Problem for Industrial Hygienists," *Industrial Hygiene Newsletter*, July 1950, 3–4, 16; H. K. Abrams, "Occupational Illness Due to Agricultural Chemicals," *California's Health*, September 15, 1950, 35–36; Irma West, "Occupational Disease of Farm Workers," *Archives of Environmental Health* 9, no. 1 (July 1964): 93 (quotations), 92–97; California Department of Public Health, Bureau of Adult Health, *Reports of Occupational Disease Attributed to Pesticides and Other Agricultural Chemicals, California, 1957* (Berkeley, CA: The Department, n.d.); Irma West, "Statement," in US Senate, Committee on Government Operations, Subcommittee on Reorganization and International Organizations, *Interagency Coordination in Environmental Hazards (Pesticides): Hearings . . ., Agency Coordination Study*, 88th Cong., 1st sess., 1963 (Washington, DC: GPO, 1964), 623, 625, 638; Irma West, "Public Health Problems Are Created by Pesticides," *California's Health*, July 1965, 12 (quotation), 11–18; California Department of Public Health, *Occupational Disease in California Attributed to Pesticides and Other Agricultural Chemicals, 1965* (n.p.: The Department, n.d.), 21; Robert Z. Rollins, "Federal and State Regulation of Pesticides," *AJPH* 53, no. 9 (September 1963): 1427–31, esp. 1428, 1430; California Governor Edmund G. Brown's Special Committee on Public Policy Regarding Agricultural Chemicals, *Report on Agricultural Chemicals and Recommendations for Public Policy* (Sacramento, CA: n.p., 1960), 26 (quotation), 30–31.

25. Pawel, *The Union of Their Dreams*, 31–39; Dunne, *Delano*, 127–36; Eugene Nelson, *Huelga: The First Hundred Days of the Great Delano Grape Strike* (Delano, CA: Farm Worker Press, 1966), 120; Frank Bardacke, *Trampling Out the Vintage: Cesar Chavez and the Two Souls of the United Farm Workers* (New York: Verso, 2011), 324.

26. US Senate, Committee on Labor and Public Welfare, Subcommittee on Migratory Labor, *Migrant and Seasonal Farmworker Powerlessness: Hearings . . . on Pesticides and the Farmworker*, 91st Cong., 1st sess., 1969 (Washington, DC: GPO, 1970), 3011–13, 3027–30, 3059–63. The union met the same opposition when it sought records in Riverside County, California, in 1969. But in this instance, its appeal of an adverse judicial decision won access by demonstrating that the county officials had not chosen to protect supposed trade secrets when growers or insurance companies wanted to see pesticide records. See "DDT Poisoning Becomes National Concern," *El Malcriado* (Delano, CA), April 15–30, 1969, 2; "New Attempt to See Poison Records," *El Malcriado*, August

15–September 15, 1969, 7, 15; Jerry Cohen, David Averbuck, and Chuck Farnsworth, "Audio Interview: Jerry Cohen/David Averbuck/Chuck Farnsworth Discuss Legal Cases, 1960s," May 19, 2009, in Farmworker Movement Documentation Project, University of California, San Diego Library, https://libraries.ucsd.edu/farmworkermovement/ufwarchives/ufwlegal/Lawyers2LeRoy.mp3.

27. Miriam Pawel, *The Crusades of Cesar Chavez: A Biography* (New York: Bloomsbury, 2014), 191 (quotations); Pawel, *The Union of Their Dreams*, 51–52; Robert van den Bosch, *The Pesticide Conspiracy: An Alarming Look at Pest Control and the People Who Keep Us Hooked on Deadly Chemicals* (Garden City, NY: Doubleday, 1978), 76 (quotation), 76–79.

28. "Court Questions Poison Injunction," *El Malcriado*, September 15, 1968, 6; "What Are They Hiding?," *El Malcriado*, February 1, 1969, 4 (quotation), 5, 11; "Economic Poisons: A Threat to Workers and Consumers," *El Malcriado*, January 15, 1969, 1; "Rain of Death and Sickness," *El Malcriado*, March 1–15, 1970, 11 (Chavez quotation). On Jose Guadalupe Posada's radical perspective and his legacy for Chicano/a activists, see Carlos F. Jackson, *Chicana and Chicano Art: ProtestArte* (Tucson: University of Arizona Press, 2009), 29–34, 67–68. On Posada and the Mexican iconography of death, see Stanley H. Brandes, *Skulls to the Living, Bread to the Dead: The Day of the Dead in Mexico and Beyond* (Malden, MA: Blackwell, 2006), 43–66, esp. 61–66. For further use of skull images, see "Don't Eat Grapes," *El Malcriado*, June 1–30, 1969, 1; "Data on DDT and Parathion," *El Malcriado*, July 1–15, 1969, 11; "Senator George Murphy Is Back in Show Business," *El Malcriado*, September 15–October 1, 1969, 1.

29. "Growers Spurn Negotiations on Poisons," *El Malcriado*, January 15, 1969, 3; "Pesticide Training Should Take Eight Weeks for Safety," *El Malcriado*, March 15–31, 1969, 10; US Senate, Committee on Labor and Public Welfare, Subcommittee on Labor, *Agricultural Labor Legislation: Hearings . . . on S. 8 . . . [and] S. 1808*, 91st Cong., 1st sess., 1969 (Washington, DC: GPO, 1970), 29 (Huerta quotation); US Senate, *Migrant and Seasonal Farmworker Powerlessness*, 3406 (Cohen quotation), 3030 (Cohen quotation), 3393, 3716, 3806 (Mizrahi quotation), 3806–8; Laura Pulido, *Environmentalism and Economic Justice: Two Chicano Struggles in the Southwest* (Tucson: University of Arizona Press, 1996), 112–19; Laura Pulido and Devon Pena, "Environmentalism and Positionality: The Early Pesticide Campaign of the United Farm Workers Organizing Committee, 1965–71," *Race, Gender and Class* 6, no. 1 (1998): 42–45.

30. Victoria M. Trasko, "Present Status of Occupational Health Programs," in ACGIH, *Transactions of the Thirtieth Annual Meeting, 1968* (n.p., n.d.), 53 (quotation), 51–55; [Ad Hoc Committee on Occupational Health Programs], "A Look at Occupational Health as a State Activity," ibid., 171–75; Nicholas A. Ashford, *Crisis in the Workplace: Occupational Disease and Injury: Report to the Ford Foundation* (Cambridge, MA: MIT Press, 1976), 51 (quotation), 49–51, 72–88; US Senate, Committee on Labor and Public Welfare, Subcommittee on Labor, *Occupational Safety and Health Act, 1970: Hearings . . . on S. 2193 . . . and S. 2788*, 91st Cong., 1st and 2nd sess., 1969–70 (Washington, DC: GPO, 1970), 1080 (Selikoff quotation); Joseph A. Page and Mary-Win O'Brien, *Bitter Wages: Ralph Nader's Study Group Report on Disease and Injury on the Job* (New York: Grossman, 1973), 69–85.

31. PHS Division of Occupational Health, *Protecting the Health of Eighty Million Americans: A National Goal for Occupational Health: Special Report to the Surgeon General of the United States Public Health Service* (Washington, DC: GPO, 1965), passim, esp. 12, 36; Ashford, *Crisis in the Workplace*, 57 (quotation).

32. US Senate, Committee on Labor and Public Welfare, Subcommittee on Labor, *Occupational Safety and Health Act, 1970: Hearings . . . on S. 2193 . . . and S. 2788*, 91st Cong., 1st and 2nd sess., 1969–70 (Washington, DC: GPO, 1970), 182–83, 685.

33. Ibid., 905, 922, 940 (Hannan quotation), 926, 935–41, 956.

34. Ibid., 632 (Nader quotations), 635–36. On the secrecy-related difficulties that the Nader Study Group experienced in investigating enforcement activities in 1969, see Page and O'Brien, *Bitter Wages*, 95–99.

35. US House of Representatives, Committee on Education and Labor, Select Subcommittee on Labor, *Occupational Safety and Health Act of 1969: Hearings . . . on H.R. 843, H.R. 8309, H.R. 4294, [and] H.R. 13373*, 91st Cong., 1st and 2nd sess., 1969–70 (Washington, DC: GPO, 1970), 940 (Burke quotation), 928, 940–99, 1006 (Hannan quotation), 1006–7, 1013–14, 1194 (Mazzocchi quotation). For the retaliatory transfer of Daniel Hannan, see Daniel Hannan to Dominick Daniels, December 5, 1969, USW Local 1557 Records, box 1, folder 2. On the failure of state and federal inspectors to provide reports to the Oil, Chemical and Atomic Workers International Union, see Les Leopold, *The Man Who Hated Work and Loved Labor: The Life and Times of Tony Mazzocchi* (White River Junction, VT: Chelsea Green, 2007), 247–48, 284.

36. US House, *Occupational Safety and Health Act of 1969*, 582 (Triggs quotation), 581–93, 1338–45. On the denial of social rights to workers in agriculture, domestic service, and other areas of the economy where people of color were concentrated, see Dona C. Hamilton and Charles V. Hamilton, *The Dual Agenda: Race and Social Welfare Policies of Civil Rights Organizations* (New York: Columbia University Press, 1997); Robert C. Lieberman, *Shifting the Color Line: Race and the American Welfare State* (Cambridge, MA: Harvard University Press, 1998). For a fatal poisoning of an uninstructed sixteen-year-old California worker, see Ruth Harmer, "Poisons, Profits, and Politics," *Nation*, August 25, 1969, 134.

37. US House, *Occupational Safety and Health Act of 1969*, 1347–49, 1354, 1366, 1372, 1374, 1376–82, 1388 (Milby quotations).

38. US, *United States Statutes at Large*, vol. 84 (Washington, DC: GPO, 1971), 1590 (quotation), 1595 (quotation), 1596, 1599. In both their compliance and standard-setting work, US Occupational Safety and Health Administration (OSHA) personnel were compelled to protect the confidentiality of trade secrets. See ibid., 1606.

39. Ibid., 1601 (quotations).

40. Ibid., 1611 (quotations), 1611–12.

5. NO NEED TO ALARM EMPLOYEES

Epigraph: US House of Representatives, Committee on Government Operations, Manpower and Housing Subcommittee, *Control of Toxic Substances in the Workplace: Hearings*, 94th Cong., 2nd sess., 1976 (Washington, DC: US Government Printing Office [GPO], 1976), 73 (Finklea quotation).

1. Ibid., 55–61; National Institute of Occupational Safety and Health (NIOSH), *National Occupational Hazards Survey*, 3 vols. (Washington, DC: GPO, 1974–77), esp. vol. 3: iv, 7; US Occupational Safety and Health Administration (OSHA), "Hazard Communication: Notice of Proposed Rule Making," *Federal Register* 47, no. 54 (March 19, 1982): 12093–94; Neal Q. Herrick and Robert P. Quinn, "The Working Conditions Survey as a Source of Social Indicators," *Monthly Labor Review*, April 1971, 16–18.

2. James T. Patterson, *The Dread Disease: Cancer and Modern American Culture* (Cambridge, MA: Harvard University Press, 1987), 231–94; Joseph K. Wagoner, "Occupational Carcinogenesis: The Two Hundred Years since Percivall Pott," *Annals of the New York Academy of Sciences* 271 (May 1976): 2 (quotation), 1 (quotation), 1–4; "Let Workers Know of Hazards," *Steel Labor*, October 1977, 20 (quotations).

3. Joseph A. Page and Mary-Win O'Brien, *Bitter Wages: Ralph Nader's Study Group Report on Disease and Injury on the Job* (New York: Grossman, 1973), 198–99, 222; Rachel Scott, *Muscle and Blood* (New York: E. P. Dutton, 1974), 93–95, 102–3; Paul

Brodeur, *Expendable Americans* (New York: Viking, 1974), 42, 47–63; Michael Alaimo, "Union on the Move: The Oil, Chemical and Atomic Workers' Efforts in Health and Safety," *Job Safety and Health*, November 1978, 28; Charles Stokes, "Request for Health Hazard Evaluation," August 18, 1976, Daniel Hannan Papers, box 2, folder 4, Historical Collections and Labor Archives, University Libraries, Pennsylvania State University, University Park; Steven Wodka, "The Effects of an Informed Work Force," in *Public Information in the Prevention of Occupational Cancer: Proceedings of a Symposium*, ed. Thomas P. Vogl (Washington, DC: National Academy of Sciences Press, 1977), 179.

4. Nicholas A. Ashford, *Crisis in the Workplace: Occupational Disease and Injury* (Cambridge, MA: MIT Press, 1976), 263–65; Page and O'Brien, *Bitter Wages*, 204 (quotation), 199–200.

5. OSHA Office of Training and Education, "Summary of Occupational Cancer Information and Alert Program," in *Public Information in Prevention*, ed. Thomas P. Vogl, v (quotation); "Discussion of What Is a Carcinogen," ibid., 41–42, 45 (Van Duuren quotation); Joseph Fletcher, "The Right to Know," ibid., 55 (quotation); Andrea M. Hricko, "The Right to Know," ibid., 69 (quotations), 68–72; David A. Wegman, "The Right to Know," ibid., 75 (quotation), 77 (quotation), 74–77.

6. Paul Kotin, "The Right to Know," in *Public Information in Prevention*, ed. Thomas P. Vogl, 62–65; Andrea M. Hricko, "The Right to Know," ibid., 68–69; Herbert W. Simons, "Educational Programs," ibid., 118 (quotation), 117–19; "Discussion of Educational Programs," ibid., 141, 144 (Simons quotation), 139 (Cornely quotation); Richard Marco, "How to Inform the Non-Union and Small Plant Workers," ibid., 154–55; Committee on Public Information in the Prevention of Occupational Cancer, National Research Council, *Informing Workers and Employers about Occupational Cancer* (Washington, DC: National Academy of Sciences Press, 1977), 7 (quotation) and throughout.

7. OSHA, "National Consensus Standards and Established Federal Standards," *Federal Register* 36, no. 105 (May 29, 1971): 10503–6, 10519–20, 10523; David P. McCaffrey, *OSHA and the Politics of Health Regulation* (New York: Plenum, 1982), 72–73, 94; Charles H. Powell and Herbert E. Christensen, "Development of Occupational Standards," *Archives of Environmental Health* 30, no. 4 (April 1975): 171–73.

8. Labels and Precautionary Information Committee (LaPIC), Manufacturing Chemists' Association (MCA), "Minutes of Meeting," June 20–21, 1972, L-729, Toxic Docs, https://www.toxicdocs.org/d/wgewdL86q3az8LGrV89d723gV, Center for the History and Ethics of Public Health, Columbia University and the Graduate Center, City University of New York; LaPIC, MCA, "Minutes of Meeting," September 13–14, 1972, L-737-38, Toxic Docs, https://www.toxicdocs.org/d/N2gaGbvNg3MKLyyKkZ8G-Z9b9w; G. Robert Sido, "Report to the Board of Directors of MCA on the Activities of the Labels and Precautionary Information Committee," January 9, 1973, 7 (quotations), Toxic Docs, https://www.toxicdocs.org/d/6eY2XVweL3GNVQ0n6qnY3x8g; LaPIC, MCA, "Minutes of Meeting," February 21–22, 1973, L-744-45, Toxic Docs, https://www.toxicdocs.org/d/Qg1q6vvxDnQ3dJgDD8Ew4L7K5; Occupational Health Committee, MCA, "Minutes of Meeting," March 23–24, 1972, OHC-60, Toxic Docs, https://www.toxicdocs.org/d/VJ0d48O9x6OpqxxxM5a1BOg7w; LaPIC, MCA, "Minutes of Meeting," June 14–15, 1973, L-754, Toxic Docs, https://www.toxicdocs.org/d/Ne87j0o07E0OmrvOO5JRQ6n68; idem, "Minutes of Meeting," January 30–31, 1974, L-771, Toxic Docs, https://www.toxicdocs.org/d/bYavKOebpw49Vx14MB1wMB1wBYM1.

9. NIOSH, *An Identification System for Occupationally Hazardous Materials: A Recommended Standard*, US Department of Health, Education, and Welfare (DHEW) (NIOSH) Publication 75-126 (Washington, DC: GPO, 1974), 7–8 (quotation), vi.

10. Ibid., 13–46; OSHA Advisory Committee on Hazardous Materials Labeling, "Report," June 6, 1975, 3 (quotations), 3–4, 6–7, 38–39, Document ID OSHA-H022A-2006-0869-0143, https://www.regulations.gov.

11. Idem, "Proceedings," April 22, 1975, 55–69, Document ID OSHA-H022A-2006-0869-0120, https://www.regulations.gov; idem, "Report," June 6, 1975, 20–21, 24–26, IIa, IIm, Document ID OSHA-H022A-2006-0869-0143, ibid. For the MCA's resistance to the United Nations warning images, see LaPIC, MCA, "Minutes of Meeting," June 18, 1953, L-50, Toxic Docs, https://www.toxicdocs.org/d/QkzmwnQdeQMNagJrymzg5OLRo; idem, "Minutes of Meeting," October 13–14, 1953, L-55, Toxic Docs, https://www.toxicdocs.org/d/xzNmY3zoNd1dqdkZ4pay0V0n6. For an early case in which the MCA endorsed application of the skull-and-bones marking for carbon tetrachloride, at least in part to meet "a public relations problem," see idem, "Minutes of Meeting," February 15–16, 1956, L-140 (quotation), L-139-40, Toxic Docs, https://www.toxicdocs.org/d/Lqkw1w35Z6Yk9OQ3EjRJMeZq.

12. OSHA Advisory Committee on Hazardous Materials Labeling, "Report," June 6, 1975, 21–24, IIa-IIs, Document ID OSHA-H022A-2006-0869-0143, https://www.regulations.gov; Joseph A. Patterson et al. to Assistant Secretary of Labor, June 13, 1975, enclosed with Document ID OSHA-H022A-2006-0869-0143, https://www.regulations.gov.

13. OSHA, "Hazardous Materials Labeling: Advance Notice of Proposed Rulemaking," *Federal Register* 42, no. 19 (January 28, 1977): 5373 (quotation), 5372–74; OSHA, "Hazards Identification: Notice of Proposed Rulemaking and Public Hearings," *Federal Register* 46, no. 11 (January 16, 1981): 4412–53; McCaffrey, *OSHA and the Politics of Health Regulation*, 123–25.

14. Gerald Markowitz and David Rosner, "'Unleashed on an Unsuspecting World': The Asbestos Information Association and Its Role in Perpetuating a National Epidemic," *American Journal of Public Health* (*AJPH*) 106, no. 5 (May 2016): 834–40; OSHA, "National Consensus Standards and Established Federal Standards," *Federal Register* 36, no. 105 (May 29, 1971): 10506; OSHA, "Emergency Standard for Exposure to Asbestos Dust," *Federal Register* 36, no. 234 (December 7, 1971): 23207–8; George H. Taylor to James D. Hodgson, November 4, 1971, Document ID OSHA-H033A-2006-0818-0003, https://www.regulations.gov. On the estimated cumulative mortality, see William J. Nicholson, George Perkel, and Irving J. Selikoff, "Occupational Exposure to Asbestos Exposure: Population at Risk and Projected Mortality—1980-2030," *American Journal of Industrial Medicine* 3, no. 3 (1982): 259–311; D. E. Lilienfeld et al., "Projections of Asbestos Related Diseases in the United States, 1985–2009: I. Cancer," *British Journal of Industrial Medicine* 45, no. 5 (May 1988): 283–91. For the scientific evidence of carcinogenicity, see Irving J. Selikoff, Jacob Churg, and E. Cuyler Hammond, "Asbestos Exposure and Neoplasia," *JAMA* 188, no. 1 (April 6, 1964): 142–46; Irving J. Selikoff, Jacob Churg, and E. Cuyler Hammond, "Relation between Exposure to Asbestos and Mesothelioma," *New England Journal of Medicine* 272, no. 11 (March 18, 1965): 560–65; Barry I. Castleman, *Asbestos: Medical and Legal Aspects*, 3rd ed. (Englewood Cliffs, NJ: Prentice Hall Law and Business, 1990), 39–130. On the broader regulatory issues and trends, see John F. Martonik, Edith Nash, and Elizabeth Grossman, "The History of OSHA's Asbestos Rulemakings and Some Distinctive Approaches That They Introduced for Regulating Occupational Exposure to Toxic Substances," *American Industrial Hygiene Association Journal* 62, no. 2 (March–April 2001): 208–17.

15. OSHA, "Standard for Exposure to Asbestos Dust: Notice of Proposed Rule Making," *Federal Register* 37, no. 7 (January 12, 1972): 468 (quotation), 466–68.

16. NIOSH, *Occupational Exposure to Asbestos: Criteria for a Recommended Standard* (Washington, DC: GPO, 1972), I-5 (quotation), I-5-6; Textile Workers Union of

America, "Statement," February 10, 1972, 5, Document ID OSHA-H033A-2006-0818-0106, https://www.regulations.gov; OSHA Advisory Committee on Asbestos Dust, "Official Report of Proceedings," February 15, 1972, 117 (Weaver quotations, Baliff quotation), 117–24, Document ID OSHA-H033A-2006-0818-0015, https://www.regulations.gov; OSHA Advisory Committee on Asbestos Dust, "Official Report of Proceedings," February 22, 1972, 110–11, Document ID OSHA-H033A-2006-0818-0016, https://www.regulations.gov; OSHA Advisory Committee on Asbestos Dust, "Official Report of Proceedings," February 23, 1972, 121 (Weaver quotation), 117–22, Document ID OSHA-H033A-2006-0818-0017, https://www.regulations.gov.

17. OSHA Advisory Committee on Asbestos Dust, "Official Report of Proceedings," February 3, 1972, 19–20, 23, Document ID OSHA-H033A-2006-0818-0013, https://www.regulations.gov; OSHA Advisory Committee on Asbestos Dust, "Official Report of Proceedings," February 22, 1972, 112–18, 132–34, Document ID OSHA-H033A-2006-0818-0016, https://www.regulations.gov; OSHA Advisory Committee on Asbestos Dust, "Official Report of Proceedings," February 23, 1972, 122–27, Document ID OSHA-H033A-2006-0818-0017, https://www.regulations.gov.

18. OSHA Advisory Committee on Asbestos Dust, "Recommendations Regarding the Proposed Standard for Exposure to Asbestos Dust," February 25, 1972, 4, 9–12, Document ID OSHA-H033A-2006-0818-0011, https://www.regulations.gov; Isaac H. Weaver to George C. Guenther, February 25, 1972 (quotations), Document ID OSHA-H033A-2006-0818-0012, ibid.

19. OSHA, "Official Report of Proceedings . . .," March 14, 1972, 77 (Wolfe quotation), 76–77, 85 (Mazzocchi quotation), Document ID OSHA-H033A-2006-0818-0153, https://www.regulations.gov; Norbert J. Roberts, "Statement," March 16, 1972, Document ID OSHA-H033A-2006-0818-0136, ibid.; Lain Tetrick, "Statement," March 14, 1972, Document ID OSHA-H033A-2006-0818-0072, ibid.

20. Bruce J. Phillips, "Views and Arguments," March 14, 1972, 5 (quotations), Document ID OSHA-H033A-2006-0818-0101, https://www.regulations.gov; OSHA, "Official Report of Proceedings . . .," March 14, 1972, 70 (Neumann quotation), 70–71, Document ID OSHA-H033A-2006-0818-0153, ibid.; E. M. Fenner, "Statement," March 14, 1972, Document ID OSHA-H033A-2006-0818-0095, ibid. For the evidence of carcinogenicity and its estimated toll, see the source cited in note 14.

21. OSHA, "Official Report of Proceedings . . .," March 15, 1972, 186 (Swetonic quotation), 191 (Swetonic quotations), 186–88, 199, Document ID OSHA-H033A-2006-0818-0154, https://www.regulations.gov; OSHA, "Official Report of Proceedings . . .," March 16, 1972, 309 (Pundsack quotation), 307–13, 330, Document ID OSHA-H033A-2006-0818-0155, ibid.; Bruce J. Phillips, "Views and Arguments," March 14, 1972, 6, Document ID OSHA-H033A-2006-0818-0101, ibid.; OSHA, "Official Report of Proceedings . . .," March 17, 1972, 421–27, 446, 458–59, 515, 527–28, 535, Document ID OSHA-H033A-2006-0818-0156, ibid.

22. OSHA, "Standard for Exposure to Asbestos Dust," *Federal Register* 37, no. 110 (June 7, 1972): 11319 (quotation), 11321 (quotations), 11319 (quotation), 11318–22; Elliott Bredhoff et al., "Brief for Petitioners . . . for Review of the Secretary of Labor's Standard for Exposure to Asbestos Dust under the Occupational Safety and Health Act," n.d., 71 (quotation), 71–72, Document ID OSHA-H033A-2006-0818-0106, https://www.regulations.gov; Asbestos Study Committee, Friction Materials Standards Institute, "Minutes of Meeting," February 16, 1973, 3 (quotation), Toxic Docs, https://www.toxicdocs.org/d/kDOpJ2zne5O7GJ7V0JwO8o01b.

23. OSHA, "Occupational Exposure to Asbestos: Notice of Proposed Rulemaking," *Federal Register* 40, no. 197 (October 9, 1975): 47658–59, 47663. This proposed reform, which also contemplated identifying asbestos as a carcinogen and expanding employees'

access to their medical records, fell victim to the business community's deepening antagonism to OSHA. On the antiregulatory drive, see Ashford, *Crisis in the Workplace*, 253; Charles Noble, *Liberalism at Work: The Rise and Fall of OSHA* (Philadelphia: Temple University Press, 1986), 99–120.

24. OSHA, "Emergency Temporary Standard on Certain Carcinogens," *Federal Register* 38, no. 85 (May 3, 1973): 10929 (quotation), 10930 (quotation); LaPIC, MCA, "Minutes of Meeting," June 14–15, 1973, L-753, Toxic Docs, https://www.toxicdocs.org/d/Ne87j0o07E0OmrvOO5JRQ6n68; OSHA, "Emergency Temporary Standard on Certain Carcinogens," *Federal Register* 38, no. 144 (July 27, 1973): 20074, 20075 (quotation); OSHA, "Standards Advisory Committee on Carcinogens: Notice of Receipt of Recommendations of the Committee and of Their Availability for Public Inspection," *Federal Register* 38, no. 173 (September 7, 1973): 24376–78; OSHA, "Occupational Safety and Health Standards: Carcinogens," *Federal Register* 39, no. 20 (January 29, 1974): 3759–97; McCaffrey, *OSHA and the Politics of Health Regulation*, 83–85. On OSHA's reticence to recognize carcinogenicity during this period, see David Michaels, *Doubt Is Their Product: How Industry's Assault on Science Threatens Your Health* (Oxford: Oxford University Press, 2008), 97–99, 127–30. As applied to vinyl chloride, some industrial representatives objected even to the weaker phrase "cancer-suspect agent." See Gerald Markowitz and David Rosner, *Deceit and Denial: The Deadly Politics of Industrial Pollution* (Berkeley: University of California Press, 2003), 200.

25. US House of Representatives, Committee on Government Operations, *Deficiencies in the Administration of the Federal Insecticide, Fungicide, and Rodenticide Act*, 91st Cong., 1st sess., House Report 91-637 (Washington, DC: GPO, 1969), 7, 9, 15, 16, 18; Rodolfo N. Salcedo et al., *Improving the Communication Adequacy of Pesticide Labels: Phase I Summary Report* (Urbana: Office of Agricultural Communications, University of Illinois, 1971), esp. 4; OSHA, "Emergency Temporary Standard for Exposure to Organophosphorous Pesticides," *Federal Register* 38, no. 83 (May 1, 1973): 10716 (quotations), 10716–17; Ashford, *Crisis in the Workplace*, 183–84, 527–28; US Environmental Protection Agency (EPA), "Worker Protection Standards for Agricultural Pesticides: Restatement of Certain Existing Standards," *Federal Register* 39, no. 92 (May 10, 1974): 16889–91.

26. NIOSH, *Occupational Exposure to Inorganic Mercury: Criteria for a Recommended Standard* (Washington, DC: GPO, 1973), 3 (quotation); NIOSH, *Occupational Exposure to Inorganic Arsenic: Criteria for a Recommended Standard* (Washington, DC: GPO, 1974), 3; OSHA, "Standard for Exposure to Inorganic Arsenic: Notice of Proposed Rulemaking," *Federal Register* 40, no. 14 (January 21, 1975): 3398, 3402; OSHA, "Occupational Exposure to Inorganic Arsenic" [Final Standard], *Federal Register* 43, no. 88 (May 8, 1978): 19628; NIOSH, *Occupational Exposure to Benzene: Criteria for a Recommended Standard* (Washington, DC: GPO, 1974), 7 (quotation), 13; OSHA, "Occupational Exposure to Benzene" [Permanent Standard], *Federal Register* 43, no. 29 (February 10, 1978): 5966; NIOSH, *Occupational Exposure to Chromium (VI): Criteria for a Recommended Standard* (Washington, DC: GPO, 1975), 8 (quotation), 7; Michaels, *Doubt Is Their Product*, 99.

27. Alan Derickson, "Surviving a 'Carcinogen Rich Environment': Steelworkers' Democratic Intrusion into the Regulation of Coke-Oven Emissions," *Journal of Policy History* 27, no. 4 (2015): 561–91, esp. 571–78. On the reshaping of social regulatory procedures, see Sidney M. Milkis, "Remaking Government Institutions in the 1970s: Participatory Democracy and the Triumph of Administrative Politics," in *Loss of Confidence: Politics and Policy in the 1970s*, ed. David B. Robertson (University Park: Pennsylvania State University Press, 1998), 51–74. On the organizational conservativism of the United Steelworkers (USW), see Lloyd Ulman, *The Government of the Steelworkers Union* (New

York: John Wiley, 1962); John Hinshaw, *Steel and Steelworkers: Race and Class Struggle in Twentieth-Century Pittsburgh* (Albany, NY: SUNY Press, 2002), 55–213.

28. Daniel Hannan, "Minutes of [USW] Coke Oven Advisory Committee Meeting," August 1, 1973, USW District 31 Records, box 30, folder 1, Research Center, Chicago History Museum; USW, "Evaluation of the National Institute for Occupational Safety and Health's Criteria for a Recommended Standard on Occupational Exposure to Coke Oven Emissions," n.d. [ca. July 10, 1973], 14, 16, USW Safety and Health Department Records, box 12, folder 9, Historical Collections and Labor Archives, University Libraries, Pennsylvania State University, University Park; James Smith, "Presentation of the United Steelworkers of America . . .," March 4, 1975, 54 (quotation), 54–56, ibid., box 23, folder: Coke Oven; OSHA, "Exposure to Coke Oven Emissions: Proposed Standard," *Federal Register* 40, no. 148 (July 31, 1975): 32278, 32280; USW, "Position of United Steelworkers of America on Proposed Coke Oven Regulations," September 30, 1975, 67, Hannan Papers, box 1, folder 5.

29. OSHA, "Informal Public Hearing on Proposed Standard for Coke Oven Emissions," December 17, 1975, 3028 (Tompkins quotation), 3030, 3042, 3100 (Robinson quotation), 3091–3103, Docket H-017, document 153.17, OSHA Technical Data Center, Perkins Building, Washington, DC; OSHA, "Informal Public Hearing on Proposed Standard for Coke Oven Emissions," December 18, 1975, 3196–99, 3246, 3231 (Pughsley quotation), 3131–32, ibid., document 153.18; OSHA, "Informal Public Hearing on Proposed Standard for Coke Oven Emissions," December 19, 1975, 3381 (Chapman quotation), 3413–23, 3437, 3446–49, ibid., document 153.19. For Pughley's suggestion to NIOSH, see Daniel Hannan, "Minutes of [USW] Coke Oven Advisory Committee Meeting," August 1, 1973, USW District 31 Records, box 30, folder 1.

30. OSHA, "Informal Public Hearing on Proposed Standard for Coke Oven Emissions," December 16, 1975, 2978 (Buchanan quotation), 2978–80, Docket H-017, document 153.16, OSHA Technical Data Center, Perkins Building, Washington, DC; OSHA, "Informal Public Hearing," December 17, 1975, 3017, ibid., document 153.17; OSHA, "Informal Public Hearing," December 18, 1975, 3243, ibid., document 153.18; OSHA, "Informal Public Hearing," December 19, 1975, 3384, ibid., document 153.19.

31. OSHA, "Occupational Safety and Health Standards: Exposure to Coke Oven Emissions," *Federal Register* 41, no. 206 (October 22, 1976): 46779–81, 46783, 46788–90; Daniel Hannan to Anthony Manguso, December 22, 1976 (quotation), USW Safety and Health Department Records, box 25, folder: Daniel Hannan—Miscellaneous.

32. Larry Ahern, "The Need for Worker Hazard Identification," in American Conference of Governmental Industrial Hygienists (ACGIH), *Labeling and Warning Systems: Proceedings of a Topical Symposium, 1977* (Cincinnati, OH: The Conference, 1978), G-1 (quotation), G-1-3.

6. NEW WORKER-ORIENTED COUNTER-INSTITUTIONS

Epigraph: Peter Greene, Sidney Wolfe, and Andrew Maguire to Morton Corn, September 27, 1976, in US House of Representatives, Committee on Government Operations, Manpower and Housing Subcommittee, *Performance of the Occupational Safety and Health Administration: Hearings*, 95th Cong., 1st sess., 1977 (Washington, DC: US Government Printing Office [GPO], 1977), 137.

1. Daniel Berman, "Guide to Worker-Oriented Sources in Occupational Health and Safety," *Occupational Health Project Report* (Medical Committee for Human Rights), August 1974, 2 (quotation); untitled item, *Safer Times* (Philadelphia Area Project on Occupational Safety and Health), January–February 1977, 2. On the emergence of alt-labor groups, see, among others, Steve Early and Larry Cohen, "Jobs with Justice: Mobilizing Labor-Community Coalitions," *Working USA* 1, no. 4 (November–December

1997): 49–57; Janice Fine, *Worker Centers: Organizing Communities at the Edge of the Dream* (Ithaca, NY: ILR Press of Cornell University Press, 2006); Janice Fine, Victor Narro, and Jacob Barnes, "Understanding Worker Center Trajectories," in *No One Size Fits All: Worker Organization, Policy, and Movement in a New Economic Age*, ed. Janice Fine et al. (Champaign, IL: Labor and Employment Research Association, 2018), 9–38; Celeste Monforton and Jane M. Von Bergen, *On the Job: The Untold Story of Worker Centers and the New Fight for Wages, Dignity, and Health* (New York: New Press, 2021). On the first generation of alternative organizations, albeit those composed mainly of retired workers, that dealt with occupational health, see Barbara E. Smith, *Digging Our Own Graves: Coal Miners and the Struggle over Black Lung Disease* (Philadelphia: Temple University Press, 1987), 76–200; Alan Derickson, *Black Lung: Anatomy of a Public Health Disaster* (Ithaca, NY: Cornell University Press, 1998), 151–62; Robert E. Botsch, *Organizing the Breathless: Cotton Dust, Southern Politics, and the Brown Lung Association* (Lexington: University Press of Kentucky, 1993).

2. Sidney G. Tarrow, *Power in Movement: Social Movements and Contentious Politics*, 3rd ed. (New York: Cambridge University Press, 2011), 199 (quotation), 195–214. On the general surge in activism in this period, see, among many others, Maurice Isserman and Michael Kazin, *America Divided: The Civil War of the 1960s*, 4th ed. (New York: Oxford University Press, 2011); David Chalmers, *And the Crooked Places Made Straight: The Struggle for Social Change in the 1960s*, 2nd ed. (Baltimore, MD: Johns Hopkins University Press, 2012); Jacquelyn Dowd Hall, "The Long Civil Rights Movement and the Political Uses of the Past," *Journal of American History* 91, no. 4 (March 2005): 1233–63; Thomas J. Sugrue, *Sweet Land of Liberty: The Forgotten Struggle for Civil Rights in the North* (New York: Random House, 2008); Tom Wells, *The War Within: America's Battle over Vietnam* (Berkeley: University of California Press, 1994); James Miller, *"Democracy Is in the Streets": From Port Huron to the Siege of Chicago*, 2nd ed. (Cambridge, MA: Harvard University Press, 1994); Sara Evans, *Personal Politics: The Roots of Women's Liberation in the Civil Rights Movement and the New Left* (New York: Vintage, 1980). On the four movements most directly related to the right to know, see Robert Gottlieb, *Forcing the Spring: The Transformation of the American Environmental Movement* (Washington, DC: Island, 1993); Adam Rome, *The Genius of Earth Day: How a 1970 Teach-In Unexpectedly Made the First Green Generation* (New York: Hill and Wang, 2013); John Dittmer, *The Good Doctors: The Medical Committee for Human Rights and the Struggle for Social Justice in Health Care* (New York: Bloomsbury, 2009); Lily M. Hoffman, *The Politics of Knowledge: Activist Movements in Medicine and Planning* (Albany: State University of New York Press, 1989); Peter B. Levy, *The New Left and Labor in the 1960s* (Urbana: University of Illinois Press, 1994); Aaron Brenner, Robert Brenner, and Cal Winslow, eds., *Rebel Rank and File: Labor Militancy and Revolt from Below during the Long 1970s* (New York: Verso, 2010); Paul F. Clark, *The Miners' Fight for Democracy: Arnold Miller and the Reform of the United Mine Workers* (Ithaca, NY: ILR Press of Cornell University Press, 1981); Smith, *Digging Our Own Graves*; Derickson, *Black Lung*, 143–82.

3. On the evolution of rights discourse and politics, see Alan Brinkley, *The End of Reform: New Deal Liberalism in Recession and War* (New York: Vintage, 1996), 3–14; T. H. Marshall, *Citizenship and Social Class and Other Essays* (Cambridge: Cambridge University Press, 1950), 1–85; Nancy Fraser and Linda Gordon, "Contract versus Charity: Why Is There No Social Citizenship in the United States?," *Socialist Review* 22, no. 3 (July–September 1992): 45–67; John D. Skrentny, *The Minority Rights Revolution* (Cambridge, MA: Belknap Press of Harvard University Press, 2002); Edward D. Berkowitz, *Something Happened: A Political and Cultural Overview of the Seventies* (New York: Columbia University Press, 2006), 133–57; Sophia Z. Lee, "Rights in the

New Deal Order and Beyond," in *Beyond the New Deal Order: U.S. Politics from the Great Depression to the Great Recession*, ed. Gary Gerstle, Nelson Lichtenstein, and Alice O'Connor, (Philadelphia: University of Pennsylvania Press, 2019), 110–23. On health rights, see Thomas Bole III and William Bondeson, *Rights to Health Care* (Dordrecht, Netherlands: Kluwer Academic Publishers, 1991); Alan Derickson, *Health Security for All: Dreams of Universal Health Care in America* (Baltimore, MD: Johns Hopkins University Press, 2005).

4. On cross-class collaboration, see, among others, Barbara Ehrenreich and John E. Ehrenreich, "The Professional-Managerial Class," *Radical America* 11, no. 2 (March–April 1977): 7–31; John D. McCarthy and Mayer N. Zald, "Resource Mobilization and Social Movements: A Partial Theory," *American Journal of Sociology* 82, no. 6 (May 1977): 1212–41. On the Workers' Health Bureau, see David Rosner and Gerald Markowitz, "Safety and Health on the Job as a Class Issue: The Workers' Health Bureau of America," *Science and Society* 47, no. 4 (Winter 1984–1985): 466–82; Angela Nugent, "Organizing Trade Unions to Combat Disease: The Workers' Health Bureau, 1921–1928," *Labor History* 26, no. 3 (Summer 1985): 423–46.

5. On the blended strategy of progressive reform, see Paul Burstein, "Legal Mobilization as a Social Movement Tactic: The Struggle for Equal Employment Opportunity," *American Journal of Sociology* 96, no. 5 (March 1991): 1201–25, esp. 1203–5; Max Felker-Kantor, "'A Pledge Is Not Self-Enforcing': Struggles for Equal Employment Opportunity in Multiracial Los Angeles, 1964–1982," *Pacific Historical Review* 82, no. 1 (February 2013): 63–94, esp. 73.

6. On business unionism, see Kim Moody, *An Injury to All: The Decline of American Unionism* (New York: Verso, 1988), 24–69; Nelson Lichtenstein, *State of the Union: A Century of American Labor* (Princeton, NJ: Princeton University Press, 2002), 141–56.

7. Oil, Chemical and Atomic Workers International Union (OCAW), *Proceedings, Ninth Constitutional Convention, 1967* (n.p., n.d.), 61 (Nader quotation), 58–61, 64–65; Les Leopold, *The Man Who Hated Work and Loved Labor: The Life and Times of Tony Mazzocchi* (White River Junction, VT: Chelsea Green, 2007), 230–38.

8. Leopold, *The Man Who Hated Work*, 247–48, 283–89; Gerald Markowitz and David Rosner, *Deceit and Denial: The Deadly Politics of Industrial Pollution* (Berkeley: University of California Press, 2003), 158–59; US House of Representatives, Committee on Education and Labor, Select Subcommittee on Labor, *Occupational Safety and Health Act of 1969: Hearings . . . on HR 843, HR 3809, HR 4294, HR 13373*, 91st Cong., 1st sess., 1969 (Washington, DC: GPO, 1970), 1179–307, esp. 1181–93, 1201, 1206, 1252, 1280–81, 1288–89, 1297–99.

9. Ibid., passim, esp. 1200–1, 1204, 1213–15; OCAW, *Hazards in the Industrial Environment: A Conference Sponsored by District 8 Council* (n.p., n.d. [1969]), reprinted in ibid., 1305 (Mazzocchi quotation), 1233–1307; Leopold, *The Man Who Hated Work*, 240–42, 245–55.

10. Ibid., 268–71, 302–11; Ray Davidson, *Challenging the Giants: A History of the Oil, Chemical and Atomic Workers International Union* (Denver, CO: The Union, 1988), 325–27; Robert Gordon, "'Shell No': OCAW and the Labor-Environmental Alliance," *Environmental History* 3, no. 4 (October 1998): 460–87; Daniel M. Berman, *Death on the Job: Occupational Health and Safety Struggles in the United States* (New York: Monthly Review Press, 1978), 191.

11. Leopold, *The Man Who Hated Work*, 292–94; Jeanne M. Stellman and Susan M. Daum, *Work Is Dangerous to Your Health: A Handbook of Health Hazards in the Workplace and What You Can Do About Them* (New York: Vintage, 1973), xxii (quotation), passim, esp. xxiii, 363–64; Jeanne M. Stellman, "A Strong and Militant Union: Key to Job Health Gains," *OCAW Union News*, October 1975, 4; Jerianne Heimendinger,

A Primer on Occupational Safety and Health Legislation (Washington, DC: OCAW, n.d. [ca. 1974], 4, 17; Phyllis Lehmann, "A Long Hard Struggle," *Job Safety and Health*, September 1975, 30 (Mazzocchi quotation), 32 (Mazzocchi quotation).

12. Ray Davidson, *Peril on the Job: A Study of Hazards in the Chemical Industries* (Washington, DC: Public Affairs Press, 1970), 15 (quotation), 15–17, 66, 54–55, 70, 72, 20, 146–48, 160–61, 180.

13. Franklin Wallick, *The American Worker: An Endangered Species* (New York: Ballantine, 1972), 1 (quotation), 3, 9, 18–19, 21, 17 (quotation), 15–17, 110 (Sellers quotation), 110–13, 140–48.

14. Joseph A. Page and Mary-Win O'Brien, *Bitter Wages: Ralph Nader's Study Group Report on Disease and Injury on the Job* (New York: Grossman, 1973), 120 (quotation), 128 (quotation), 129 (quotation), 115–36, 221–26, 243 (quotation), 242–51, 185–89, 256 (quotation). On the scorched-earth politics of Nader and his followers, see Paul Sabin, *Public Citizens: The Attack on Big Government and the Remaking of American Liberalism* (New York: Norton, 2021).

15. Rachel Scott, *Muscle and Blood* (New York: E. P. Dutton, 1974), 60–61, 91–97, 238, 290–91.

16. Paul Brodeur, *Expendable Americans: The Incredible Story of How Tens of Thousands of American Men and Women Die Each Year of Preventable Industrial Disease* (New York: Viking, 1974), esp. 30, 55–73, 163, 180–83.

17. Howard Kohn, "Malignant Giant: The Nuclear Industry's Terrible Power and How It Silenced Karen Silkwood," *Rolling Stone*, March 27, 1975, 42–46, 58–62; B. J. Phillips, "The Case of Karen Silkwood: Mysterious Death of a Nuclear Plant Worker," *Ms.*, April 1975, 59–66; Leopold, *The Man Who Hated Work*, 312–35, esp. 332; Howard Kohn, "The Case of Karen Silkwood," *Rolling Stone*, January 13, 1977, 30–39. For David Burnham's reporting in the *New York Times*, see, among his other articles, "Death of Plutonium Worker Questioned by Union Official," November 19, 1974, 28; "Plutonium Plant under Scrutiny," November 20, 1974, 19; "FBI to Study Plutonium Factory Critic's Death," November 21, 1974, 30; "Atom Case Death Linked to a Second Car," December 24, 1974, 4.

18. Willard S. Randall and Stephen D. Solomon, "54 Who Died," *Philadelphia Inquirer*, November 26, 1975, Today sec., 13 (unidentified workers' quotation), 12–50; Willard S. Randall and Stephen D. Solomon, *Building 6: The Tragedy at Bridesburg* (Boston: Little, Brown, 1976). For the provocative Naderite discoveries, see US Senate, Committee on Commerce, Subcommittee on the Environment, *Toxic Substances Control Act: Hearings . . . on S. 776*, 94th Cong., 1st sess., 1975 (Washington, DC: GPO), 58–69, 343–50 (Health Research Group, "Cancer in the Workplace—A Report on Corporate Secrecy at the Rohm and Haas Co., Philadelphia, Pa.").

19. Vincent K. Pollard, "Nixon, the Business Community and the 1970 Job Safety Law," *Weekly News Letter* (Illinois State Federation of Labor), March 25, 1972, 2; "OSHA's Failure," *Health Rights News* (Medical Committee for Human Rights [MCHR]), December 1972, 11; Dave Kotelchuck, "Industrial Health and the Chemical Worker," *Science for the People*, May 1972, 10–14, 26; Frank Mirer, "Occupational Health: Time for Us to Get to Work," *Science for the People*, November 1972, 4–7.

20. Ben Wisner, "Advocacy and Geography: The Case of Boston's Urban Planning Aid," *Antipode: A Radical Journal of Geography* 2, no. 1 (August 1970): 25–29; David H. Wegman, Leslie Boden, and Charles Levenstein, "Health Hazard Surveillance by Industrial Workers," *American Journal of Public Health* (*AJPH*) 65, no. 1 (January 1975): 26–30; David H. Wegman, Gilles P. Theriault, and John M. Peters, "Worker-Sponsored Survey for Asbestosis: Detection of Occupational Lung Disease without a Control Group," *Archives of Environmental Health* 27, no. 2 (August 1973): 105–9.

21. Industrial Health and Safety Project, Urban Planning Aid, *A Unionist's Guide to the Occupational Safety and Health Act of 1970* (Cambridge, MA: Urban Planning Aid, 1971), 6 (quotation), 6–8; Industrial Health and Safety Project, Urban Planning Aid, *How to Look at Your Plant* (Cambridge, MA: Urban Planning Aid, 1972), 3 (quotation), 13, 25–33; "Union Wins Health Clauses," *Survival Kit*, December 1972, 2; "Worker's Noise Meter Brings Results," *Survival Kit*, ibid., 1, 7; "Editorial," *Survival Kit*, April 1974, 2 (quotation); Occupational Health and Safety Project, Urban Planning Aid, *Solvents* (Cambridge, MA: Urban Planning Aid, n.d. [ca. 1973]); Peter Orris, "Frank Wallick UAW CACOSH 1972 [sic, ca. April 1973] Medical Committee for Human Rights," *YouTube*, https://www.youtube.com/watch?v=JezeaxKuNj0; Industrial Health and Safety Project, Urban Planning Aid, *Contract Clauses for Occupational Health and Safety* (Cambridge, MA: Urban Planning Aid, n.d. [1976]).

22. Donald Whorton, "Overview of Labor Occupational Health Project," *LOHP Monitor*, October 1974, 1 (quotation); Bob Fowler, *A Guidebook for Local Union Health and Safety Committees* (Berkeley, CA: Labor Occupational Health Project, 1974), esp. Appendix: "Health and Hygiene," 5 (Gary Sellers, "A Worker's Bill of Health Rights"); Morris Davis, *California Negotiated Clauses for Occupational Health and Safety* (Berkeley, CA: Labor Occupational Health Project, 1975); Andrea Hricko, "Cal/OSHA Developments: The Workers Right to Know," *LOHP Monitor*, August–September 1975, 3; Andrea Hricko, "Worker's Rights under the Asbestos Standard," *LOHP Monitor*, January 1976, 1–2; Sidney Weinstein, "Health and Safety Conference Draws Local Trade Unionists," *LOHP Monitor*, February 1976, 4; Andrea Hricko, *Working for Your Life: A Woman's Guide to Job Health Hazards* (Berkeley, CA: Labor Occupational Health Project and Public Citizen's Health Research Group, 1976), E-6-9; Jeanne Mager Stellman, *Women's Work, Women's Health: Myths and Realities* (New York: Pantheon, 1977).

23. Daniel M. Berman and Teamsters Local 688, "A Union Program on Job Health and Safety," August 24, 1971, 11 (quotation), 1 (quotation), Medical Committee for Human Rights Records, box 41, folder 469, Kislak Center for Special Collections, Rare Book and Manuscripts Library, University of Pennsylvania, Philadelphia; Daniel M. Berman, "A Program on Job Health and Safety on a Limited Budget," December 1971, ibid., folder 468. On Teamsters Local 688, see Robert Bussel, *Fighting for Total Person Unionism: Harold Gibbons, Ernest Calloway, and Working-Class Citizenship* (Urbana: University of Illinois Press, 2015), esp. 45–46, 166, 168–69.

24. Daniel M. Berman to Pat[ricia Murchie], October 9, 1971, MCHR Records, box 41, folder 469; Patricia Murchie to Daniel M. Berman, October 17, 1971, ibid.; Joe Goodman, "Medical Committee Meets in Kentucky," *Guardian*, November 24, 1971, 8; *Occupational Health Project Report* (MCHR), no. 1, December 22, 1971; MCHR, *Occupational Safety and Health* (Chicago: The Committee, n.d. [1971]); [MCHR], "Occupational Health Task Force," n.d. [ca. January 1972], n.p. (quotation), MCHR Records, box 41, folder 471. On earliest interest in occupational health at MCHR and the politics of those interested, see MCHR, "Organizational Newsletter," August 19, 1971, MCHR Records, box 41, folder 468; Daniel M. Berman to author (email), December 29, 2021, copy in author's possession; Ronda Kotelchuck and Howard Levy, "MCHR: An Organization in Search of an Identity," *Health/PAC Bulletin* 63 (March–April 1975): 20, 23.

25. University of Illinois School of Medicine, United Auto Workers, and MCHR, "Health in the Workplace: A Working Conference," January 7–8, 1972, MCHR Records, box 41, folder 468; "On-the-Job Health Needs Get New Breed Priority," *UAW Washington Report*, January 17, 1972, 2; Gregg Downey, "Occupational Health Issue May Be Rallying Point for Doctors and Unions," *Modern Hospital*, February 1972, 40 (Jordan quotation), 39–42; Dan Berman, "Organizing for Job Safety," *Science for the People*,

July–August 1980, 11; "Chicago Conference," *Occupational Health Project Report*, no. 2, n.d. [ca. January 1972].

26. Phyllis Cullen, "You Might Give Me Five More Years of Life," *Health Rights News*, March 1972, 9 (Williams quotation); "MCHR Meets Labor," *Health Rights News*, March 1972, 10 (Buff quotation); United Steelworkers Local 1865 et al., "Health in the Workplace: A Working Conference in Ashland, Kentucky," March 3–4, 1972, MCHR Records, box 41, folder 468.

27. Donald Whorton, "Occupational Health," *Health Rights News*, March 1972, 12 (quotation); Dittmer, *The Good Doctors*, 248–49; Daniel M. Berman, *A Job Health and Safety Program on a Limited Budget* (Chicago: MCHR, 1972); [Daniel Berman], "Urban Planning Aid, Inc.," *Occupational Health Project Report* no. 4, n.d. [ca. March 1972], n.p. (quotation); [Daniel Berman], "Pamphlets," *Occupational Health Project Report* no. 4, n.p.; [idem], "Available Materials," *Occupational Health Project Report* no. 5, n.d. [ca. April 1972], n.p.; [Daniel Berman], "Report on the MCHR convention," *Occupational Health Project Report* no. 6 (June 1972): 2–3, 4–6; Daniel Berman, "On the Importance of Money (or We're Broke)," *Occupational Health Project Report* no. 6 (June 1972): 11; Wallick, *The American Worker*, 163 (quotation), 162–63; Peter Orris, "Dan Berman MCHR CACOSH Conference 1972 [sic, ca. April 1973] Medical Committee for Human Rights," *YouTube*, https://www.youtube.com/watch?v=vkHDfH5ldPc.

28. [Daniel M. Berman], "How to Organize an Occupational Health Conference," 1972, n.p. (quotations), Daniel M. Berman Papers, box 2, folder 63, Archives and Special Collections, University of California, San Francisco, Library; Allegheny County Labor Council et al., "Health in the Workplace: A Working Conference on Occupational Health and Safety," December 1–2, 1972, MCHR Records, box 41, folder 472; "Occupational Health: The Mounting Militancy of Medical Activists," *Occupational Hazards*, March 1973, 55 (quotation), 57 (quotation), 55–57; John Bradley, "Meeting Notice: Pittsburgh Area Committee on Occupational Safety and Health," n.d. [ca. January 9, 1973], Political and Social Activist Movements Collection, box 1, folder 7, Archives Service Center, University of Pittsburgh, Pittsburgh, PA.

29. [Daniel M. Berman], "Collective Bargaining Demands on Health and Safety," *Occupational Health Project Report*, December 1972, 1 (quotations); District 12, Amalgamated Meat Cutters and Butcher Workmen, "Amalgamated Meat Cutters' Resolution on Health and Safety," *Occupational Health Project Report*, December 1972, 1–5; Will Shortell, "How to Run an Occupational Health and Safety Task Force," *Occupational Health Project Report*, March 1973, 3 (quotation, emphasis in original).

30. Daniel M. Berman, "The Worker's Right to Know," *Health Rights News*, April 1973, 12 (quotations); untitled item, *Occupational Health Project Report*, August 1973, 2; Daniel M. Berman, untitled editorial, *Occupational Health Project Report*, February 1974, 2; [Daniel M. Berman], "List of Projects and Continuing Information Sources," *Occupational Health Project Report*, 7; Daniel M. Berman, "Guide to Worker-Oriented Sources in Occupational Health and Safety," *Occupational Health Project Report*, August 1974, 1–29. On the involvement of radical elements in the legal profession in movement work, see Luca Fulciola, *Up Against the Law: Radical Lawyers and Social Movements* (Chapel Hill: University of North Carolina Press, 2022). On MCHR's demise, see Dittmer, *The Good Doctors*, 251–64.

31. Phyllis Lehmann, "The Worker's Right to Know," *Job Safety and Health*, June 1974, 10 (quotations), 9–10; Don Whorton, *Byssinosis* (Chicago: MCHR, n.d. [ca. 1973]), 7 (quotation).

32. Daniel M. Berman, "Report on MCHR's National Occupational Health Project," October 15, 1974, MCHR Records, box 42, folder 473; "Pittsburgh Area Committee on Occupational Safety and Health," April 1973, Berman Papers, box 4, folder 117; Charles

Grese, "Meeting Highlights," *1557 Labor Journal* (USW Local 1557, Clairton, PA), September 1973, 1; Pittsburgh Area Committee on Occupational Safety and Health, "Red Lung: Lung Diseases of Steelworkers," n.d. [ca. January 16, 1974], Political and Social Activist Movements Collection, box 1, folder 7; Daniel Hannan to Adolph Schwartz, January 22, 1974, Hannan Papers, box 2, folder 7; Berman, *Death on the Job*, 190–91; Berman, "Organizing for Job Safety," 13 (quotation).

33. Philadelphia Chapter, MCHR, "Minutes, Meeting," February 23, 1975, MCHR Records, box 50, folder 579; Rick Engler to author (email), January 30, 2022, with attachment "Engler interview," January 21, 2022, as revised," in author's possession; Philadelphia Committee on Occupational Safety and Health, "An Introduction to Occupational Safety and Health," n.d. [ca. June 19, 1975], MCHR Records, box 50, folder 579; Engler to Steering Committee et al., July 1, 1975, Berman Papers, box 4, folder 115; PhilaPOSH, "Health and Safety Problems in Your Plant," n.d. [ca. October 2, 1975], MCHR Records, box 50, folder 580; Berman, "Organizing for Job Safety," 11–12.

34. Richard Engler, *Oil Refinery Health and Safety Hazards: Their Causes and the Struggle to End Them* (Philadelphia: PhilaPOSH, 1975), 27 (quotation), 2, 9–10, 23–30; "Who We Are," *Safer Times*, March–April 1976, 1 (quotation), 1–2; "Briefs," *Safer Times*, March–April 1976, 7; PhilaPOSH, "It's Your Right to Know," n.d. [ca. 1976] (quotation), Rick Engler Collection on New Jersey Worker and Community Right to Know Act, box 1, folder 5, Special Collections and University Archives, Rutgers University Libraries, New Brunswick, NJ.

35. "A Conference on Job Health," *Safer Times*, March–April 1976, 8 (quotation); "Workers Confront OSHA," *Safer Times*, May–June 1976, 1; "Workers Speak Out at PhilaPOSH Conference," *Safer Times*, May–June 1976, 6; [Engler?], "Background on the Philadelphia Area Project on Occupational Safety and Health," n.d. [ca. April 1976], 1 (quotation), 1–3, Berman Papers, box 4, folder 113.

36. Jim Moran, "Birth of a Safety Committee," *Safer Times*, May–June 1976, 5; "Area Chemical Workers Force Plant Cleanup," *Safer Times*, April–May 1977, 1, 6, 7; "OSHA Task Force Will Report," *Safer Times*, March 1977, 2.

37. Engler, *Oil Refinery Health and Safety Hazards*, 22–24, 26; Engler to author, January 30, 2022, with attachment; untitled item, *Safer Times*, January–February 1977; Jim Rensen, "Lee Workers Fight to Know," *Safer Times*, January 1978, 3, 8; "OSHA Task Force Will Report," *Safer Times*, March 1977, 2; Jim Moran, Rick Engler, and Mary Aull, "1977 PhilaPOSH Annual Report," January 22, 1978, 3, Berman Papers, box 4, folder 113.

38. Engler to author, January 30, 2022, with attachment; Moran, Engler, and Aull, "1977 PhilaPOSH Annual Report," 3, 8, Berman Papers, box 4, folder 113; Dudley Burdge, "An Action Proposal on Our Right to Know," n.d. [ca. May 23, 1977] (quotations), Engler Right to Know Collection, box 1, folder 5; PhilaPOSH, "It's Our Right to Know!," n.d. [mid-1977], ibid.; Rensen, "Lee Workers Fight to Know," 8; Jim Moran to Dave Snapp, July 14, 1977, Rhode Island Committee on Occupational Safety and Health Records, box 1, folder: COSH Conference #1, Manuscripts Division, Rhode Island Historical Society, Providence, RI. On Moran's firing, see "What's What in PhilaPOSH," *Safer Times*, November 1976, 4.

39. [Dave Snapp], "COSH Meetings—Philadelphia," July 29–31, 1977, RICOSH Records, box 1, folder: COSH Conference #1; Bob Holt to All Coordinating Committee Members, August 17, 1977 (quotation), RICOSH Records, box 4, folder: Right to Know Outreach.

40. [Dave Snapp], "COSH Meetings—Philadelphia," July 29–31, 1977, RICOSH Records, box 1, folder: COSH Conference #1; Jim Moran, Jim Bessen, and Dudley

Burdge to Health and Safety Activists, n.d. [ca. August 1977], RICOSH Records, box 1, folder: COSH Conference #1; Moran to Trade Unionist, August 10, 1977, RICOSH Records, box 4, folder: Right to Know Outreach; Debby Levenson, "Minutes of Phila-POSH Membership Meeting," November 15, 1977, Berman Papers, box 4, folder 116; Jane Diamond to COSH Groups, August 17, 1977, RICOSH Records, box 4, folder: Right to Know Outreach; MassCOSH, "Is Your Job Making You Sick?," n.d. [ca. November 1977] (quotation), RICOSH Records, box 3, folder: COSH Work on Right to Know; Diamond, "Minutes from COSH group meeting," April 29, 1978, RICOSH Records, box 3, folder: COSH Work on Right to Know; Moran to All COSH Groups, October 14, 1977, RICOSH Records, box 3, folder: COSH Work on Right to Know; Joseph O'Brien and Moran to Ray Lederer, September 16, 1977, RICOSH Records, box 4, folder: Right to Know Outreach; James J. Florio, "Florio Feels OSHA Action Can Help Protect Workers from Exposure to Dangerous Chemicals," October 24, 1977 (quotation), Engler Right to Know Collection, box 1, folder 5.

41. Jim Moran, Jim Bessen, and Dudley Burdge to Health and Safety Activists, n.d. [ca. August 1977], RICOSH Records, box 1, folder: COSH Conference #1; Peter A. Greene to Eula Bingham, November 3, 1977, RICOSH Records, box 4, folder: Right to Know Outreach; Greene to Moran and Rick Engler, November 28, 1977, RICOSH Records, box 3, folder: COSH Work on Right to Know; PhilaPOSH, "It's Our Right to Know!," Berman Papers, box 4, folder 113.

EPILOGUE

Epigraph: Eula Bingham, "The 'Right-to-Know' Movement," *American Journal of Public Health (AJPH)* 73, no. 11 (November 1983): 1302 (quotation).

1. Ibid.; Harriet Applegate, "The Cincinnati Story," in Caron Chess, *Winning the Right to Know: A Handbook for Toxics Activists* (Philadelphia: Delaware Valley Toxics Coalition, 1984), 69–75.

2. Tim Morse, "Dying to Know: A Historical Analysis of the Right-to-Know Movement," *New Solutions* 8, no. 1 (1998): 117–45; James C. Robinson, *Toil and Toxics: Workplace Struggles and Political Strategies for Occupational Health* (Berkeley: University of California Press, 1991), 108–46; Susan G. Hadden, *A Citizen's Right to Know: Risk Communication and Public Policy* (Boulder, CO: Westview, 1991); Brian Mayer, *Blue-Green Coalitions: Fighting for Safe Workplaces and Healthy Communities* (Ithaca, NY: ILR Press of Cornell University Press, 2009), 98–132; Brian Mayer, Phil Brown, and Rachel Morello-Frosch, "Labor-Environmental Coalition Formation: Framing and the Right to Know," *Sociological Forum* 25, no. 4 (December 2010): 746–68.

3. Barry Bluestone and Bennett Harrison, *The Deindustrialization of America: Plant Closings, Community Abandonment, and the Dismantling of Basic Industry* (New York: Basic Books, 1982); John P. Hoerr, *And the Wolf Finally Came: The Decline of the American Steel Industry* (Pittsburgh, PA: University of Pittsburgh Press, 1988); Kim Moody, *An Injury to All: The Decline of American Unionism* (New York: Verso, 1988); B. I. Castleman and V. Navarro, "International Mobility of Hazardous Products, Industries, and Wastes," *Annual Review of Public Health* 8 (1987): 1–19; Kim Phillips-Fein, *Invisible Hands: The Making of the Conservative Movement from the New Deal to Reagan* (New York: Norton, 2009), 150–262; David Vogel, *Fluctuating Fortunes: The Political Power of Business in America* (New York: Basic Books, 1989), 148–289, esp. 140–41, 158–59, 269; Charles Noble, *Liberalism at Work: The Rise and Fall of OSHA* (Philadelphia: Temple University Press, 1986), 99–206.

4. David Burnham, "Agency Lists but Does Not Notify Workers Exposed to Carcinogens," *New York Times*, April 25, 1977, 18; Editorial, "The Government's Deadly Omission," *New York Times*, April 25, 1977, 22; Ronald Bayer, "Notifying Workers at Risk:

The Politics of the Right-to-Know," *AJPH* 76, no. 11 (November 1986): 1352–56; Daniel M. Berman, *Death on the Job: Occupational Health and Safety Struggles in the United States* (New York: Monthly Review Press, 1978), 1–4; Paul Brodeur, *Outrageous Misconduct: The Asbestos Industry on Trial* (New York: Pantheon, 1985); *Silkwood*, directed by Mike Nichols (1983; New York: ABC Motion Pictures); Sanjoy Hazarika, "In Hospitals of Bhopal, the Suffering Goes On," *New York Times*, December 5, 1984, A12; William Robbins, "Near West Virginia Plant, the Talk Is of Escape," *New York Times*, December 9, 1984, 22; Stuart Diamond, "The Disaster at Bhopal: Workers Recall Horror," *New York Times*, January 30, 1985, A1, A6; Steven R. Weisman, "Bhopal a Year Later: An Eerie Silence," *New York Times*, December 5, 1985, 5. For the Superfund Amendments and Reauthorization Act of 1986, of which Title III was Emergency Planning and Community Right-to-Know, prompted by the Bhopal disaster, see US, *United States Statutes at Large*, vol. 100 (Washington, DC: US Government Printing Office [GPO], 1989), 1613–782, esp. 1728–58. Other notable exposés of this period include Samuel S. Epstein, *The Politics of Cancer*, rev. ed. (Garden City, NY: Anchor, 1979), 76–150; *Song of the Canary*, directed by Josh Hanig and David Davis (1979; San Francisco: Manteca Films).

5. Seth Frazier, "Right to Know: A Winning Campaign," *Safer Times*, January–February 1981, 3; Mayer, Brown, and Morello-Frosch, "Labor-Environmental Coalition Formation"; Chess, *Winning the Right to Know*, esp. 2, 37–67; Charles E. Ellison, "What You Don't Know Can Hurt You: The Politics of Right-to-Know in Cincinnati," *Social Policy* 14, no. 3 (Winter 1984): 20, 23, n10.

6. US House of Representatives, Committee on Government Operations, Manpower and Housing Subcommittee, *Performance of the Occupational Safety and Health Administration: Hearings*, 95th Cong., 1st sess., 1977 (Washington, DC: GPO, 1977), 75 (Bingham quotation), 79; Noble, *Liberalism at Work*, 134; Sidney M. Wolfe and Lori Abrams, *1983 Survey of Fourteen Union Safety and Health Programs: Comparisons with 1976 Survey* (Washington, DC: Health Research Group, 1984); James C. Robinson, "Labor Union Involvement in Occupational Safety and Health, 1957–1987," *Journal of Health Politics, Policy and Law* 13, no. 3 (Fall 1988): 453–68, esp. 458–61.

7. Anita Kaplan, "Labor and Community Demand the Right to Know," *Safer Times*, October–November 1980, 3, 10; Chess, *Winning the Right to Know*, 4–5, 38, 71, 74, 81, 86–88.

8. US Occupational Safety and Health Administration (OSHA), "Access to Employee Exposure and Medical Records," *Federal Register* 45, no. 102 (May 23, 1980): 35212–303; OSHA, "Hazards Identification: Notice of Public Rulemaking and Public Hearings," *Federal Register* 46, no. 11 (January 16, 1981): 4412–53; OSHA, "Hazards Identification: Withdrawal of Proposed Rules," *Federal Register* 46, no. 30 (February 13, 1981): 12214; OSHA, "Hazard Communication: Final Rule," *Federal Register* 48, no. 228 (November 25, 1983): 53280–348; Hadden, *A Citizen's Right to Know*, 22–23; OSHA, "Hazard Communication: Final Rule," *Federal Register* 52, no. 163 (August 24, 1987): 31852–86; Daniel M. Berman, "Workers' Initiatives for Occupational Health and Safety in the United States: The COSH Groups and the Unions," January 1990, 31 (quotation), 31–32, Staughton and Alice Lynd Papers, box 72, folder 869, Archives, Youngstown Historical Center of Industry and Labor, Youngstown, Ohio. For another case of this reform process, see Charles R. Shipan and Craig Volden, "Bottom-Up Federalism: The Diffusion of Antismoking Policies from U.S. Cities to States," *American Journal of Political Science* 50, no. 4 (October 2006): 825–43. On the right-to-act movement, see, among others, Rick Engler, *A Job Safety Bill of Rights* (Philadelphia: PhilaPOSH, 1984); Rick Engler, *Fighting for the Right to Act in New Jersey* (Trenton: New Jersey Right-to-Know and Act Coalition, 1992); Craig Slatin, "Health and Safety Organizing: OCAW's Worker-to-Worker Health and Safety Training Program," *New Solutions* 11, no. 4 (February 2001): 349–74.

Index

Abrams, Herbert, 77–85, 98, 152, 177n36
access to information: asymmetrical, 2, 101, 122; bureaucratic infighting over, 4, 35–36, 38, 53–57, 170n38; democratization of, 4, 11, 40, 88, 141, 153; PHS on, 4, 20, 38–39, 47, 50–51, 87–88, 91; for prevention of hazards, 10–12, 43–45, 52; state regulations on, 40–48, 87, 88, 90, 96–97; in workers' compensation cases, 19, 46–55, 87, 167n18. *See also* right to know; transparency
ACGIH (American Conference of Governmental Industrial Hygienists), 67–68, 76, 86–87, 93, 111, 121, 146, 180n2, 182n14
AFL-CIO (American Federation of Labor and Congress of Industrial Organizations), 54, 74, 115, 118, 146
African American workers. *See* workers of color
Agriculture Department (USDA), 68–70, 103, 120
Ahern, Larry, 123–24
Albrecht, C. Earl, 91
Aldrich, Mark, 22
AMA (American Medical Association), 16–17, 49, 64, 71–75, 77–78, 83, 98
American Chemical Society, 18, 32, 44, 60–61
American Public Health Association, 49, 78, 146
Andrews, John, 17, 18, 158n18
Apfelbach, George, 10
arsenic, 4, 8, 13, 16–17, 41, 60, 68, 120
asbestos: carcinogenicity of, 108, 114–19, 189n20, 188n14, 189–90n23; ignorance of hazards, 2, 118; OCAW request for investigation of, 133; OSHA standard for, 5, 115–19; product liability lawsuits by victims of, 149; pulmonary function tests and, 135; warning labels for, 115–18
asbestosis, 46, 115, 116, 118, 149
Ashford, Nicholas, 102

Baier, E. J., 92–94
Baker, Harvey, 81
Baliff, Jack, 115
Baskerville, Charles, 61

Bates, Josephine, 20
benzene, 16, 25–26, 32, 41, 45, 52, 61, 66, 93, 121
Berman, Daniel, 125, 136–37, 139–42, 149, 152
Beyer, Clara, 58
Bhopal disaster (1984), 149–50, 199n4
Bingham, Eula, 145, 146, 148, 151, 152
Bingham, Hiram, 61
Black, John, 46–47
black lung disease. *See* pneumoconiosis
Bliss, W. L., 12
Bloomfield, J. J., 51, 87
Bohme, Susanna, 60
Bowditch, Manfred, 87
Boyle, Thomas, 102
Bremner, Robert, 38
Brennan, Marlin, 91
Brodeur, Paul, 132–33, 149
Brown, George, 74
Buchanan, Louis, 123
Buff, I. E., 139, 142
Burdge, Dudley, 145
Burke, Frank, 86, 92, 105
Burke, Walter, 103
Burke, William, 41
Burnham, David, 133, 194n17
Burnham, Grace, 31
Button, Art, 138

CACOSH (Chicago Area Committee on Occupational Safety and Health), 138–39, 141, 143, 145
Campbell, R. W., 29
cancer and carcinogens: bladder cancer, 83, 108; coke oven emissions as, 92, 95, 96, 123; education on, 109–10; exhibit at ICWU convention, 84; identification of, 2, 63–65, 108, 173n11; leukemia, 121; lung cancer, 1, 63–64, 95, 115, 122, 133; OSHA standards for, 5, 119–21, 133–34, 190n24; right to know and, 108–10, 133–34, 148; warning labels for, 63–65, 115–19. *See also specific substances*
capitalism, 3, 18, 22, 28–29, 60, 156n5, 158n21
Carnegie, Henry, 13

201

202 INDEX

Carson, Rachel: *Silent Spring*, 89, 99, 181n6
Chandler, W. L., 59
Chaney, Lucian, 28
Chapman, Willie, 123
Chavez, Cesar, 99–100
chemical industry, 12–13, 18, 23, 26, 31, 41, 43–44, 59–62, 65
Chesley, A. J., 50
Chess, Caron, 150
Clark, Marion, 23
class-bridging process, 5, 77, 127, 150, 193n4
coal mining, 31, 36, 39, 90–95, 126, 134, 137, 139
Cohen, Jerry, 99–101, 104
Commoner, Barry, 88
confidentiality, 48, 50–51, 88, 168n24. *See also* trade secrets
Conley, Bernard, 71, 77
Conner, John, 70
Cope, George, 102
Cornely, Paul, 110
COSH (coalitions on occupational safety and health), 125–27, 134–48, 150–52
COVID-19 pandemic, 2, 155n3
Craig, Jeff, 95
Cumming, Hugh, 49–50
Curtis, Thomas, 74

Daniel, Pete, 69
Darlington, Thomas, 21
Daum, Susan, 129–30, 142
Davidson, Ray, 130–31
Davis, Michael, 21–22
Davis, Morris, 136
DeBlois, L. A., 28, 33
discrimination. *See* nativism; racism
DLS (Division of Labor Standards), 49, 52–58, 171n41
DoL (Labor Department), 35–36, 38–40, 57, 102–3, 105, 128
Doyle, Henry, 82
Dublin, Louis, 41–42
DVTC (Delaware Valley Toxics Coalition), 150, 151

Eastman, Crystal, 28
Eckardt, Robert, 109
education and training: on cancer, 109–10; in chemical industry, 18, 41, 44, 62; by company doctors, 37, 42, 46, 56; dust hazard campaign, 52; employer responsibility for, 53, 62, 72, 172n6; English language classes, 22–25, 29, 41; by health stewards, 76; on industrial hygiene, 9, 18, 40–41, 54; by labor unions, 56, 84–85, 129; on lead poisoning, 14, 31; New Directions program, 150–51; OSHA on, 109–10, 113, 119–20, 143; on personal hygiene, 21; on pesticides, 89, 99, 100, 104; PHS endorsement of, 171n41; on prevention of hazards, 55; Read the Label program, 72; of workplace committees, 84
Egilman, David, 60
Elkins, Hervey, 67
engineering controls, 10, 16, 27–29, 37, 53, 55, 93–94, 97, 171n41
Engler, Rick, 142–43, 152
environmental movement, 88–89, 126, 129, 131

Falk, Leslie, 90
FIFRA (Federal Insecticide, Fungicide, and Rodenticide Act of 1947), 68–69, 78, 103
Fineman, Herbert, 95
Finklea, John, 107
Fishbein, Morris, 54
Fletcher, Joseph, 110
Flexner, Jean, 53
Florio, James, 146
FOIA (Freedom of Information Act of 1966), 88, 128
Ford, C. E., 21
Ford Motor Company, 23–24
Fowler, Bob, 136
Frear, Donald, 76–77
French, Chester, 74
Fuess, J. T., 73

Gafafer, W. M., 51
Gernon, James, 40
Gibbons, Harold, 136
Goe, Robert, 79–80
Gordon, Newell, 44
Govea, Jessica, 99
Graff, Wesley, 48–49
Graham-Rogers, Charles, 12–14
Granch, A. G., 59
Gray, Albert, 47–49, 55
Greenburg, Leonard, 52, 54
Greene, Peter, 125, 127, 146
Guenther, George, 116

Haas, Andrew, 116
Haines, Walter, 10
Hamilton, Alice, 4, 8–11, 19–22, 26–28, 32–35, 42, 46, 57, 63, 138, 147, 152
Hanna, Hugh, 28
Hannan, Daniel, 94–96, 102–3, 105, 121, 123, 142, 152, 186n35
Hanson, William, 8, 17
Hardage, Harold, 130

Hayes, Wayland, Jr., 72
Hayhurst, Emery, 9–10, 14–17, 32
Heagy, Albert, 69–70
health hazards. *See* occupational health hazards
Health Research Group, 114, 117, 119, 125, 133, 144, 146
Hechler, Kenneth, 139
Henderson, Charles, 10
Higgins, Edwin, 37
Hill, Sanford, 66, 67, 70
Hitchner, L. S., 72
Holmes, Howard, 95
Holt, Bob, 145
Hotchkiss, Samuel, 36
Howell, Roger, 90
Hricko, Andrea, 110, 136
Hueper, Wilhelm, 63–64, 82, 84, 95, 179n50
Huerta, Dolores, 100, 104
human rights, 77–78, 152. *See also* MCHR
Hunter, O. Benwood, Jr., 74
hygiene. *See* industrial hygiene; personal hygiene

ICWU (International Chemical Workers Union), 80–84, 102, 123, 144
ignorance of hazards: in chemical industry, 31, 43; dangers resulting from, 1, 110; friends and enemies of, 2–3; Hamilton on, 33–35; immigrant workers and, 8, 9, 12–13; medical profession and, 16–17, 19; perpetuation of, 2, 33, 36, 37, 99, 133
Illinois Commission on Occupational Diseases, 8–11, 16, 17, 29, 33
immigrant workers: advocacy for, 3, 9; agricultural, 72, 98, 120; Americanization of, 21–25, 27, 159–60n29; in chemical industry, 12–13, 23; English language classes for, 22–25, 29, 41; ignorance of hazards, 8, 9, 12–13; illiteracy of, 11, 23, 24, 30, 72, 113, 120; interpreters for, 16, 26, 29; labor unions and, 18, 31; language barrier for, 7, 10, 13, 15, 22, 26, 41, 71–72, 98, 120; mining and, 23, 31; nativism and, 7–8, 15, 33; as service workers, 85; in steel industry, 29–30; turnover rates among, 32–33; victim blaming and, 28, 29
industrial hygiene: education on, 9, 18, 40–41, 54; investigations into, 17, 86–87, 122; model regulatory code for, 76; preventive medicine in relation to, 78; state programs for, 46–47, 50–56, 101, 168n24; trivialization of, 22, 54
industrialization, 7, 11, 16, 33, 36. *See also specific industries*

information access. *See* access to information
Inland Steel Company, 1, 122, 123
International Brotherhood of Teamsters, 136–39, 195n23
International Ladies Garment Workers Union, 18, 31, 158n20

Jennings, Paul, 103
Johns, Roosevelt, 122
Johns Manville Corporation, 79–80, 83, 110, 118, 149
Joint Board of Sanitary Control, 18, 31, 37, 43, 158n20
Jones, Roy, 49
Jordan, Frieda, 138

Kane, Bill, 151
Karasek, Matthew and Stella, 10
Kelley, Florence, 33
Kerr, Lorin, 181n7
Kohn, Howard, 133
Kotin, Paul, 110

labels. *See* warning labels
labor unions: decline of, 149; education by, 56, 84–85, 129; immigrant workers and, 18, 31; membership growth, 57, 171n40; occupational health expertise for, 80, 178n43; in OSHA standard-setting process, 130; right to know and, 5, 80, 84–97, 99–103, 122, 127–33, 139–41; strikes, 54, 80, 97–101, 129, 132, 134, 143–45. *See also* workers; *specific unions*
Lanza, Anthony, 37–38
Latinx workers. *See* workers of color
lead poisoning: ignorance of, 4, 9, 12, 19, 35; investigations of, 78–79; personal hygiene and, 22; PHS secrecy on diagnoses of, 39; prevalence of, 8, 9, 157n3; prevention of, 12, 21, 37, 52; reporting requirements, 17, 42; Standard Oil (1924), 44, 167n16; warnings about, 11, 14, 16, 25–26, 31, 40–41, 45
Legge, Robert, 79, 98
Lieben, Jan, 91, 182n10
Lloyd, William, 96
LOHP (Labor Occupational Health Project), 136
Lynch, James, 14

Mackison, Frank, 112
Maguire, Andrew, 125, 127, 144
Marco, Richard, 110–11
Markowitz, Gerald, 35, 53, 57, 114, 176n31
Mawhinney, W. C., 93
Mayers, May, 42

204 INDEX

Mazzocchi, Anthony, 103, 117, 127–30, 133, 139, 142–43, 152
MCA (Manufacturing Chemists' Association), 4, 61–74, 112–13, 119, 130, 173n7, 173n11, 188n11
McBride, Andrew, 44
McCord, C. P., 54, 56
McGorkey, Mary, 54
MCHR (Medical Committee for Human Rights), 137–42, 195n24
Meeker, Royal, 27
Mellon, Andrew, 39
mercury, 16–17, 20, 41–42, 120, 128, 135
Michaels, David, 2, 117
Milby, Thomas, 104
mining industry, 23, 31, 36–37, 79–81, 90–91. *See also* coal mining
Mitchell, Walter, 82
Mizrahi, Lee, 101
Mock, Harry, 19
Monsanto Chemical Company, 83, 84, 179n48
Moran, Jim, 145, 146, 197n38
Morley, Sheldon, 99, 100
Moses, Marion, 68
Murphy, Walter, 70–71
Murray, James, 55
Murray, Raymond, 75

NACA (National Agricultural Chemical Association), 69, 71, 72, 77
Nader, Ralph, 102–3, 125, 127–28, 131–33, 186n34, 194n14, 194n18
Nale, Thomas, 67–68
National Cancer Institute, 64, 82, 84, 109
National Safety Council, 20, 26–30, 39
nativism, 7–8, 15, 33
Nelson, Harry, 52
Neumann, Charles, 117–18
Newman, Bernard, 27
Newton, Byron, 38
New York Division of Industrial Hygiene, 14, 31, 40–44, 47, 52, 61
New York State Factory Investigating Commission, 11–14, 18, 61
NIOSH (National Institute for Occupational Safety and Health), 105–6, 108–13, 115, 120–22, 143, 149

O'Brien, Mary-Win, 131–32
OCAW (Oil, Chemical and Atomic Workers Union), 91, 103, 109, 117, 119, 127–33, 142, 186n35
occupational health hazards: confidentiality of study results, 48, 50–51; industrialization and, 7, 11, 16, 33, 36; investigations of, 4, 8–18, 23, 25, 38–39, 47–54, 78–79, 86–96; NIOSH evaluation of, 105, 109–11; prevention of, 10–12, 19–26, 29, 31, 36–38, 43–45, 52, 55, 94, 164n4; reporting requirements, 16–17, 42; self-regulatory regimes, 59, 65, 110; transparency and, 7, 14, 34, 40, 53, 106–8; vernacular terminology used for, 32; victim blaming and, 22, 28–29, 37–38, 56, 72, 109. *See also* access to information; engineering controls; ignorance of hazards; right to know; warnings about hazards; *specific industries, substances, and conditions*
Occupational Safety and Health Act of 1970, 5, 104–5, 107, 127, 128
Osborn, Stanley, 47, 49
OSHA (Occupational Safety and Health Administration): asbestos standard, 5, 115–19; business community's antagonism toward, 190n23; on carcinogens, 5, 119–21, 133–34, 190n24; citations issued by, 105, 109, 128; coke oven emissions standard, 1, 5, 121–23; criticisms of, 134, 135, 140, 141; education and, 109–10, 113, 119–20, 143; functions of, 104–5, 132; Hazard Communication Standard, 5, 114, 144, 148, 152; pesticide standard, 120; right to know and, 109–10, 113, 119–23, 125, 144; Standards Completion Program, 111; trade secret protection by, 186n38; union involvement in standard-setting process, 130; warning labels and, 113–15, 118, 119
Overlock, M. G., 26

Page, Joseph A., 131–32
Parran, Thomas, 54, 62
Patterson, Francis, 45
Pawel, Miriam, 99–100
Peirce, Paul, 16
Perkel, George, 118
Perkins, Elna, 56
Perkins, Frances, 49, 52, 55, 168n25
personal hygiene, 15, 21–22, 36–37, 144
pesticides, 60, 68–72, 76–78, 88, 98–101, 103–4, 120, 184n26
PhilaPOSH (Philadelphia Area Project on Occupational Safety and Health), 110, 125, 142–46, 150, 151
Phillips, Bruce, 117
PHS (Public Health Service): on access to information, 4, 20, 38–39, 47, 50–51, 87–88, 91; ACGIH and role of, 180n2; Chemical Products Agreements Committee, 61–62,

INDEX 205

65; Chemical Products Labeling Committee, 65; on confidential reporting practices, 168n24; corporatism and, 47, 168n21; on education of workers, 171n41; on industrial hygiene, 35, 56; investigations by, 38–39, 47–51, 81–82, 90–91; on nonoccupational health problems, 55–56; on prevention of hazards, 36–38; proposal for expanded powers, 101–2; relationship with DoL, 35–36, 38–40; scientific research by, 35, 38–39, 82, 165n6; Social Security Act and, 49–50
Plasterer, James, 93, 94
pneumoconiosis: activism and, 134, 137, 139; diagnostic findings, 79, 83, 91, 95, 181n7; ignorance of hazards, 36, 37; prevalence study of, 90; preventive measures, 31; workers' compensation and, 122
pollution, 82, 93, 95, 129–31, 150, 179n47
Posada, Jose Guadalupe, 100, 185n28
Powell, Charles, 112
Pratt, Edward, 12, 14
Price, George, 12–14, 18, 21, 37
privacy. See confidentiality
Proctor, Robert, 2
Pughsley, Eugene, 1, 122–23, 191n29
Pundsack, Fred, 118

racism, 7–8, 33, 103
Randall, Willard, 133–34
right to know: ACGIH endorsement of, 76; AMA ethical code on, 83; carcinogens and, 108–10, 133–34, 148; COVID-19 pandemic and, 155n3; environmental movement and, 88–89; hazard data and, 38–39, 47–54, 79, 86–96, 116, 122–23, 131, 141, 151; labor unions and, 5, 80, 84–97, 99–103, 122, 127–33, 139–41; legislation on, 5, 88, 96–97, 105, 107, 148, 150–52; medical exams/records and, 1, 19–21, 39, 78–79, 97, 103, 115–19, 122–23, 131, 141, 151, 165n7; origins and expansion of, 14, 16, 40, 43, 59, 88; OSHA regulations and, 109–10, 113, 119–23, 125, 144; pesticide use and, 99–101, 104; warning labels and, 74, 75, 78, 98–99. See also access to information
right-to-know movement, 125–53; alt-labor groups in, 126, 147, 191–92n1; blended strategy of, 127, 193n5; class-bridging process in, 5, 127, 150, 193n4; COSH groups and, 125–27, 134–48, 150–52; emergence of, 4, 5, 125–27, 192–93nn2–3; Hamilton and, 4, 8, 9, 147, 152; infrastructure of, 150–51; legal assistance in, 141, 196n30; mobilizing

support for, 130–34, 138; OCAW and, 127–33, 142; political and economic environment for, 149; tactical repertoire of, 151–52; unfinished business of, 153
Roberts, Floyd, 71
Roberts, Norbert, 117
Roberts, Peter, 24, 29, 160n32
Robinson, Wayne, 122
Rodrigues, John, 80
Rollins, Robert, 98–99
Roos, Lester, 41
Roosevelt, Franklin, 49.54, 55
Root, E. K., 46–47
Rosenau, Milton, 78
Rosencrantz, Esther, 79
Rosner, David, 35, 53, 57, 114, 176n31
Rostand, Jean, 89
Rudman, Frank, 92, 94

Safety First movement, 23, 24, 29, 31
Samuels, Sheldon, 118
Schereschewsky, Joseph, 20, 27, 37
Schudson, Thomas, 88
Scott, Rachel, 132
Scott, William, 95
Selby, C. D., 20–21, 39
Selikoff, Irving, 101
Sellers, Christopher, 38
Sellers, Gary, 131, 136
Sexton, Richard, 75–76
Shafer, Raymond, 97
Shaffer, C. Boyd, 112, 113
Shapp, Milton, 97
Sheehan, John, 102, 140
Shortell, Will, 141
Sido, G. Robert, 112
silicosis, 13, 15, 32, 36–37, 41, 48, 52–53, 79, 95
Silkwood, Karen, 133
Silverman, Harriet, 31
Simons, Herbert, 110
Smith, Charles, 77
Smith, Edward, 89
Smith, Gordon, 90
Smith, James, 122
Social Security Act of 1935, 36, 49–50, 103, 168n26
Solomon, Stephen, 133–34
Stagner, Jack, 130
Standard Oil tetraethyl lead disaster (1924), 44, 167n16
steel industry, 1, 5, 10–11, 29–30, 37, 91–97, 102, 121–23. See also US Steel
Stella, Antonio, 13

206 INDEX

Stellman, Jeanne, 129–30, 136, 142
Sterner, J. H., 73
Swetonic, Matthew, 118

Tarrow, Sidney, 126
Tetrick, Lain, 117
Textile Workers Union, 115, 116, 118, 132
Thompson, Frank, 24
Thompson, R. L., 47
Thompson, W. Gilman, 18, 29, 60–61
Tompkins, Bobby, 122
trade secrets, 67–68, 88, 91–92, 99, 101, 104, 110, 138, 184n26, 186n38
training. *See* education and training
transparency: advocacy for, 3–5, 53, 58, 77, 87–88, 147–52; managerial, 76, 176n31; occupational health hazards and, 7, 14, 34, 40, 53, 106–8; in public policy, 76, 88, 102; resistance to, 42, 46, 48, 57; trade secrets as barrier to, 88. *See also* access to information; right to know
Triangle Shirtwaist Factory fire (1911), 11
Triggs, Matt, 103–4
Tyler, D. A., 93

UAW (United Auto Workers), 87, 102, 131, 138, 143–45, 151
Uehlein, Julius, 96–97
UFWOC (United Farm Workers Organizing Committee), 5, 97–101, 104, 127, 184n26
UMW (United Mine Workers), 89–91, 181n7
unions. *See* labor unions
UPA (Urban Planning Aid), 134–36, 139, 142
URW (United Rubber Workers), 132, 144, 145
US Steel, 10, 11, 28–30, 90, 92–94, 97, 103, 123
USW (United Steelworkers), 5, 86, 92–97, 102–3, 108, 121–23, 127, 142, 190–91n27

van den Bosch, Robert, 100
Van Duuren, Benjamin, 109–10
Vela, Marcos, 149
Vogt, John, 12–14

Wagoner, Joseph, 108
Walker, Nicholas, 74
Wallick, Franklin, 131, 136, 140
Walworth, Herbert, 87
warning labels: ACGIH on, 111; advocacy for, 83; for carcinogens, 63–65, 115–19; expansion of scope, 62–63, 68; legislation on, 60, 65–66, 75, 152, 172n2; OSHA and, 113–15, 118, 119; for pesticides, 68–72, 78, 98–99, 103–4, 120; privatization of, 4–5, 59, 61, 65, 75; Read the Label program, 72; symbols on, 61, 71–72, 74, 75, 113; trade secrets and, 67, 68; uniformity of, 66–74
warnings about hazards: by company doctors, 19; duty to warn and, 60, 61; employer responsibility for, 11; limitations of, 11, 26, 27, 30–31, 45; multilanguage, 9–11, 14, 16, 23–27, 29, 40–41, 45, 98, 120–21, 161n35; NIOSH on, 112–13, 115, 120–21; oral messages, 22, 24, 46, 120; pictorial, 26, 30, 113, 188n11; placement of, 5, 8, 116; in safety rule books, 26, 29. *See also* warning labels
Washburn, Elliott, 8
Watkins, James, 37
Watson, C. H., 20
Watson, Lani, 6
Watson, Warren, 62
Weaver, Isaac, 115–16, 119
Wegman, David, 110
West, Irma, 87, 98, 99, 152
White, Joseph, 37–38
Whorton, Donald, 136, 138, 139, 142
Williams, Haven, 92
Williams, Lionel, 139
Wilson, Nolie, 123
Windfelder, John, 145
Winslow, C.-E. A., 18
Wodka, Steven, 128, 133
Wolfe, Sidney, 117, 125, 127
Woll, Matthew, 54
workers: agricultural, 72, 97–101, 103, 120, 186n36; alt-labor groups, 126, 147, 191–92n1; carelessness of, 22, 23, 28, 29, 37, 43, 109; participation in hazard-control programs, 80–81, 86, 87; personal hygiene of, 15, 21–22, 36–37, 144; self-help and, 5, 128–29, 132, 136–37, 143, 151; social rights and protections for, 103, 126, 186n36; turnover rates among, 32–33; women, 17, 32, 133, 135, 136. *See also* access to information; education and training; immigrant workers; labor unions; occupational health hazards; right to know; workers of color
Workers' Bill of Rights, 131, 136
workers' compensation cases: access to information in, 19, 46–55, 87, 167n18; agricultural workers and, 103; labor union advocacy and, 31; legislation on, 22, 24, 44–46; mining and, 31, 79–80, 90–91; in steel industry, 97, 122, 123
Workers' Health Bureau, 31, 61, 127

workers of color: activism of, 123; advocacy for, 3; agricultural, 101, 103, 186n36; coke oven emissions and, 1, 92, 95, 96; COVID-19 pandemic and, 2; mining and, 79, 81; racism and, 7–8, 33, 103; as service workers, 85; turnover rates among, 32–33; victim blaming and, 28

Yaffe, Charles, 88
Young, Arthur, 28
Young, Quentin, 138
Young, Robert, 29

Zemprelli, Edward, 94
Zimmer, Verne, 49, 53, 55

www.ingramcontent.com/pod-product-compliance
Lightning Source LLC
Chambersburg PA
CBHW021856230426
43671CB00006B/411